Because He's Jeff Goldblum

Because He's Jeff Goldblum

The Movies, Memes, and Meaning of
Hollywood's Most Enigmatic Actor

TRAVIS M. ANDREWS

PLUME

PLUME

An imprint of Penguin Random House LLC
penguinrandomhouse.com

LIBRARY OF CONGRESS CATALOGING-IN-PUBLICATION DATA

Names: Andrews, Travis M., author.
Title: Because he's Jeff Goldblum: the movies, memes, and meaning of
Hollywood's most enigmatic actor / Travis M. Andrews.
Description: First. | [New York] : Plume, [2020] | Includes bibliographical references.
Identifiers: LCCN 2020007121 | ISBN 9781524746032 (hardcover) | ISBN 9781524746049 (ebook)
Subjects: LCSH: Goldblum, Jeff, 1952- | Goldblum, Jeff, 1952—Anecdotes. |
Goldblum, Jeff, 1952—Appreciation. | Actors—United States—Biography.
Classification: LCC PN2287.G5785 A64 2020 | DDC 791.4302/8092 [B]—dc23
LC record available at https://lccn.loc.gov/2020007121

Printed in Canada
1 3 5 7 9 10 8 6 4 2

BOOK DESIGN BY LAURA K. CORLESS

Dedicated to Jeffrey Lynn Goldblum.
So that maybe he'll read the damn thing.

CONTENTS

Let's say . . . I become a star. What happens?
People magazine sends some nasty
schmuck like me to do some interview.
Big fucking deal.

—Jeff Goldblum as *People* journalist
Michael Gold in *The Big Chill*

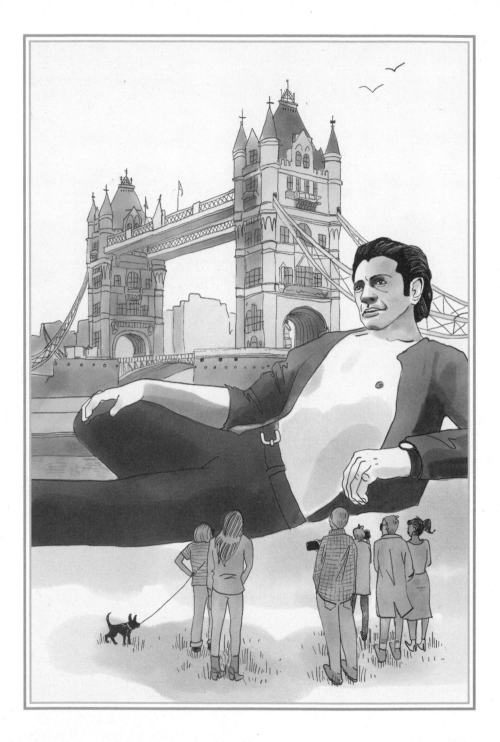

1.

Goldblum, Erected

ook, this is going to be a strange book. I'm sorry about that, I
truly am, but there's no way around it. This isn't by design.
The nature of the subject simply demands such treatment.
Jeff Goldblum is a strange character with a strange story. Consider
his 2009 death scare. *Great* place to begin, right? On the day Michael
Jackson actually died, Goldblum fictitiously died. In an early Internet
death hoax, reports of his falling off a cliff in New Zealand while
filming an episode of *Law & Order: Criminal Intent*—you know, the
show that's very much set in New York City, a place that looks *exactly*
like New Zealand—began circulating online. He, obviously, did not
fall off any cliffs, much less die, and Dick Wolf did not film his show
in the same place as *The Lord of the Rings*. The actor didn't die, but
for a while, many people thought he had died. (As the *Guardian* insightfully noted at the time, the gag "underlined his cult status: Goldblum was obscure enough to make it believable, and loved enough to

make it upsetting.") He thought the rumor was "nasty" and has discussed "the mill of information-spreading that is not based on facts," saying, "That can be alarming and poisonous, and we should be very vigilant about rejecting it." But at the same time, he appeared on *The Colbert Report* to goof on it. That contradiction might not make sense (yet) but it fully explains Goldblum's approach to acting and to life, which can be (and often is) paraphrased as "live truthfully under fictional circumstances." He's unknowable, strange, and enigmatic, but in the very best way. One reporter said trying to isolate the capital-T Truth about him is "like trying to nail jelly to a greased piglet." That pretty much sums it up. Only a fool would attempt such a thing, particularly as an entire book. Luckily for you, my publisher, my agent, and (maybe?) myself, I've always been a fool. A quick survey of my family and friends will prove that. So my deepest apologies in advance, but this is going to be a weird ride. Case in point: the first chapter, which just so happens to be the chapter you are currently reading, begins with a 330-pound, 25-foot-tall, bare-chested Goldblum.

Take a gander:

The sun dipped slowly into the river Thames in the late afternoon of July 19, 2018. It was one of those perfect midsummer days, in which the sky was bluer than Frank Sinatra's eyes and the air was as still as a wax museum, while the sun languidly set over the water in a glorious display. This serenity is usually what draws all the late-afternoon joggers, dog-walkers, and picnicking new lovers to Potters Fields Park. But that night, the sunset might as well have been an afternoon screening of the movie *Cats*, because no one bothered to so much as offer it a cursory glance.

Instead, everyone's eyes were locked on an art installation recently erected in the grass, where it would remain towering over visitors for a week. The thing was massive, the size of Paul Bunyan, if Bunyan were (a) a real person and (b) slightly better dressed. More than one onlooker's sexuality was called into question, as were a few relationship choices. It's frankly incredible the joggers didn't run into each other. How many glasses of wine overflowed as an idle hand kept pouring while its connected pair of distracted eyes was locked on the chiseled map that made up the statue's abs?

Some young folks only slightly recognized the figure, but anyone who came of age in the 1990s knew immediately what delicious flesh they beheld: that of Dr. Ian Malcolm, i.e., Jeff Goldblum's sexy, dino-doubting mathematician from *Jurassic Park*. Here, as in the movie, his shirt hung open as he reclined on one cocked arm like a swimsuit model from the 1960s, staring out into the great unknown, even though his leg had just been mauled by a Tyrannosaurus rex.

So, naturally, everyone did what everyone does in the face of spectacle these days: they whipped out their phones and took awkwardly framed photos of that statue while thinking of clever quips to write on Instagram and trying to find the proper hashtag.

There was a certain irony to the statue. After all, in *Jurassic Park*, his character famously decries the idea of bringing back dinosaurs, believing that something could go terribly wrong. And here he lay, two decades later, looking perfectly preserved, the size of a dino himself.

"This monstrously large Jeff Goldblum is how I like to imagine the man himself in his true form," Helen McClory, who wrote a slim volume of flash fiction about our man called *The Goldblum Variations*, told CNN at the time. "Or how he would have appeared in the age of megafauna."

"Life doesn't have nearly enough large statues of men as sex symbols, so it redressed the balance a little," she later told me. "I never got to see it in person, which is sad. I hope it's touring about and I might get to, one of these days."

Unfortunately, the statue was coming down on July 26, and Goldblum was busy recording a jazz album in the United States (much more on this later, I promise). He didn't have time to saunter on down to the park to look at a gargantuan representation of his younger self, so he didn't get to see it in person.

Months later, while promoting said jazz album, Goldblum appeared on *The Graham Norton Show* alongside Jamie Lee Curtis.

"I didn't know it was going up. I found out the day it went up," Goldblum told Norton, still visibly excited by the absurdity—which has been something of his lifeblood over the decades.

Norton responded that there was a surprise in store for the actor and walked across the stage to what appeared to be an end table draped with a dark cloth, which the host quickly whipped off. Goldblum's jaw fell open when he saw what sat beneath: his own noggin, only much, much, much larger, now removed from its body, which had recently sprawled out before London's Tower Bridge.

Norton picked up the statue's head, and he began wobbling under its weight like a cartoon character. Goldblum jumped out of his seat and was quickly replaced with the head.

"Look at that thing!" he exclaimed. "Look at that thing. Oh, my golly."

"You can post it on *Face*book," Curtis gleefully interjected.

"True or false: a pun is the lowest form of humor," Goldblum ribbed back without taking a pause.

The entire time, a papier-mâché head, larger than an average eight-year-old, sat on the couch and stared blankly into the audience.

Perhaps the strangest part of the statue episode was that Goldblum wasn't the first actor to be praised in such fashion, but it was the first time that anyone really noticed or cared. In 2013, a twelve-foot-tall statue of Colin Firth appeared in the middle of the Serpentine, a lake in Hyde Park, London. It showed Firth as Mr. Darcy from *Pride and Prejudice*, complete with a soaking-wet white shirt clinging to his well-defined arms and chest. Yet it didn't create much buzz. The *Hollywood Reporter* offered one of the more energetic quotes about the statue: "It makes swimming a bit more interesting, and I think the swans like it."

Goldblum as a subject, though, has the inherent power to make oddities go viral. It seems there's just something about Jeff Goldblum.

Take the Croydon Salvos store in Australia.

While the whole Goldblum statue saga played out, a much smaller—and, one might say, more personal—Goldblum shrine was being erected in the Australian charity store. It's part of the shop's running gag in which they fill every picture frame on display with photos of a different celebrity each month. Normally, this occurs under the radar, amusing only local fans. But this time felt different.

The store, in which a variety of Goldblums stared out of every picture frame, became known to the world through a visitor who documented the whole shebang on Twitter in September 2018. Quickly, the story went viral, being picked up by outlets as varied as *Time*, the *Nerdist*, and *Travel and Leisure*. And of course, BuzzFeed. Things then took an even stranger turn when other people started chiming in that, yeah, this isn't actually all that uncommon. Johnny Haeusler in Berlin, Germany, quickly shared a photo of his office's bathroom (the men's, presumably). The green tile of one wall was only visible around the edges of dozens upon dozens of photos of Goldblum at various stages in his life.

Now, if you were to tell this pair of stories to someone who had the misfortune of never having heard the name Jeff Goldblum—perhaps this person had lived under a literal rock, meaning this person was recently dead and somehow resurrected into the world having missed Goldblum's decades-long career—then they would probably gawk at you a moment, ask the obvious question ("The world still has sculptors with this sort of time on their hands?"), and then inquire as to the identity of the art's subject.

"This Goldblum fella," this recently undead person might say, "I guess he's probably a huge movie star or something?"

"Well, he *was*," you'd reply. "Like, twenty years ago. I mean, he still has some big roles every once in a while, but he's not really a leading man any longer. In fact, now that I think about it, he never really was a *leading* man per se, but he was a really likable character actor. I can name at least four movies in which he's appeared, though that doesn't sound like that many, now that I'm saying all of this out loud. By the way, how on earth did you manage to come back from the dead? That seems *way* more important than why this actor is so beloved, right?"

"Oh, well, then maybe he's embarked on a stunning second career of some sort. Is that it?"

You would probably begin puzzling over this question, finally answering that though the actor still appears from time to time in big movies, by the end of the 2010s, his big passion was . . . playing jazz piano.

"So he must have been the most famous jazz musician at the time, right?"

You would then be placed in the bewildering position of having to reveal that until recently only his most die-hard fans knew he even played jazz piano in the first place and that casual culture consumers were surprised by the whole endeavor. That it was one of those tidbits of trivia that get lost in a sea of information, something that most people might have once known as a solid cocktail party anecdote but had faded from memory. And that until he recently released his first album, most people had no idea he was a talented musician who had been playing for decades.

In fact, you would be forced to conclude, there is absolutely no discernible reason why Goldblum should be as wildly popular as he is.

And yet, he is.

In some ways, before writing this book, I was an outlier. In fairness, I had a rough start with Goldblum. I was eight or nine years old the first time I saw him on-screen, and he scared the ever-living shit out of me. My babysitter chose to leave me unsupervised and sit in the other room, flirting with her boyfriend over the phone, and *The Fly* came on television. I couldn't look away. For weeks, I was plagued with horrible visions of a half-Goldblum, half-housefly creature leaning his head into my room right as I was falling asleep. Of course, these days, some people might welcome such a midnight visitor. Rest assured a young me was not among them.

Given the tremendous range of Goldblum's filmography, I suspect many of you have similarly distinct memories of first seeing the actor. Maybe he represented an exciting life in the city if you first caught him as *People* magazine journalist Michael Gold in *The Big Chill*. Maybe seeing him in *Jurassic Park* as that chiseled brainiac led to an early sexual awakening. Or maybe, like me, he just scared the crap out of you when his DNA merged with that of a common housefly. One way or another, Goldblum was a formative part of childhood for more than one generation of Americans.

But while I had long been aware that seemingly everyone loved Goldblum, I was never quite sure *why they still did*. It seemed as if his time had passed. Sure, after the whole *The Fly* incident, I began watching his movies. I respect him as an actor and even adore some of his more bizarre performances, particularly his character in *Thor: Ragnarok*, to which he brought some seriously surreal, off-kilter energy as the fabulously dressed Grandmaster (who, in one deleted scene, appears to make out with alien tentacles). And Wes Anderson movies always appeal to me about 10 percent more if Goldblum appears in them.

But the fact that he is a living meme? That, I never understood.

The day the statue appeared, I was sitting in the newsroom of the *Washington Post*, where I work as a reporter for the Style section. I like to believe I excel at my job, but I couldn't understand why the statue existed, much less why it was being so celebrated. After all, that statue of Firth had appeared in the past to such little fanfare. (Sorry, Firth!)

I asked several of my Style colleagues the same question, only to be met with the same answer.

ME: I just don't get it. Why are people so nuts for Jeff Goldblum?
MORE INFORMED PERSON: Because he's *Jeff Goldblum*!

Understanding this was the correct answer, but still unsatisfied with it and vaguely bored, I decided it'd be fun to figure out why Goldblum is so universally famous, so beloved, and so devoid of controversy, scandal, and haters. It seemed like a better usage of my time than watching the middle portion of *Goodfellas* on TBS for like the fiftieth time.

The story of his fame has three potential beginnings. One is a familiar tale, beginning in West Homestead, Pennsylvania, that includes a dream of acting and a move to New York City. The second is unique, involving a number of dinosaurs, houseflies, big screens, and sex appeal. The third would seem downright bizarre in any other decade, for it involves the actor's watching you poop.

Strangely, it's this third story that cemented him as a modern-day hero.

The late-stage careers of aging actors in the new millennium generally follow a few well-worn paths. Some retire, others burn out, and others still have their careers sunk by scandal. But the most common one involves stars' aging like fine wines. As they earn stately wrinkles and regal gray coiffures, many former heartthrobs take on Serious Oscar-bait roles or choose to play against type in popcorn flicks—while mostly remaining out of the spotlight, particularly the sort of spotlight that comes with the viral social media stunts that have become the bread and butter of modern fame. (Think Adam Sandler crashing a wedding photo shoot. Or Tom Hanks crashing a wedding photo shoot. Or Will and Jada Pinkett Smith crashing a wedding photo shoot. Or . . . well, you probably get the point.)

Colin Firth, a contemporary of Goldblum, is a prime example. Always an earnest actor, Firth continued taking on weighty roles as he entered his fifties in movies such as *A Single Man*, *The King's Speech*, and *Tinker Tailor Soldier Spy*. In recent years, he began taking (or reprising) safe roles in popular comedic franchises, such as the *Kingsman*, *Bridget Jones*, and *Mamma Mia!* series, where he could use the gravitas his dignified wrinkles afforded him to shine.

As a result, Firth has become a reliable actor, someone who can help carry a weak movie and who adds a certain depth and complexity to ambitious ones. But his reliability also means he feels like a safe choice, making him dependable but not necessarily exciting. You'd never catch Firth popping up on, say, a Comedy Central gag show about puppets making crank calls, but that's exactly where you'll catch Goldblum, who regularly appeared on *Crank Yankers*. That might be one reason why the fanfare surrounding Firth's larger-than-life Hyde Park statue paled in comparison to the ballyhoo surrounding Goldblum's.

The other path available to movie stars seeking a second act is best epitomized by the latter-day career of Bill Murray—if it can be called a career. Unlike Firth (or George Clooney, Brad Pitt, Michael Keaton, Michael Douglas, or [*insert male star of yesteryear here*]), Murray has, in recent years, become better known for his absurd antics than for any movies he's been in since his big Serious swing *Lost in Translation* (2003). During the past few decades, the comic has taken to appearing in unexpected places, where he'll do something charming before disappearing again into the ether, like some unknowable but lovable ghost. The best known of these stunts is when he reportedly sneaks up on unsuspecting people and whispers, "I'm Bill Murray. No one will ever believe you," and then runs off.

While that might be the stuff of urban legend—the inherently clever setup of the bit is that no one can ever prove nor disprove it—he's been captured on-camera plenty of times doing things like crashing a bachelor party to offer the groom-to-be marital advice or joining a surprised couple for their engagement photos. Each time, celebrity bloggers rush over each other to tell the story of crazy Bill Murray. The "news" then begins circulating on social media to the point where mainstream outlets such as *USA Today* and CNN decide to pick up the story, further cementing Murray's stardom without the actor's so much as making an official statement, shooting out a tweet (he's not personally active on social media, in any case) or, of course, appearing in a new project.

It's irresponsible to ascribe intention, and there's no real way to figure out why Murray revels in such larks. Maybe he gets a personal kick out of making other people happy, or maybe it's simply how he keeps himself entertained after achieving a level of stardom most working actors only dream of. Whatever the reason, it has kept his name in the headlines and thus kept him relevant years after his peak. Younger audiences may have never seen *Meatballs*, *Stripes*, or even the original *Ghostbusters* (a film that, fun fact, Goldblum was up for but ultimately didn't get), but they probably know Murray's name from Twitter stories and viral videos.

Goldblum is similarly popular in those digital spheres. He's a great interview, often displaying a mixture of intellect, wit, and open-heartedness that the Internet tends to eat up. His unique fashion sense, fueled by a personal stylist, has helped him become a mainstay in men's magazines like *Esquire* and *GQ*. These days that means not only does he grace covers and is endlessly profiled, but he (and his sartorial choices) are constantly circulating on platforms like Instagram and Snapchat.

But unlike Murray, it never seems like Goldblum is trying to remain relevant or make headlines. And unlike someone like Firth, it never feels like he's taking a particular role because it's safe. If anything, he seems to pursue things that are *unsafe*, at least career-wise. At the moment this sentence is being written, Goldblum is currently in the midst of touring behind his first jazz album. Jazz isn't exactly a popular genre these days, but Goldblum doesn't seem to give a damn. He loves it, so he's going to pursue it. And it works. The album debuted at the top of the jazz charts, moving at least three thousand units in the first week (not bad in the digital age, especially for a jazz album). Perhaps the publicist of Universal's Decca Records, which released his album, said it best. "As far as I can tell, everyone loves Jeff Goldblum," Decca director of A & R Tom Lewis said in a statement. "He's a fantastic jazz pianist, a great band leader and just about the loveliest man in the world. His love of jazz is infectious and whenever he plays, he makes you feel very happy. If we can take Jeff's music into people's homes, then we will be helping, in our own small way, to make the world a happier place."

And it's true. In the process of writing this book, I spoke with dozens upon dozens of people. Many of them had great cause to like him, but a handful of others (like, say, an ex-fiancée) might have taken the opportunity to pull a few skeletons out of the old closet or to at least throw a little shade. But, no. Everyone had nothing but kind words to say, no matter how lengthy or brief their connection. Here are a few incredibly random examples!

When I reached out to Craig Kilborn, the former host of *The Late Late Show* and *The Daily Show*, his immediate response was, "Big fan of Jeff and he's an old friend—he's one of the real nice guys in Hollywood . . . love Jeff."

Added Kilborn, "Jeff was one of my favorite guests—wonderful enthusiasm and a quirky sense of humor. I was fortunate to get to know him off-camera—a real nice guy—a gentle soul as we like to say. He's very healthy—careful what he eats—and a stylish dresser. And, of course, we both love jazz."

Chris Bradley, who codirected Goldblum in the brilliant, absolutely bonkers half-documentary/half-mockumentary *Pittsburgh*, said, "Everywhere he goes, people just light up. They want to be a part of whatever he's doing."

Bradley has one memory that really helps define what makes him so likable: "One moment that really sticks with me when I think about Jeff is [from when] we were filming this scene in Times Square. It was the middle of the day, super-crowded, and people noticed that it was Jeff Goldblum. And so they came over while we were filming, and we took a break for a minute."

Some fans ran over saying things like "Oh, Jeff, I'm a big fan. Can we take a quick photo with you?" Bradley recalled. "And he says, 'No. No, no, no. Let's take our time with it. Let's take a good photo.' That's such a Jeff way to look at things: Let's enjoy everything. Let's not rush through this. Let's do it right. I think that kind of pervades everything he's done."

It isn't just colleagues or friends who sing his praises, either. In 1968, during his first year as an educator, a then-twenty-three-year-old Bruce Broglie taught mechanical drawing in tenth grade to Goldblum at Calhoun Junior High School—and he still remembers the actor with a deep fondness. He keeps a yearbook from that year as a memento. It's nothing fancy: just sturdy paper held together by a plastic binding comb. The deeply serious eyes of a young Goldblum stare out from the page through thick, black-rimmed glasses. His hair lies flat on his head. Unlike the way he wears it today, it's not styled—it's almost dorky, for lack of a better word. But there's no mistaking him.

Broglie, his voice filled with warmth, remembered a teenage Goldblum as "a little on the lanky side" and "lean as can be."

"As best I can remember it, he was kind of a quiet kid with a studious kind of look, like a professor. He was a good kid, never had any issues with him," Broglie said, adding as if in astonishment, "Never dreamed he would become a famous actor."

Broglie described the young actor as someone with "good values" who was "on a good path."

"I could tell you he tried to put firecrackers in the principal's pocket, but that didn't really happen," he added with a chuckle.

So, as Kanye West once rapped, what's the basis? Just what is behind all this widespread veneration?

Ronald Allan-Lindblom, the former artistic director of the Pittsburgh Playhouse and Point Park University's Conservatory of Performing Arts who met Goldblum when the actor was starring in a play in his hometown back in 2004, has a theory.

"My impression of Jeff and his work is that Jeff has never tried to be anyone other than who he is," he said. In other words, Goldblum is authentic, at least insofar as a celebrity can be "authentic." He gives off the impression—one confirmed by those who have worked with him—that he only does what he wants to do, and he only wants to do things he finds interesting. So while he may lean into a certain image of himself, it's because he finds that image interesting.

But at the same time, he's unknowable. As McClory said, "He's a bit of an enigma as a person: for all that he seems accessible and warm and friendly, there is an aura of mystery to him. It's hard to imagine him doing prosaic things like buttering toast—in my mind at least, he would imbue even that with some kind of flair. In terms of his career, he is known for some iconic roles and for generally adding pizzazz to whatever film he is in, so he's not just known as 'famous for being famous,' a kind of hollow celebrity. He seems like a living meme—something unexpected, usually wonderful, or puzzling, with a uniquely strong image."

They're both onto something.

By doing only what interested him (let's put it this way: the guy went from *Jurassic Park* to a stint on *Law & Order: Criminal Intent* to *Tim and Eric's Billion Dollar Movie* to a tiny arc on *Glee*), Goldblum has created an image of himself as genuine—either inadvertently (thus authentically, which some who know him believe to be the case) or purposefully (but skillfully enough to make it seem inadvertent, which others believe to be true and which would be a tremendous feat requiring one to spend one's entire life in the role of oneself, rather than just being oneself). Either would be an impressive accomplishment. It's no easy task to come off as "real" in the social media age, but it's also an achievement that is uniquely Goldblum, a man who forewent an almost guaranteed decade or two of superstardom to follow his own weird, confounding muse.

So, how did he pull this off?

Let's find out, but I have an idea to start with: because he's *Jeff Goldblum*.

INTERLUDE #1

Behind the Writing, or Inside the Writer's Studio / An Introduction to Interludes / And Also an Interview with Jeff Goldblum That Never Actually Occurred

This seems like as good a place as any to explain how this book was put together. The part I did, not the literal binding process, obviously, which I know nothing about and would need a Goldblum character to explain to me. Here's the general formula: I spent about a year consuming every interview the man has ever given, reading every piece ever penned about him, speaking to dozens upon dozens (upon dozens, and so on, and so forth) of his friends, his collaborators, his colleagues, journalists who covered him, and the like. I also spoke with experts on films and fame and all that good stuff. When appropriate, quotes were edited for clarity and brevity, which is a fancy journalist way of saying I removed all the *umm*s and *like*s and *uhh*s and such. The stories and anecdotes and quotes and laughs and tears contained herein come from that research. You can see which interviews and pieces I referenced and quoted by chapter in the bibliography, which is that boring section in the back that will trick you into thinking this book is a *little* longer than it really is. Sorry about that.

Despite the best efforts by the author (hey, that's me!), Jeff Goldblum was not involved in the creation of this book—though his manager was extremely kind when breaking my heart and informing me he wouldn't be. That means it's *unauthorized*, making this the most punk rock a celebrity biography/consideration/examination/celebration can be. Given, though, our subject's penchant for jazz music, we'll approach it as a literary version of that genre. This will prove to be less confusing than it sounds. There will be tangents. Oh, there will be tangents. Sometimes this book will focus deeply on projects you might never have heard of (but that are generally more interesting than the ones you *have* heard of). Goldblum will not be wearing his shirt (textually) for much of the book, which will hopefully entice some readers.

If I had to come up with some sort of saccharine mission statement for this whole enterprise, something to discuss during book club, then it would go a little like this: I hope your takeaway is that it's possible, perhaps even more likely, to become a beloved (and, more important, happy) Famous Person by generally doing the right thing and being your authentic self. Awww, I know, I know. But it's true. If there were a second mission statement, then it would be that I hope I managed to cut out all the boring bits. Let's be honest: biographies can feel a lot like being forced to grow, cultivate, and eat your vegetables! This one will hopefully feel more akin to a Netflix binge accompanied by a pint of Häagen-Dazs. Yes, I clearly have high standards. Finally, it is my deepest hope that Goldblum will read this book and decide he loves it and then tell everyone to read it, thus propelling it to the top of the *New York Times* bestseller list and ensuring that I will get to write many more books, which would make my mother and my girlfriend happy, which is really the whole point of doing this anyway, right?

Before we go any further, though, let me tell you about libel! Early on in journalism school, everyone learns about a little thing called libel. Basically, that refers to printing false statements that damage a person's reputation and is a great way to get sued and fired and defamed and all that good stuff. But here's the thing. Goldblum has given interviews to just about everyone in the world but yours truly, and this is a book about him, so to not have an interview with the man just didn't sit right. So, my deepest apologies to the wonderful professors at my alma mater Louisiana State University, but I've decided to just go ahead and make one up. I mean, I've watched, read, and listened to so many interviews with the guy that I think I can basically imagine how an interview would go. To be completely clear, here's a disclaimer: THIS IS A WORK OF FICTION. THIS INTERVIEW IS NOT REAL. PLEASE DO NOT SUE ME, MR. GOLDBLUM, AS YOU HAVE WAY MORE MONEY AND POWER AND ALL THAT THAN I DO.

Anyhow, I'm pretty sure an interview would go something like this . . .

JEFF GOLDBLUM: Ahh, so nice to meet you, Travis. Can I call you that? Travis? Hold on one moment.

TRAVIS MAGNER ANDREWS: Well, yeah, I mean, it's my name . . .

JG [to waiter]: Yes, yes, I'll have the fish here . . . but I'd like you to take the oil you would use to cook it, mix it with some butter, and give that to another table. Instead, cook my fish in spinach and coconut water if you don't mind. Also, if you could substitute the fish itself for jackfruit, I'd be [purrs] mighty obliged.

JG [to me]: Now, with that out of the way, we can focus on *us*! Tell me, if you will, how did you come to write a book about me?

TMA: Well, I wrote a piece for the *Washington Post* about you, and a wonderful agent, Laurie Abkemeier, called out of the blue and said the world needed a Goldblum book. I've always wanted to write a book and would like to publish some fiction later, so it seemed like a good idea...

JG: Can I offer some advice? It's this: you should never be careerist. I'm not and look where I've gotten. See, when I was a child, I harbored this secret desire to be an actor, and every day after taking a shower, I'd scribble on the bathroom—

TMA: Oh, no, I'm aware of that. Don't worry. I'd rather chat about where you've gotten. I'm curious as to—

JG: Well, as my acting teacher Sandy Meisner always said, "You're only interesting to the point that you're interested," and he also said, "It takes twenty years to call yourself an actor," so I feel I'm on the verge of my best work yet. Would you like a Halls?

TMA: I haven't asked a question.

JG: Oh, let me see those hands! You know, you look like a young Seth Rogen *[purrs]*.

TMA: Uhh, is that... meant to be insulting?

JG: Oh, no, no, no! Look what you've done with your little beard, especially this patch in the middle of your chin where there's no hair. How original! It's like an anti-soul patch! And *[taking my hand]* look at these fingers.

TMA: Could you put down my hand? I'm a little self-conscious, I have to admit, since they're kind of short and stubby and—

JG: Ahh, just like beautiful vegan Vienna sausages! How exquisite, and *sooooooo* strong from all that clicky-clack, clacky-clack-clack *[pantomimes typing]*.

TMA: I don't think this is going well.

JG: Oh, sure it is. You know, this all reminds me of Michael Corleone doing . . . *something.*

TMA: What reminds you of Michael Corleone?

JG *[while purring]:* ***Everythiiiiiing.*

TMA: Okay, look, so this isn't going great. But I need to ask. My buddy Colin Daileda and I wrote this pilot about a newsroom called *Interns*, and we'd love for you to—

JG: Hey, did you ever see that movie *The Paper* with Michael Keaton? He's from my hometown, Pittsburgh, did you know? Anyway, doesn't that sound terrific, this *Interns* project, just marvelous, you know, but I have to get a ring fitting before swinging by a vegan dairy farm on my way home. First, though, would you like to see a magic trick?

TMA: Those don't seem like real—

[Jeff Goldblum begins to exit while performing a magic trick involving a rope, when he spots a piano. He sits down and plays for seventeen hours, never resuming this interview.]

The Origin Story

Jeff Goldblum is an entire universe unto himself.

To reduce the man to a label as simple as "Hollywood superstar" would be an injustice. No, much like our pal Walt Whitman, he contains multitudes. For the moment, let's set aside his accomplished jazz career, his considerable romantic history, and his enviable dexterity as the world's most delightful talk show guest (rivaled only by Norm Macdonald). Let's set aside the delightful way he talks, always improvising, almost like the jazz he plays, which naturally means setting aside the delicious* fact that he once began a Q & A by saying this: "I must ask, what is, what's 'Q' in reference to? 'Q,' I know in James Bond movies there was a 'Q' and he was the funny guy

---

*Goldblum has such an affinity for using "delicious" as an adjective that it has quickly wormed its way into my own writing. What can I say? It truly is a pretty delicious modifier!

who gave him all the gadgets. Wait a minute, does it have something to do with that? No. Maybe it's 'Q' for 'question man.'"

Which means we also must set aside the fact that, when the letters "Q" and "A" were then defined for him, he responded, "Ohh, so you're doing a show called Q, and I'm doing a show called A. . . . We'll mix them up like chocolate and peanut butter and see how they go together."

What's most impressive is how the lanky actor has become an ever-evolving part of the English lexicon.

Seriously.

A great part of the research for the book you are currently reading came in the form of poring through decades' worth of writers' grasping to decipher this walking riddle of joy, and one thing became quickly and abundantly clear: writers *love* to change his last name into an adverb, adjective, noun, or—in the rare but thrilling instance— verb. Seriously, they love it more than describing what female celebrities are eating and wearing, making oblique sports references for no apparent reason, and quoting David Foster Wallace.

A few common tropes for writers—myself included, I won't lie— are discussing the Goldblumian nature of his persona, musing about his Goldbluminess, and terming things Goldblum-esque. Because there's simply no other way to describe a man who is so wholly himself.

Every universe, of course, must begin somehow. So what was the Big Bang igniting the Goldblumverse?

Goldblum was born in 1952 in West Homestead, a small borough eight miles to the south of Pittsburgh better known for pumping out factory men and steelworkers than quirky Oscar-nominated actors with a penchant for tickling the ivories. (Goldblum described

the area as "smoky and evocative," and while it was definitely the former, it's easy to argue it wasn't the latter.) And when I say small, I
mean *small*. The borough (really an extension of the city) is about one
square mile and that square mile contained the Goldblum family,
which consisted of patriarch Harold Leonard Goldblum, matriarch
Shirley Jane Goldblum, and four children: Jeff; his two older brothers, Rick and Lee; and his younger sister, Pamela.

To many in the area, the sextet represented the picture-perfect
family, a modern-day equivalent of the Cleavers. Harold worked as a
doctor to the area's steel-mill workers, often making house calls, while
Shirley mostly tended the home, a brick Colonial with a baby-grand
Steinway in the living room and a multicolored upright in the basement. Many decades later, when the actor became popular enough to
publicly remember his childhood, he tended to emphasize nice small-
town details that make it sound like something out of *The Donna
Reed Show*. He talked about going to Joe Jerry's candy story "with
that great candy that wasn't retro then" or his frequent visits to a diner
called "Estok's, where [he] had lunch every day, a BLT and coconut
custard pie or a cheeseburger." He explored the dinosaur exhibits at
the Carnegie Museums with his pops and trounced through the nearby
woods at Chatham College with Pamela, where the two sat by the fish-
pond there while munching on cream cheese and olive sandwiches.*

---

*Strange as it might sound, the many sandwiches of his childhood often pop up in the Gold-
blumverse. During a Reddit AMA, he was presented with a simple question: "What's your favorite sandwich?" This was his typed response, verbatim:

Ooooooooh. SANDWICH. OH MY GOSH.
Oh my gosh.
I love sandwiches.
*When I was a kid, every day I had a bacon lettuce tomato sandwich. Then at some point I switched
to tuna fish sandwiches. Then turkey and swiss with russian dressing. Now I try to stay in the
healthier vein, but I love every moment of my sandwich life.*

He and his childhood best friend, Buddy Dee, played a game they dubbed Mill, seemingly after the steel mills in the area. The rules were simple: they would dig holes in the woods. And . . . that's it. Chutes & Ladders is more complicated (but probably less fun).

At home, he often sat in his bed, listening to the trains rush through West Homestead. He once described that sound as "a lonesome-hollow, plaintive sort of thing," because he's Jeff Goldblum, and that's the alluring way Jeff Goldblum talks about ordinary things. That "zzz-oooo" noise "was very evocative of the promise of poetry and the future," he added, because of course he did.

This almost innocuous image of familiar innocence wasn't lost on those who knew the family, at least those who knew them from afar.

David Beistel, friends with his older brother Lee, recalled visiting the house, his nostalgia-tinged voice filling with excitement as he described shooting pool in their back room or hanging around the family's actual pool during the city's balmy summers.

There were, as Beistel was quick to point out, a few particularly notable things about the Goldblums to the community. For one, they were Jewish ("He was the first Jewish person I ever met"). Harold's father, a Russian Jew, had emigrated to the United States bearing the last name Povartsik. He "had a little candy store and sold some luggage, didn't really want to learn to drive and that kind of stuff." Goldblum's mother, meanwhile, had been born to an Austrian Jewish father. All of which would have been a moot point if their home had been in Squirrel Hill, along with most of Pittsburgh's Jewish population, but they were in West Homestead. Goldblum said, "I was the only Jewish fellow in school . . . I was a little bit unlike other people."

He also made it clear that this "otherness" didn't deeply affect him, that he doesn't want to make more of it than it is. So, by all accounts, this seemed like your typical American family.

But, as is always the case, as perfect as the family seemed, there was more bubbling beneath the surface. Goldblum's own recollections certainly hint at some odd goings-on in that house on Lynnwood Drive. He once described that part of his life as "a whole Philip Roth novel that I'll only skim the edges of."

It's difficult to decipher quite what that means, especially since he tends to speak about it in a manner that can best be described as charmingly evasive. But whatever that means, it's likely a big factor in what made Goldblum so, well, Goldblumy.* As he put it, "There were seeds of my strangeness early on, but I wasn't in possession of that until much later."

Those seeds may have come from his parents. Beistel never saw Harold around much during his visits. The house calls and that darn Hippocratic oath kept him busy. Goldblum's own recollections of his father are mostly positive. He remembers Harold as a "very authentic, real sort of guy with a big work ethic. Lovely." The two bonded at Steelers games, and Goldblum remains a rabid fan of the black and yellow.

But he also recalls Harold's temper. In 1992, *People* ran a profile of the actor that stated, "Jeff was raised on a diet of fear."

"There were beatings with belts, and there was always the threat of a beating," he told the magazine. "It was terrible and abusive. I hate the whole system of being quiet and keeping in line. By the time you're I don't know how old, life has chained you up in some way."

Years later, his memories of his dad appeared to have softened, even if the through-line remained the same. He has bluntly said, "I wish I hadn't said that," referring to the alleged beatings, adding that *maybe* they happened once or twice. He walked it back even further when he told Marc Maron of his dad: "Sometimes, he'd blow . . . and he'd whip off his belt sometimes." This time, though, the statement

---

*See, I told you I've succumbed to doing it, too. What can I say? I'm only human, after all.

came with a clarification. "The threat was always there. . . . [But] it's not that he beat us. I'm not saying that."

The true star of the Goldblum clan, though, was Shirley. That's who really titillated Beistel, as he recalled to me decades later: "She was a force of nature," he said. "In my estimation, she's the most beautiful, classy woman I ever met in my entire life . . . and she could swear like a sailor." He added, "Jeff was the apple of his mother's eye."

Sharon Eberson, who has covered the arts for the *Pittsburgh Post-Gazette* for years, had another phrase for Shirley, dubbing her a "wild woman."

Wild or not, she certainly seemed to embody some of the most endearing, enduring, and endemic stereotypes of the 1960s. "She would vacuum the house naked," Goldblum said. "Our general credo was the human body is—in the new freedoms, this is in the new freedoms era—fine and dandy." She "also was given to a complicated and probably unrealized sexuality, I'm just guessing," he added. She also grew marijuana in the backyard and, according to Goldblum, "smoked a lot and wanted to smoke with us. She wanted to be part of the youth-culture thing. She was kind of youth obsessed." After all four children left the house, she became a sex therapist and then a local radio personality.

Meanwhile, there was Goldblum, an athlete, yes, but also a self-described "geek"* who was generally quiet in his youthful years and

---

*The term *geek* followed him well past middle age, which isn't surprising considering his most popular acting credits involve dinosaurs, aliens, and *multiple roles as a scientist*. Only reinforcing this notion is the fact that he partnered with National Geographic for a series titled *The World According to Jeff Goldblum* in which he explores the history of everyday objects. Though, when confronted with the term in 2016, he balked. "Do you know what the original definition of a geek was?" he asked. "A geek was a circus freak who would bite the heads off chickens. I am not a geek." (Writer's note: Knowing this fact doesn't really help his case. Deep down, I think we all know he's a total geek.)

dreamed of escape. "Teenagers coming into their interesting years. I was separating myself out," he said, "getting my own identity. Then in 11th and 12th grades at West Mifflin North, I stayed to myself and just planned on getting out."

Instead of being the overtly social guy we know now, the young Goldblum spent the time consumed by the arts, which his parents introduced him to. Both Harold and Shirley had creative aspirations of their own. Harold wanted "to rise up and to be an American—he was going to either be a doctor, as one did, or an actor," Goldblum said. So he tried to do both, kind of. He "stuck his head in the back of [an acting] class of Carnegie Tech, which it was then called . . . and said, 'It was out of my league,' whatever that means." Shirley, meanwhile, put her dreams aside to raise her four children.

The couple would take frequent cultural pilgrimages to New York City, returning with new jazz albums and bright yellow *Playbills* that enticed their young son. He would listen to the albums while his father detailed facts about the musicians. They particularly enjoyed the homegrown Erroll Garner. Harold would tell his son, "Listen to this guy. He sits on a phone book. Listen how he pauses and what he does with octaves."

As a boy, Goldblum was particularly drawn to the theater, seeing productions like *Beauty and the Beast* and *Hansel and Gretel* at the Pittsburgh Playhouse, a venue Allan-Lindblom said was "held together with duct tape and determination." He enjoyed them well enough, but it was his first taste of adult theater, the comedic *Beyond the Fringe*, that made him sit up and take notice. "I remember getting sweaty, thinking, 'I'm going to jump up and get involved in the show!' I didn't, but it was a close thing. I was stage-struck. . . . There's nothing as powerful as live theater, the innocence and poetry of it."

Even blockbuster films tickled his fancy.* When he was around eleven years old, he went to what he called his "first Event Movie," 1963's *King Kong vs. Godzilla*, in a multistory movie palace. "All three balconies were packed. Kids were screaming. Popcorn boxes were flying. You couldn't hear a thing. It was a semi-riot. I still dream about it."

His parents didn't just expose him to the arts but also promoted them, enrolling their children in lessons of all stripes from a young age. When Pamela was eight and Jeff was ten, for example, they took Tam O' Shanter art classes on Saturdays at the Carnegie Museum of Art from Joseph Fitzpatrick, the legendary instructor who taught artists such as Annie Dillard, Andy Warhol, and Mel Bochner. Fitzpatrick would lecture the children before giving them a drawing assignment, encouraging them to spend time sitting on the museum floors and studying the work hanging in those halls.

"He gave us a space where it was safe to be our most creative," Pam Goldblum said of the always besuited Fitzpatrick. But that doesn't mean he was lenient, as evidenced by the formal dress code he insisted upon. "God forbid you should wear jeans," she added.

Fitzpatrick, whom Goldblum called "a wonderful, classy, elegant, talented guy who was different from anyone in Pittsburgh whom [Goldblum had] come in contact with," made quite the impact on the boy. As journalist Cristina Rouvalis wrote, "the biggest honor for any student was to have your art selected as one of the outstanding works and be invited to recreate it the following week on stage."

Naturally, one week, Goldblum's piece was chosen, and the moment in the spotlight stuck with him. "There were thousands of kids

---

*For any students reading this for tenth-grade American lit: this is called FORESHADOW-ING. Don't say I told you.

in this thing, and eight or ten got called up to reproduce a picture from the week before on an easel in front of everybody and then talk about it," he recalled, before adding one of his signature understatements: "The first time I got picked was a memorable school experience."

Meanwhile, he was taking piano lessons, first with a local instructor named Tommy Emmel. He didn't take his studies too seriously at first, what with their monotonous chord memorization and dreadful scales exercises. But then his teacher "gave [him] an arrangement or two of something syncopated." He said, "I don't think I even knew that word before. It was 'Alley Cat.' There was something about that that just stirred my innards, mysteriously and naturally. And then 'Deep Purple' and 'Stairway to the Stars,' with interesting chords that really got to me, and I was like, 'Jeez, I gotta just sit and practice until I know this thing, because I love it.'"

As he grew more obsessed with jazz, he and his parents found an instructor who gave lessons at a professional level, local jazz pianist Frank Cunimondo. By that point, Cunimondo was something of a local legend, who could be found playing his music in clubs around the country and even on television, such as on *The Tonight Show Starring Johnny Carson*. Though he now teaches at the University of Pittsburgh, at the time he only gave lessons to those who solicited him and were serious about the craft.

"He was a great student and had a lot of natural talent. He always came to his lessons totally prepared and with a smile," Cunimondo said. "He's a very special person; I realized that when he studied with me. As soon as he would come for a lesson, the studio would brighten up. He was always smiling, always had a joke to tell. Very unusual person for his age, very mature."

Goldblum holds his many mentors in a sort of respectful reverence, always being sure to mention them in interviews even now, some fifty-plus years later. In this case, Cunimondo returns the affection.

He said that he sees his former student "on the tube nearly every week" and has spoken to him here and there over the years. His takeaway: fame didn't do a damn thing to change the teenager he knew.

"The time he studied with me, he was the same as he is now. Hardly anything has changed, except his haircut is a little gray. But he's the same person, with the great personality he has: cheerful, very happy, energetic and with a great sense of humor. I don't think he ever had a bad day in his life."

Though piano lessons struck a chord* with Goldblum, he proceeded to follow every muse that appeared, which soon led to the tap and jazz dancing lessons through which he began to realize one of the more enjoyable aspects about being involved with the arts: the women. The revelation came backstage during a performance when he was around thirteen years old and shared a dressing room with the girls. As Goldblum recalled to his hometown newspaper years later: "And I remember some wide fishnet stockings and thinking, 'This is a good thing, to be in show biz!'"

But liking the idea of show business and actually fostering a burning desire to be an artist of the screen are on widely different ends of the same spectrum. Who among us growing up *didn't* like the idea of show business? Since I can remember, I've imagined myself wielding an electric guitar and belting out insane solos while singing introspective songs to thousands that divulge some deep truth about both the world and myself. And I'll admit it: I still do. But guitar lessons lasted all of three weeks when I figured out that switching from a G to an A hurt my stubby fingers, and the only song I could learn to play was "Seven Nation Army."

The difference, in other words, is huge. It's easy to see a movie and

---

*I know, I know. I'm sorry. This isn't even the last time I'll do this.

want to be the thing you've just seen. That's why there's no place more dangerous than the highway the weekend a new *Fast and Furious* movie hits theaters. But desiring something enough to spend a lifetime pursuing it is a whole different beast.

Goldblum seems to have pinpointed the moment everything changed and he shifted from the first category to the second, though the story, which he tells often, is slightly suspect. Sure, he always presents himself as the real-deal, authentic person truly showing that primary, private, *real* self. "I'll tell you anything; I'm an open-faced sandwich,"* he said when he appeared on *WTF with Marc Maron*, a podcast that's become an (in)famous place for Famous People to expose their struggles and darkest secrets. And he may well mean that. But he's still a celebrity, and one of the first notes in the Celebrity Instruction Guide is to find a relatable story from your past and hone it into a precise little nugget of empathetic faux openness, one that's always available to be dropped in an interview as an easily remembered origin story. (Think: Bruce Wayne witnessing the murder of his parents but way less traumatic.)

This sort of origin story might appear shallow or glib, but it's a necessary evil, a product of having to answer the same question hundreds of times over a few decades. Whether or not it's 100 percent true doesn't matter. These stories form our image of him through repetition. It's like listening to a song on a worn-out album that skips here or jumps there. That version *becomes the song*. Some of those nuggets can never be fact-checked, but Goldblum has said them so many times in places like *People, Entertainment Weekly,* and the *New York Times* Style section, at this point they're capital-T Truth.

This one involves a shower, a bathroom mirror, and a finger. And,

---

*See? Sandwiches, again!

yes, I know Goldblum tends to activate the dirtiest part of most psyches, and I know I just created in your mind's eye the image of a young, svelte Goldblum in a steamy shower doing things I refuse to put on the page, but please pull your head out of the gutter. The story is more like an aspirational children's story than checkout-line smut.

But which story is real? Honestly, Goldblum has told the anecdote to so many publications during his decades-long career, you could toss a dart at a stack of magazines and would have a good chance of hitting it. So let's pick one. How about the (delightful) version he told *GQ*'s then–editor in chief Jim Nelson on the magazine's *Mad Influence* podcast?

"I wanted to be an actor when I was like ten years old. My dad had said if you find something you love to do [then] that may be a lighthouse and a compass, et cetera et cetera, for your vocational choice, and around fifth grade I took part in this summer camp . . . they put me in this drama program, and I did the show.* And after, I was so exhilarated. My parents said, 'How'd ya like that?' And I was like [Goldblum noises], 'Yeah, I really liked it.'

"But I kept it secret, but it was then that I developed this notion and obsession and passion and idea that I was gonna be an actor."

Note: That's not the story. That's the prequel. It's better than those *Star Wars* prequels, so quit acting so disappointed. Here's the actual story, from the same interview, the one with the shower et al.

"Around ninth and tenth grades, I took this other summer course at Carnegie Mellon University. . . . Then we had real professors from the college that year and students from all over the country. I felt

---

*He once wrote of his first performance: "My first play was *Belle of the Balkans* in summer camp. It was a spoof of a Gilbert and Sullivan operetta. I played the lead character. I wore plaid shorts and had a camera around my neck. The audience laughed a bit, and I was exhilarated. Acting became a passionate obsession."

enlivened and inflamed by that. This is my thing. And at that point, I started to write on the shower door every morning when it steamed up, 'Please, God, let me be an actor.' And then I'd wipe it off before anybody could see it, because it was still a secret. But I had this, you know, I was like I need to do this very badly. . . . The fuel from that seed has possibly attracted this life that I've managed to affect."

The many, many iterations of this story differ slightly. In some retellings, he wrote, "God, let me be part of this," referring to the acting world he encountered at Carnegie Mellon (which, fun fact, included a young Ted Danson, who made Goldblum feel as if he belonged at CMU the day he said, "Hello, Jeff," as the eager young boy introduced his folks). In others, it's more of an active plea dripping with the desperate need to act, along the lines of "Please, God, *make* me an actor." But the two constants are (a) he wanted to be an actor from the depths of his soul, no matter what, and (b) he didn't feel comfortable telling anyone yet, because telling anyone might ruin the whole thing.

Part of his inclination toward secrecy might have been that he wasn't really in it for the fame. Being stopped on the street by rabid fans waving pens and photographs at him, wishing for an autograph? That's not what acting is to Goldblum, and it certainly wasn't then. Instead, he felt it could become a "spiritual, humanistic, soulful, magical, mystical journey. Not, 'Hey, love me, love me, I need to be loved.' It was about something else."

Music was also something else. While it was another medium that transported him, as it still does and likely still will until he sails off this mortal coil, he felt more comfortable sharing his passion for it with others than sharing acting.

He always had, after all. Visitors to his house, such as Mildred

Snitzer, a friend of his mother's after whom he would later name his jazz band on a whim, remembered a prepubescent Goldblum tinkering away at the ivories when she would come visit the house for dinner every Tuesday night after being widowed.

By his midteens, he had gained enough confidence in his musicianship that he wanted to play for crowds, leading to the practical question of where one finds crowds willing to listen to a teenager play any piano, much less jazz, in the suburbs of Pittsburgh. West Mifflin North was an option, and his classmates remember his playing during morning assemblies. (Whether or not he played "Hey Jude" or "Come Together" in the gym at a pep rally after the basketball team took home the championship, while his classmates gathered in a swaying, joyous circle, remains a focal point of debate among the alumni of the class of 1970. That's not surprising, considering the patina of fame and time begins to obscure everything at some point.)

Playing a school auditorium might suit an amateur musician, the kind who joins a cover band as an excuse to toss back some cold ones, have a good time, and get in with the ladies. But that's not who Goldblum was (or is (save, maybe, for the ladies)). He's always been an Artist first and foremost, to the point where later in his life he would fret that he had become a "song and dance man." (He worried so deeply that he called his sister and asked, "Am I trying to work my way down the rungs of sophistication and substance?" She responded, "Music, beyond language, comes from someplace deep in yourself and can be offered to somebody in a place that's impactful," a response he deemed "encouraging.")

So he decided to get some more adult gigs. It's another story he enjoys telling and, as a result, has recounted many, many times over. Here's how he told it to Dave Itzkoff of the *New York Times* in 2014:

"I'd shut the door, sneakily, and take the Yellow Pages and look up cocktail lounges around Pittsburgh. I thought I was a scam artist of some kind—I said, 'Hey, I hear you need a pianist there.' Many places would say, 'We don't even have a piano.' Some places would say, 'Well, come over and play, and we'll see.' And I got a couple of jobs that way. Now I'm 15, 16. These are ripe years for the idea of getting involved with show folks and girl singers, too."

At some point, most aspiring actors outgrow their hometown. This was not the case for Goldblum. He was more pushed out. Despite his summers in their theater program, he wasn't accepted to the drama school at CMU. Though the city had given him a rich training in and enviable exposure to the arts, it had given up on him, at least for the time being. If he was to live as an artist, he needed to leave—but he needed a push.

Cue several mentors suggesting he head out to that sleepless city. Lou Snitzer, brother-in-law of the aforementioned Mildred at the time, was one of them. As she told it: "My [second] husband had a brother, Lou, who was one of the old-time talent agents. . . . My husband says, 'Why don't you look up my brother, Lou? Maybe he can give you some tips on how to get into the business.'

"Well, Jeff did that. Lou said, 'Go to New York. Get your feet wet there. And go to school. Then, maybe you'll hit Hollywood.'"

He left home at the ripe young age of seventeen and headed to the big city with dreams of being an actor.

"Lou was right, of course," Goldblum said. "If not for that I wouldn't have gotten away from my family, wouldn't have studied with Sandy Meisner, and then that summer gotten my first job in Central Park and lost my virginity.* So, thanks, Lou Snitzer!"

It's a perfect origin story, when you think about it. An eccentric

---

*Okay, look: I know that's a hell of a thing to drop out of nowhere, so just trust me when I say that we'll *definitely* be revisiting this particular awakening.

mother and a stern father, both of whom wanted to act but never had the chance. A secret passion welling up inside a shy kid, one who felt somewhat othered in his West Homestead neighborhood. A tremendous amount of artistic training waiting to be unleashed. A great disappointment that would turn out to be a blessing in disguise.

It would be difficult to craft a more perfect origin story. So, is it apocryphal? The answer to that is impossible to ascertain, at least until we have time-traveling technology, and even then, to prove part of it, we'd have to plant a camera in a teenage Goldblum's bathroom—and I certainly have no aspirations of landing in jail for breaking both American and time-traveling law.

The fact is that it doesn't matter if it's bullshit. We create our life stories by piecing together bits of our past into a coherent narrative. Goldblum has been a master of the press since his early days, shaping an aspirational story that's enjoyable to believe and believable enough to be enjoyable. So even if it's a little too neat, even if it's not exactly *true*, it's undoubtedly the *truth*.

A Brief but Necessary Interlude
About the Inimitable Acting Teacher
Sanford Meisner

To understand Jeff Goldblum is to understand Sanford Meisner. There was arguably no more important person to the actor's professional, and, in some ways, personal, life than Meisner.

Goldblum had already taken the step of moving to New York City at the age of seventeen, and he wasn't going to let something silly like his being a minor stop him from achieving his dreams, even though he wasn't old enough to take classes. So, taking advice from one of his summer instructors, Mordecai Lawner, he fudged his age to enroll in classes under the famed Meisner at Neighborhood Playhouse School of the Theatre in Manhattan.

For the uninitiated, the late Meisner was one of the most vaunted master drama instructors of the twentieth century. The legendary—and legendarily tough—teacher was a member of the New York City theater collective called the Group Theatre, alongside Harold Clurman and Lee Strasberg, all of whom roughly followed the teaching of Russian theater practitioner Konstantin Stanislavski—before creating their own methods.

Strasberg grew obsessed with Stanislavski's idea of affective memory, the idea of an actor's mining true memories for emotion to then transfer onto a character. It's a central tenet of Method acting, a system that Strasberg was so highly influential in creating, he has been dubbed the "father of Method acting in America."

Meisner, though, pushed against affective memory, instead thinking an actor should develop a character's own emotional landscapes by living in "imagined circumstances." "Actors are not guinea pigs to be manipulated, dissected, let alone in a purely negative way," he said of Method acting. "Our approach was not organic, that is to say, not healthy."

Instead, he created his own approach. His philosophy is often summed up thus, as Ranjiv Perera—the head teacher at the Sanford Meisner Center, the last school founded by the late master, in Los Angeles—told me: "Most acting approaches are too technical and too heady and put the actor into his head instead of making it completely about the other actor . . . The foundation and basis of good acting is human connections, because acting is really about dramatic and heightened moments of life, and when those happen, people feel and experience things—but also connect with the other person."

"You don't have to play at being the character; it's right there in your doing it," Meisner wrote in his utilitarianly titled *Sanford Meisner on Acting*. "It's all right to be wrong, but it's not all right not to try."

Traditionally, actors would study under him for two years, during which they'd participate in several exercises that would help them fully embody the method of "how to really focus on each other."

As a result, "the fundamental traits that people say Meisner actors have is that they're very organic and spontaneous and, most fundamentally, really connected to the other actor."

Despite how admired by and influential to his students the teacher was, to say he could be tough to study under would be an understatement. Perera described him as "a terrifying force of nature," for example. With his froglike croak of a voice, the result of a laryngectomy in 1970, he fired the sharpest daggers in the business, all for the sake of finding excellence in every student.

Here are a few, erm, testimonials (for lack of a better word) he's received over the years:

He was kind of an aloof guy. I met him when I was in the Army, and I said, "Gee, what would be worse: to go fight in Korea or go study under Sandy Meisner?" —ROBERT DUVALL

He was not my father. He was nobody's father. He was your teacher. He was your mentor. He had standards, and you better cut it, or you weren't back. But that was the reality of the world you were preparing yourself for. —SUZANNE PLESHETTE

I don't think I was ever comfortable. I think it was two years of stress and strain, almost unrelieved. Some moments were better than others. Once in a while, you would do improvisation and get a slight nod of approval from Sandy, and that would be a red-letter day. And there were other days when it was disaster. —GREGORY PECK

He always wore a long camel's-hair coat, and the way he held his cigarette was the sexiest thing I ever saw. And that cigarette ash would get longer and longer until it was longer than the unsmoked part. We would just wait for that damn ash to fall while we were all in total agony about whether he would call us up and torture us about our inability to act. He was completely enthralling to listen to, witty and dark, funny and cruel. I never act on stage, partly

because he gave me the lead in Dark of the Moon *one time, and
when I walked onto the stage he said, "Don't enter like Doris Day."*

—DIANE KEATON

He may have been tough, but he was among the best. As Elia Kazan
once said, "Take it from a director: if you get an actor that Sandy Meisner has trained, you've been blessed."

Goldblum is clearly among those blessings. He brings his former
teacher up constantly, and it explains a lot about him. Here, in a nut-
shell, was his takeaway from Meisner: "This improvisation entails what
he calls working off of the other person, so that you're not bedeviled by
self-consciousness and imprisoned with self-consciousness, which is a
natural byproduct of being witnessed and wanting to do good and
make an impression or be interesting, being worthy of other people's
interest. [It's all] based on the principle you're interesting to the extent
that you're interested."

Judging from decades' worth of profiles, this is clearly a quality
Goldblum imbued himself with, carrying it far beyond the stage. More
often than not, when he sits down for an interview, he immediately begins asking the reporter questions, rather than the other way around.
As a result, he's earned a reputation in some journalistic corners as
being coy and evasive, as if it's an act. Maybe it is an act, maybe not.
Regardless, there *is* something truthful about the way he acts. The line
between fact and fiction can be as thin as an atom, especially when
following a technique that requires you to be true to a character regardless of what's happening around you. So it doesn't feel so much
like his potentially cagey behavior is manufactured, but rather, the
Meisner technique has simply become part of Goldblum's DNA. Is he
acting? Probably somewhat. Who the hell among us isn't?

We could dive much deeper into the Meisner technique, of course, but there are other books about that written by much smarter (or, at the very least, nerdier) people than me. So just know that, if you have to boil it down (as many often do), then the Meisner technique gives actors "the ability to live truthfully under the given imaginary circumstances."

Now back to our regularly scheduled programming.

The Early Days

This chapter should probably kick off with some tired aphorism about New York City. Something about how it's a place where anything can happen and often does. A faux-deep line about how it's the city that forces tough life lessons (and quickly!) on unsuspecting newcomers. How anyone can be anything in the Big Apple if only you dream enough or some bullshit. All of that's true to some degree of course, as Goldblum—after getting "a box of an apartment at Sutton Place on East Fifty-Seventh Street" at seventeen years old—would realize during the roller coaster of his first couple years there, ones that arguably changed the direction of his life (even beyond the teachings of Sandy Meisner).

Much of what the city could teach him, though, had previously been imparted by his older brother Rick. Sure, his parents shared their various cultural appreciations with him, but it was Rick who sat the boy down and played Thelonious Monk for him for the first time, when the pianist was on the cover of *Time* in 1964.

After finishing high school, Rick got a "cool pad" in Pittsburgh and fell deeply into the sixties counterculture. Naturally, his younger brother would visit and soak everything up with glee. One time, Rick "said, 'Here's some hash.'" Goldblum recalled, "I'd never had anything before, and he put on *Magical Mystery Tour* and maybe *Sgt. Pepper* and maybe *The White Album*.* I didn't know what the heck was going on. It was like tripping on acid." Not to mention, "he was already kind of a handsome guy, with girls,† so he was kind of guiding me. I looked up to him terrifically."

Unfortunately, Rick's embrace of the counterculture would soon lead to tragedy. Goldblum described him as "a kind of truth-seeker and adventurer and a Hemingway-esque, wanna-be writer." So at twenty-three, Rick found himself at the mecca for such people: in "North Africa, like *Casablanca*, in Morocco." It made sense, since he was "kind of an early hippie, beatnik, bumming around on a beach kind of thing."

There, Rick contracted a virus that spread throughout his body and shut down his kidneys. He died before having a chance at the life he wanted, leaving his young brother, essentially a child who had just moved to the toughest city in the nation, to grapple with loss and mortality—things he shouldn't have thought about for many decades to come—alone.

"Rick was a huge influence on me. Who knows how I'd be different

---

* By the Beatles, obviously. If you don't know this, it's extremely confusing that you own or have borrowed this book.

† For proof that this is true: When Mildred Snitzer was interviewed as a centenarian, as in when she was more than one hundred years old, she said twelve words about Rick. Five of them were: "He was a handsome guy."

if he had lived? It's like chaos theory tells us—a butterfly flapping its wings can change the weather across the globe," he said later.

Butterfly wings, indeed. He said, "I realized the importance of getting a grip, because life is fragile." It seems important to note this is the same year that he took LSD once and mescaline, better known to most as peyote, a few times. He wasn't a huge fan: "It made me think in spectacular and miraculous ways, but it was brain messy. I wanted my full wits about me. I was very serious about acting."

If nothing else, that last sentence is certainly not bullshit.

Still grieving and only partially through his training at the Neighborhood Playhouse in 1971, a young Goldblum auditioned for Mel Shapiro and John Guare's new rock musical, *Two Gentlemen of Verona*, part of Joseph Papp's Shakespeare in the Park series. (And by "auditioned," I mean he showed up because the Neighborhood Playhouse got a call that there was a spot for a tall actor.) Shapiro and Guare put together the book, with the former directing and the latter penning the lyrics of this screwball, often somewhat improvisational take on Shakespeare's famous play.* Galt MacDermot, best known for writing the music to *Hair*, took care of the rock arrangements.

They were immediately taken with the young actor, partially because he seemed nothing like an actor. (This is a good place to discuss just how freakishly tall Goldblum is. Most actors are on the shorter side, appearing taller on-screen than they do on the street. The go-to cocktail party anecdote for proving this is that both Tom Cruise and Al Pacino are only five foot seven, while Goldblum is basically a

---

* A taste of how (in some ways) loose the production was: "John [Guare], he would be sitting on the bus or whatever, and he'd come into rehearsals with stuff written on shopping bags. And I believe he would never say he did but I'M SAYING HE DID," Jonelle Allen, one of the leads, said, laughing. "Ideas on shopping bags and pieces of paper. And I was like, 'This man is mad! A mad genius!'"

colossus at six foot four. Add in his angular limbs and lengthy torso, and he looks like someone who would be more at home on a basketball court than a stage. In still photographs, he almost resembles a clumsy giraffe, even though he's as graceful as a cheetah.)

"We were amused by him," Shapiro told me through a thick New Yawk accent. "He was very odd, offbeat, and we were looking for that in the whole cast. We didn't want any traditional Broadway look or sound, and he made us laugh. And anyone who made us laugh in those days, we pretty much hired."

Their appreciation for him went deeper than that, though.

"I remember vividly when we were casting, and he came in and he looks so much like not an actor. I mean, he was very tall and gangly but sort of graceful. But what I was most taken with is he mentioned that his brother had just died recently," Guare told me. "I felt the death of his brother had made Jeffrey suddenly decide to be an actor *now*. He just took a different path. I felt his brother's death was very involved in his auditioning for the show."

As tragic as the situation was, it set him apart.

"One of the things that touched Mel and I about him was how the death of his brother just came up without any self-aggrandizing way, not searching for pity," Guare added. "It was just a man at a crossroads, and I think that's part of what made Mel and I say, 'Let's take him on.'"

Plus, of course, Guare said, "There was no one in the cast that looked like him. He was just original, and there was something about him that [Shapiro] and I both just trusted." Added Shapiro, "He has that wonderful body, which is very expressive. He'd make a great clown,* or a great mime."†

---

*SOMEBODY MAKE THIS MOVIE NOW.

†OR THIS ONE.

So there he was in the summer of 1971, cast in a rock musical version of *Two Gentlemen of Verona*. Alongside the three leads,[*] Raul Julia, Clifton Davis, and Jonelle Allen, he began rehearsing for the summer staging at the Delacorte Theater in Central Park.

As a result, he left the Neighborhood Playhouse and his studies with Meisner to begin his career as an actor. But while the casting was a vital step, he was still only an actor on his tax returns. He will be the first to say, as he often has, "Meisner used to say that you can't even consider yourself an actor until you have worked at it for 20 years. Then you can say you have the innards of an actor."

Though said innards were missing, he did have a job. And let's be honest, sometimes a job is the most important aspect. Fake it 'til you make it and all that. Looking back at his rise years later, he said, "It was pretty fast. Maybe it wasn't as meaningful as it might have been to somebody who'd struggled more, but it was a charge."

But his costars in the show remember his taking every advantage of his role. Even though he was merely in the chorus (with, as luck would have it, a then-also-unknown Stockard Channing), he absorbed as much information as he could, a theatrical sponge, while keeping his mouth shut.

"Jeff's job was to carry me off- and onstage in his arms. The funny thing about him was he was always so quiet and always so shy, especially while carrying me," Jonelle Allen later said. "So much so that through the years, when I'd see him or hear him talking or whatever, I'd think, 'That can't be the same guy!' because this was a guy who was afraid to pick me up in his arms."

He may have been bashful to some degree, "but he was watching

---

[*] Diana Davila joined the cast a week before it hit Broadway. Oh, and spoiler alert: when you get to the end of this section, the musical hits Broadway.

47

Raul Julia. He was watching [Allen]. He was watching Clifton Davis." Allen said, "He was always like a little hawk. He was watching. He was observing. And he was learning. So what I thought was shyness was him being meticulous."

(One other reason she doesn't always recognize him, she added with a laugh, was "he grew into *that nose*.")

"He was very studious, really following and listening," Shapiro agreed. "You could see him learning." As a result, he was somewhat forgettable to his costars. Clifton Davis's manager told me that "Jeff was a joy to work with and [Davis] has nothing but good to say about him, but that is about it." He didn't remember any stories or anecdotes about the man. That was true of many people involved with the production—"I have no memories of him in the show because he was always watching," Guare said. "He was watching Raul Julia, who was so spectacular, and trying to figure out his role in this brand-new world he had suddenly committed to." As anyone who has seen the man on television in the ensuing years might have guessed, this was one of the last times Goldblum would be a silent observer. His time with *Two Gentlemen* is a quiet relic showcasing just how seriously he took the craft.

He did, however, manage to let loose a little on opening night. It must have been exhilarating, performing in front of such a large audience for the first time—in New York City, no less! But what happened afterward was probably far more thrilling. He went out to dinner with some of his fellow cast and crewmembers, and . . . then his night kept going, ending with, as the common parlance goes, the eighteen-year-old's becoming a man.*

---

*See! I *told* you we'd return to this! If you say nothing else about this book, you can at least say I kept my promises. Yes, it might be strange if someone asks if you can recommend this book, and you respond, "Well, the author keeps his promises." But, then again, this is a strange book.

"There was this woman who seemed exotically older to me," Goldblum told *NME*. "I think she was in her late 20s. Nine or 10 years older than me. She worked in the costume department. She'd been married and was now separated, living in a loft in some place like Tribeca or SoHo. This was all exotic to me. We'd flirted a little bit. After the meal she said: 'Let's share a cab home.' In the cab there was some, uh, um . . . kissing. She said: 'Come to my house.' We went there, and, well, I won't go into all the details but that's where I lost my virginity."

And the next morning, as he put it, he felt "another mosaic piece was laid into the final thing, certainly." He said, "I told her, just before we did it. I said, 'I've gotta tell you, I've never done this before.' She seemed to like that. She said: 'Really? Really?'"

The show—which Allen described as "absolutely magical . . . lightning in a bottle," adding, "We were all a part of something we didn't know we were a part of. I think that's how it is when something's good"—moved to Broadway later that year, offering Goldblum a nice launching pad for a career in theater. And, as we know, Goldblum has repeatedly returned to the stage (usually with better results than the ill-fated *The Music Man*).

If he had stuck with theater, of course, this book probably wouldn't exist. He instead became a Hollywood A-lister, a fact that still awes both Guare and Shapiro, though simultaneously they're not surprised.

"He was so unlike an actor that I was always impressed that of all the people in that cast, he was the one who had the biggest career," Guare said. "He brings an incredible reality to his roles. Not a naturalistic reality, but it's as if he just is not pretending. He's so skilled, but his skill is invisible. It's like he just wandered in off the street, just wandered in from some place."

Not to hammer this point home too much, but it becomes brilliantly clear that Goldblum stands out in both men's minds nearly fifty years later, as Shapiro told me nearly the same exact same thing, complete with the walking-in-off-the-street simile, in an entirely different conversation: "It's a wonder he became an actor, because he doesn't look or do anything like an actor should. Which I guess is why he's so successful. He doesn't look like a person acting. He looks like a person who makes you think, 'Why is he there?' He looks like he walked in off the street."

Allen said, "When we did *Two Gentlemen*, none of us knew who he'd be."[*] Goldblum didn't either. But then there was his serendipitous appearance in the off-Broadway production *El Grande de Coca-Cola*, which Robert Altman witnessed.[†]

His rocket was about to launch.[‡]

---

[*] Allen said that, despite what he became, when she ran into him years later in Malibu, he was that eighteen-year-old again. "The funny thing was that even though he was becoming established by then, he still dealt with me like my guard who was afraid to talk to me and who carried me off- and onstage," she said. "Tell him it's okay to talk to me now!"

[†] As you've probably surmised, this is *so, so* important.

[‡] Yeah, yeah, I heard it too the second I typed it. But I promised a textually shirtless Goldblum, and this is kinda in keeping with that, right?

A Battle for the Title of Biggest Jeff Goldblum Fan, Even Though None of the Contestants Know They're in a Battle for the Title of Biggest Jeff Goldblum Fan

Well, the title kind of gets to the point, so let's go!

MIKE McKELVEY

The Pittsburgh-based tattoo artist jokingly thought that the city's official "Jeff Goldblum Day" in 2004 wasn't enough, so he decided to hold his own, one filled with T-shirts, trivia, and Goldblum-themed tattoo specials in 2018. Other small businesses got in on the fun, and some fans even got Goldblum's face tattooed on their bodies (a shockingly common thing to do). "I'm still holding out hope that Jeff Goldblum just shows up," McKelvey told a local paper at the time. "He has a charismatic quirkiness about him."

Alas, Goldblum did not appear, but the resulting mini-fest was successful enough to warrant another the following year. Only this time, things got interesting: the man himself made a surprise visit. Shock rippled through the shop, shock that can best be summed up by the words of attendee Sara Harvey, who posted a photo of herself and Goldblum on Twitter with the caption: "Jeff Goldblum looked me in the eyes and I forgot how to use my face."

Not many fans can lure the object of their fandom to their very own shop, so McKelvey seems like an early favorite for this entirely made-up award that no one but me cares about. But, spoiler alert, since he's the first one on this list going from bottom to top, you already know he didn't win. Good try, man.

SETH FREEDLAND AND AMY MARSH, CIRCA 2016

What is fandom if not wanting to bathe in the essence of a celebrity as often as possible? The only caveat is that "as often as possible" isn't *always*, an issue Seth eliminated when he asked the Huntley Hotel in Santa Monica if they could fill his room with framed photographs of the actor, of whom his girlfriend Amy counts herself as an enormous fan. The request "was kind of out of the ordinary," David Cohen, the director of the hotel's front office, told ABC News at the time. "But we just wanted to meet it because it was within our realm to do."

What customer service! Five stars!

"Jeff Goldblum holds a special place in my girlfriend's heart. She's a big fan. Amy's foundational affection for Goldblum is the scene in *Independence Day* when he and Will Smith are victoriously walking away from the smoking wreckage in the desert, smoking cigars and laughing as their women jump into their arms. If this whole thing has an origin point, it's that single scene," Freedland told the outlet, adding Amy "was equal parts astonished and delighted. At one point, she grabbed the shirtless Goldblum photo and made a thunderstruck face."

Proof of their fandom? They took the photographs home. Bringing his face into their own (temporary) abode certainly earns a few points.

Extra points for his saying both "thunderstruck" and "foundational af-fection" in the same interview.

AMANDA SCHINKE

Goldblum's an actor, so Schinke decided to watch everything he's ever appeared in and to rank those performances in a variety of categories in a Tumblr blog aptly titled *Watching Every Jeff Goldblum Movie*. There's the Goldblum presence (how much is he in it?), Goldblum hot-ness (self-explanatory), Goldbluminess (we've discussed this word so much that if you don't know what it is at this point, I request you burn my book immediately because you do not deserve it), and Total Gold-blum Rating (a composite of the aforementioned).

The project began in 2010. "I had watched a few Jeff Goldblum mov-ies in close succession and I was talking with a coworker about the notes he pretty consistently hits in his movies—he plays a scientist or a journalist, a shot is clearly framed to show off how tall he is, he delivers a monologue with a quick melodic patter, he plays the piano, those kinds of things," the Brooklyn resident told me via email. "My coworker, who might have just not wanted to talk about Jeff Goldblum anymore, told me to start a blog, so I did. Since this was in Tumblr's heyday, I did it on Tumblr."

She said, "Either nobody would read it, or . . . I would end up with a book deal (after all, this was the era of FAIL Blog and F U, Penguin). Instead, I've ended up with a modest 800ish followers who seem con-tent with my extremely sporadic content."

It's not easy upholding this level of fandom, but Schinke pushes through anyway. As she explained, "On a personal level, the issue with having a half-ironic niche interest and being Extremely Online about it is that, for people who don't know me very well—like old high school or college friends, or my coworkers—it's the one thing they remember about me. So any time Jeff Goldblum ends up in pop culture news, half a dozen people are going to tell me about it or tag me on Facebook, so then my Facebook activity is wall-to-wall Jeff Goldblum and more people think of me as the Jeff Goldblum person. (To be fair, I probably did not help this by giving my 25th birthday a *Come as Your Favorite Jeff Goldblum* theme.)"

On the upside, though, she concluded, "I always hear when there's a Goldblum-centric event to hit up. Alamo Drafthouse did a four-movie Goldblum marathon that I went to; Nitehawk Cinema did a Goldblum film series; and Videology (which has since closed) did a Jeff Goldblum trivia night, which I won."

Major points for the sheer amount of time and dedication here.

EVAN GOLDBERG

It's impossible to know if Goldberg, the screenwriter and director who co-penned *Superbad, Pineapple Express,* and *This Is the End,* is truly a fan of the tall guy, but he certainly should be. As the story goes, Goldblum sat next to a woman named Lisa Yadavaia on a flight. He noticed her finishing a book and, Goldblum being Goldblum, offered to read it aloud to her. The odd experience made it back to Yadavaia's boyfriend, who just so happened to be Goldberg. The writer called Goldblum and asked him to come on over to his house one morning and read a poem he'd written for Yadavaia, one that doubled as a proposal.

The two married not long after, which I *presume* would make them lifelong fans. If nothing else, it must make anniversaries weird.

Placing your *proposal,* one of the five most important things you'll do in life, in the hands of the object of your/your partner's fandom? Definitely earns a few points.

CONAN O'BRIEN

The two always shared a flirtatious relationship—and that's putting it mildly—but when Conan invited the actor to his podcast, things reached a new level. O'Brien asked if he could sit in on Goldblum's therapy sessions, asked repeatedly about his sexual awakenings, moaned in unison with the actor, and said, "I think it's good that there are other people in the room. If there weren't other people, it would be (a) more exciting, (b) scarier."

Finally, he asked Goldblum to dinner. When the actor suggested bringing their families, O'Brien bemoaned the idea, saying, "Wives, they can get in the way."

I mean, this seems obvious. Conan, you might have *also* declined my request to chat, but I remained impressed with your dedication. For that, you earn the award of Biggest Jeff Goldblum Fan. It's better than hosting *The Tonight Show*.

I promise.

Who Needs a Mantra, Anyway?

Careers, according to writers, take the form of one of two things: a rocket ship or a roller coaster. What can I say? We're a creative bunch! Goldblum's could easily be seen as either, so here's the part of the book where I take off my journalist hat (one of those nerdy bowler-ish things with the little piece of paper exclaiming "PRESS" sticking out of it) and place on my critic hat (one of those idiotic floppy golf hats*) to try to decipher what exactly Goldblum's career tells us.

One thing is certain: it was . . . both. Really it was like a rocket

---

*Not, obviously, idiotic if you're, you know, a *golfer*. Also, when the bad reviews start rolling in saying he "tried to do too much" or *whatever*, I'm going to blame this one joke in interviews. I think it'll work. Goldblum returns to his own personal well of jokes again and again, mostly poking fun at himself for being such a ladies' man. This is, like, the same thing. Right? *Right?*

strapped to a roller coaster that blasted off before anyone checked the stability of either the projectile or the tracks it would fly along with abandon. Chuck Klosterman, the cultural critic and prolific author known for such books as *Sex, Drugs, and Cocoa Puffs*; *Killing Yourself to Live*; and *But What If We're Wrong?*, theorized that it was all a purposeful accident, which fits well with Goldblum's insistence that he's never been a careerist. "He accidentally played this perfectly. Like, he could never have done this on purpose, but the way it worked out is almost ideal. You look at his first films, from *Death Wish* up to *Annie Hall*, he has these very small roles in culturally interesting movies that are now interesting when you watch because you don't expect him to be in them. Then there's a period where he's in these really massive movies, where he certainly made a ton of money and probably still makes money to this day from them," Klosterman told me, noting that in those blockbusters, he's added value. Anyone could have played the parts, but he brings something special that helps us remember what could easily have been nonmemorable roles without negatively affecting the films themselves, since his role is a stock character anyway (which he takes to another level). "That allows the rest of his career to basically just be acting, and he could kind of pursue films that didn't necessarily have a natural trajectory. There's no obvious reason why somebody who's in *The Big Chill* is also in *The Fly*. It's not like you make *The Big Chill* to be cast in *The Fly*."

As Sean Fennessey, the chief content officer of the Ringer and host of the movie podcast *The Big Picture*, put it to me, "I view him as a bridge guy. He's one of the few people who has been able to create a thirty-plus-year career for themselves without having to be a star, sort of remaining beloved and present, if not in the center of the frame. Which is rare. He also somehow managed to be unsullied by his participation in the IP wars of the last fifteen years and still found unique and strange parts in interesting films. I also feel like just in the last few years, the kind of cult of him as a celebrity has emerged in a unique way. I don't really remember him having a big reputation as a famous person until the dawn of the Internet. That's when people got that much more interested in the very unique, anxious, specific energy he had."

But in this chapter, we're focusing on the beginning, which started out as a fucking rocket. I apologize for the language,* but honestly, it's apropos. I can't imagine a single Southern, Christian grandmother who wouldn't employ the filthiest existing language if it would somehow gift her grandchild this career debut. There aren't many people who say at seventeen years old, "I think I'll become an actor for real," and then go on to do exactly that. Well, to be fair, there was that *one week*. The one where Goldblum worked the only "real" job he ever had, if you're the kind of person that subscribes to the notion that playing music, acting, directing, and toiling in the arts isn't actually work, which would probably make you the same kind of person prone to saying the phrase "Get a job, hippie!"

He sold office supplies, and it almost killed him.†

Goldblum's burgeoning movie career brought him to sunny Los Angeles in the early 1970s, where he figured he should try to nab a steady income. Most actors struggle, after all. Little did he know at the time that his life path would just skip past the subsisting-on-a-single-banana-and-half-a-can-of-beans cliché that most of his peers would live out.

---

* Mostly to my mother.

† This feels like hyperbole, but it's how he tells it!

"When I came to California in '74, I said, 'I should get a job and get some more money,' or something like that,'"* he told *Vanity Fair*.

"I got a job selling pencils and pens and stationery equipment over the phone. . . . They said, 'Don't use your own name.' It was kind of a scam; it was a boiler room operation of sorts. We called up correctional institutions back East. So early in the morning, we'd get up and say, 'Hi, this is Joe [fake name]. We're from Washington, D.C. We had a government program fall through, so we had a whole surplus of magic markers and pens. Do you use the green or the red?' You know, this horrible sales technique." Once he found out what they used, he then asked if he could send them some. "Well, after a week, I'm such a sensitive type, I wound up in the hospital. Maybe coincidentally, maybe not."

Rest assured, he never worked in sales again. And, unless something catastrophic occurs, he never will.

So aside from that, we're talking about a rocket to begin, one with a seemingly unlimited amount of fuel and an incredible compass that pointed straight north to the best (and, as time would prove, most influential) directing talent in the business—almost by accident. As the man himself said, "I was never particularly careerist, anyway. I was after this wild-hearted, romantic, creative adventure. I'm a lucky guy. . . . I intersected with important directors in some of their most important movies."

That's putting things mildly.

During his first nine years in the industry, before breaking out in Lawrence Kasdan's *The Big Chill*, he worked with luminaries such as Michael Winner, Robert Altman, Woody Allen, David Cronenberg, and Philip Kaufman.

---

* His phrasing here is truly revealing, showing how little he thought about money, even then, in the early days. Must be nice!

"I've become aware I'm particularly, uncommonly lucky, some-how," Goldblum acknowledges. That said, some of his roles aren't ex-actly what you'd call Goldblum-esque, particularly his screen debut. When you think of the man, what are the first adjectives that come to mind? I'll give you a moment. Really. To give you time to think, this next paragraph will be complete and utter tripe—and I don't mean a cow's first or second stomach.

Since I basically forced myself to burn a paragraph while you think, here's another fun bit of trivia you can use: If you watch enough of Goldblum's late-night appearances, which are truly spectacular, you notice he has an affection for throat lozenges. Most of the time, he ex-presses this abiding interest by offering other people a nice, cooling Halls or whatnot. One time in 2013, though, he appeared on Conan O'Brien's eponymous TBS show, seemingly to compliment Conan's bare abs. (The late-night host had just appeared naked in the shower with Chelsea Handler for a sketch, and Goldblum couldn't get over how cut he was. "How have you achieved that, because I happen to know, by the way, if you don't, that you're turning fifty years old to-morrow.* And you've got a six-pack or a twelve-pack or whatever.") As Goldblum began flirting with Conan, as he does every time he ap-pears on the show, he caught his breath. "I almost choked on my Halls cough drop!" he said after spitting it out. When Conan called him out for eating "candy," Goldblum was quick to point out, "It was a Halls! I thought being a little mentholated would give me some vocal warmth." Naturally, Conan accused him of lobbying on behalf of the brand, prompting Goldblum to say, "One has many lozenge choices, and there are many good ones. Fisherman's Friend is nice. Very strong."

---

*Let's just skip over the fact that he might have told Conan that *Conan* doesn't know he's a day away from a milestone birthday. Sure, maybe he was telling the audience, but we can never be sure with Goldblum.

Later, when he guest-hosted *The Late Late Show with James Corden*, he opened his monologue by throwing lozenges to the crowd, as if he were Oprah giving out new cars. So, you know, take that for what you will. There's a 90 percent chance you're craving a lozenge right now.

Okay, anyway! The adjectives, I'm guessing, are "tall," "smoky," "sexy," "fit," "kind," "generous," "nice," "gracious," "stylish," "suave," and, most important, "cool."

Those are good adjectives, because they all describe the actor who is so beloved, a bunch of you bought this book just to learn more about him. But here's the thing: his first role that made it out into the world was the diametric opposite of any of those adjectives, except tall, I suppose.

Put bluntly, he portrayed a nameless, nihilistic murderer and rapist—and he used his few minutes on-screen to do the two things that murderers and rapists tend to do—in Michael Winner's 1974 revenge flick *Death Wish*. No Goldblum charm. No intellectual curiosity. Not even any reason for evildoing other than pure wickedness.

It's like if you started dating somebody and only discovered years later that they used to wear Crocs. Sure, it might *seem* meaningless in the grand scheme of things, but the reality of this person that kept you so giddy your heels were perpetually over your head has suddenly changed entirely. That such a brief appearance could so fundamentally alter his appeal speaks volumes to the dominant feeling we have for the man: glowing and respectful admiration.

While Goldblum undoubtedly earned, and excelled in, the role, it came with a side order of serendipity, at least for Winner. Controversy embedded itself in the basic concept of *Death Wish*—that's kind of the point. But it contained the potential to easily become racially charged, as a newspaper would put it, or *racist*, as the rest of us would. To wit: it was about an older white guy going around New

York City and looking for muggers to kill. Without careful casting, the optics could go south, and quickly.

"When we made *Death Wish*, most of the muggings in New York were committed by blacks and Hispanics because at that point they were the deprived people," the late Winner, never one to mince words or strive for political correctness, told *Vice* in 2009. "The studio was nervous about how we were going to portray these muggers and they told us that we had to be very careful with how we cast them."

At the time, Frank Yablans ran Paramount, the studio producing *Death Wish*—and he clashed with the director. Winner wrote in his biography, "Yablans was concerned we shouldn't appear anti-black. I thought that was anti-black in itself. Because he was saying that blacks were so debauched a race that they'd support black muggers and not wish to see them killed by Charlie Bronson."

Nonetheless, he took his charge and began auditioning potential muggers. They came into his office in small groups, and—there's no polite way to put this, so let's use Winner's words—"had them play a scene where they had to rape a chair."

"It was the first audition that I'd ever had for a movie," Goldblum later recalled. He was given the basics of a scene and "they said, 'Just improvise with a couple other guys.'" "There were fifty other horrible-lookin', mean guys kind of pumping themselves up into a state of hysteria and malevolence. I went in and did what I could. There were no women there, victims, but we pretended to be not nice," he added in a *Vanity Fair* video interview, while pantomiming slashing the air with a knife. "And they liked me for it, I guess."

The auditions certainly sound exciting, for lack of a better word. Wrote Winner: "There was a young man with a knife and dark glasses who looked very odd. Suddenly he took out the knife as if he was going to attack me. One of the other actors jumped on top of him!

A major scuffle ensued in my small office. It was very silly because the fellow with the knife was only play-acting, but you don't draw a knife in a crowded office in New York. There was one young man who was particularly loose and brilliant in auditions. I went to Frank Yablans and Dino [De Laurentiis] and said, 'You don't have to worry about the blacks. I've just chosen the chief mugger in the film. He's a Jew! You won't have trouble from them!' They said, 'Who is he?' I said, 'You've never heard of him. Jeff Goldblum.'"

The actor's first role lasts all of a couple minutes, but it's unforgettable.

So, what happens?

Glad you asked.

In an effort to seek forgiveness from my mother for that terrible language I used earlier (sorry again, Mamabear), I've replaced a particularly tough word he uses with the word "coconuts" in the dialogue below. Here's a hint: the word contains five letters (including an "s" at the end, since it's plural in his usage). All these letters appear in "coconuts." It does not include the second "c" or either "o," and you've got to rearrange the letters a bit. Got it? Okay, good. I'm extremely proud of having saved my mama from further embarrassment.

The scene:

The very first time audiences ever see Goldblum on-screen, he's midair. Freak #1 (or "Unus," as we'll call him, because it's Latin for "one" and a hilarious-looking word) leaps between aisles of a grocery store, a blanket of loose chips hugging his lanky body. He's a bundle of pure frantic energy, never quite standing still. For a second, he rounds another aisle and points—we finally get a full view of the man. Stringy hair bursts from under something like an ascot cap, likely made of suede but with small brown points like a crown, what radio host Jesse Thorn dubbed a "Jughead hat" and Goldblum described as a "jerry-rigged crown out of felt" that he picked out himself. A brown leather jacket, zipped to the top and far too small, hugs his torso (the way so many today wish they could), while too-short jeans do the same to his legs. A yellow ascot chokes his neck, and one of those potato chips sticks out of his mouth like a cigarette. He points down an aisle at a pair of wealthy-looking women.

He and the other two freaks do weird things like throw a frozen turkey around and continue spilling potato chips all over the linoleum floor of the fluorescent-lit grocery. The trio hit the cash register to buy five loose cans of Schlitz beer and one tall canister of spray paint, which one of them waves in the face of a police officer. Unus holds his middle and index fingers to his mouth and makes a physical reference to cunnilingus with his tongue toward the disgusted cashier.

The trio eventually discover the address of those well-dressed women and arrive at the building. One of the freaks says, "I'm going to do a thing," and begins spray-painting a wall, but Unus says, "Shit, man, we got business." Then they pretend to be a grocery delivery service and trick their way inside.

That's when things break bad.

Unus grabs Hope Lange's Joanna Kersey in a chokehold and says, "Nobody gets hurt, Mother. Just hold still. Don't move." When asked about the purpose of his visit, Goldblum's Unus says—and this is true and actually in a movie that you can watch—"Don't jive, Mother. You know what we want."

She does not.

He promises not to hurt her if she hands over some dough, and he looks for her purse while one of his fellow freaks scrawls swastikas in spray paint above the grand piano in the living room.*

---

*Shockingly, Goldblum's character doesn't play this piano. This might be the last time he doesn't sit down to bust out a few chords in a movie.

"Shit, you only got four bucks," he says, returning with Kersey's purse. When she says that's all they have, he responds, "Rich people like you? Shit! We want money, Mother. Now get it!" Then he lifts up his elbow and jacks her in the face, as one of the other freaks says to Kathleen Tolan's Carol Toby, "How'd you like to get fucked? I'm going to stick you in the ass," while forcefully stripping her top off.

Goldblum's freak, meanwhile, mounts Kersey and begins beating her, yelling, "Goddamn rich *coconut*. I kill rich *coconuts*."

The point doesn't need to be belabored further. Eventually Goldblum's character rips his pants off and forces himself into Toby's mouth while yelling, "Open your goddamn throat."

"It's a brutal scene," Goldblum remembered. "I did something in the movie that I did, sort of, in the audience, which was be very jazzed-up as if I'm on crystal meth or something . . . street-disturbed, freakish."

It's horrible, disgusting, and nearly unbearable to watch. Most of all, it's shocking to see *Goldblum* doing all those things. Our Goldblum. Mr. *GQ*. Mr. *Jazz*. Mr. Internet Daddy.

But once you recover from the shocking brutality of the scene, the feeling of disgust is replaced by one of admiration and, in a strange way, one of nostalgia. "I was thrilled to get a part," he said. "I was scared but excited." But as Goldblum's career progressed—and, more important, as his fame grew—he became choosier in his roles. Unlike many actors, that didn't necessarily mean avoiding what some might consider "low culture," such as Comedy Central shows or network procedurals or video game voice work. Instead, though he would likely never admit this, it meant he chose roles that better suited his brand while simultaneously attempting to fulfill his artistic interests. That, of course, isn't surprising. All Famous People do this to some degree. With a certain brand of fame comes the power to write your own public story, to create your own character. So naturally

Goldblum would continue to craft and strengthen his half-savvy, sexy, slightly self-effacing, ultra-charming, aloofly self-aware, and half-serious actor persona.

That he would hone his brand—and one glance at his Instagram leaves no question as to whether he's doing so intentionally—is natural. I know what you might be thinking. Earlier I argued that what we all love so much about him is his authenticity, which might seem antithetical to the idea of his curating an image. But the idea of never taking another role like Freak #1 to uphold a certain public image* isn't inauthentic. Consider this: Every situation in which we've seen actor Jeff Goldblum is inherently inauthentic. Every situation in which we've seen *any* actor is inherently inauthentic. We like celebrity profiles and books like this one because most of them promise authenticity and insight. The lucky few might grasp at the latter, but none deliver on the former, because the former does not exist in the world of fame. So the basic definition of *Authentic* is forced to change, to some degree. Being Authentic means sticking to your brand, because there's a kernel of Truth to it. That's why it felt so insane when Hugh Grant was arrested for soliciting prostitutes but it felt par for the course when Kevin Spacey was repeatedly accused of sexual assault. People teach us who they are, even within a constructed reality. And one thing you can say about Goldblum is that he's never wavered from the persona he created as a young man. Sure, the clothes and the style have changed, but no one can pretend to be something he is not for that many decades without being something of a genius. So not choosing flat roles like Freak #1 throughout his career in order to maintain the image we have in our minds and hearts of Jeff Goldblum isn't inauthentic. It's completely the opposite. Brand building

---

*Which, again, remains a theory—though one that's pretty easy to argue.

can be done sincerely, otherwise no kindhearted nonprofit organization would ever accomplish anything. And consider this: the reason you're reading this book right now is probably because you're much more enamored with Jeff Goldblum's creative and cultural persona than curious what street he lived on in 1976.

And he's aware of that.

So, yes, he'll still take on dark characters but never *flat* ones (save, of course, for when he basically reprised the mugger role in *St. Ives* a couple years later, only this time he was called "Hood #3" and Bronson got to kick the shit out of him). He always adds something to flesh them out, even if just slightly. In 1990, he played a serial killer version of Satan in *Mr. Frost*, but he imbued even that character with subtle charm and charisma, just enough so no one walked away from the theater with sour thoughts of the real-world Goldblum. And in 2019, he portrayed Dr. Wallace Fiennes, a lobotomist loosely based on the real-life physician Walter Freeman, in *The Mountain*. But while he didn't employ that binary gee-shucks/ladies'-man charm, he did tap-dance throughout the film, playing a dark, complicated character with a healthy dose of humanity. That's exactly what makes his very first performance so striking: there isn't an ounce of the Goldblum charm in it. Freak #1, whom we've affectionately named Unus, is pure, guttural evil. And Goldblum, a truly terrific actor, a fact that gets somewhat lost in his Goldbluminess, proves just how horrific true nihilism can be. Which brings in the nostalgia factor. The actor/public persona we've ended up with is a gift, no doubt, but it's difficult not to wonder (at least as a fun thought experiment) what would have happened if he went the criminal route. It's hard to imagine the world's embracing him in quite the same way if he, say, murdered innocent people in his every film.

Goldblum himself is glad he didn't choose to wander that route, of course, though he was prompted by a . . . well, let's say odd and racist agent who told him, "'Well, if you changed your name from Gold-blum to Hernandez, you could get a lot of bad guy parts, because a lot of these, sort of . . .'" the actor said, trailing off. He, of course, declined the offer.

In the end, most of his fans are probably glad too. The online uproar over his playing a lobotomist was loud enough. Just imagine if someone approached you and said, "Did you hear about the new Goldblum movie? He plays a totally unrepentant murderer and rapist with zero charm and no redeeming qualities and says the word *coconut* a lot."

Let's just say he probably wouldn't sell many jazz albums after that.

Goldblum doesn't talk about his *Death Wish* role too often. What would there really be to talk about anyway? But he does enjoy telling one story, because he didn't earn just a career out of his few minutes of screen time but also some poignant, if simple, advice.

Winner, who passed away in 2013, was not the kind of man one would deem "easy to work with" or who always offered particularly eloquent or detailed direction. Let's put it this way: Dinah May, his longtime assistant, wrote a book titled *Surviving Michael Winner: A Thirty-Year Odyssey*. What more do you need to know?

Still, he gave Goldblum a strange gift.

"As I look back on it, I could have done a lot better. I don't know what I did that may have been striking. But I *was* excited. Like I say, I had this fire in my belly from the start. So being on a set was like 'Yeah, let's go' or something like that but [also] 'Jesus, I don't know what I'm doing; this is scary,'" Goldblum recalled. Making it more frightening still was Winner, "the British director, he was known for being abusive and kind of a screamer." He went on, "So as I did my first camera rehearsal, we're skulking up some back stairs to get to this apartment door, he screams at me in front of everybody, 'Goldblum, start acting *nooooooooooooow.'* . . . So I burned with shame and sort of anger, but then I started acting. As it turned out, it wasn't the worst direction in the world. There's not much more to say, really. Start acting now, and that's it. . . . Start pretending and keep pretending."

And so he has, ever since.

The next few years brought a smattering of small roles, including another stint working with Winner in a bit part in his 1977 horror movie *The Sentinel.* The role may not stand out in Goldblum's oeuvre, but it does point to a recurring theme that spans the actor's entire career: directors both admire his talent and adore working with him so much that they repeatedly return to him. Lawrence Kasdan, for example, cast him in both *The Big Chill* and *Silverado.* Philip Kaufman worked with him in *Invasion of the Body Snatchers* and *The Right Stuff.* Wes Anderson has returned to him thrice. The list goes on, but no one worked with him more times than the legendary Robert Altman.*

While *Death Wish* was his first movie to hit theaters, it wasn't his only movie released in 1974. The other, arguably a bigger step in his young career, came about thanks to Goldblum's role in the play *El Grande de Coca-Cola.* Remember our foreshadowing, kids? Well, as he told it, "Robert Altman came one night, sort of by a fluke. He was in New York and scouting for actors. There was a blizzard, and he just came across the street to the Plaza and saw the show and liked me."

That's like hitting the lottery. "Robert Altman was a larger-than-life major film artist and innovative human force," said Alan Ru-

---

*At the time of this writing, in 2019. Wes Anderson could very well surpass Altman in time.

dolph, a director who often worked with Altman as an assistant or second assistant director. "Creatively and socially, his process and persona were as singular and groundbreaking as his work. There was nothing like it. Altman was the mesmeric center of a self-contained renegade film-making universe. His private office chamber/bar/salon was stimulating and stimulated, a constant egalitarian parade of film luminaries and new discoveries." The director, hot off 1970's *M*A*S*H* and 1973's *The Long Goodbye*, decided he wanted to work with the young actor. So, a few short weeks later, he gave Goldblum a call, asking him to play a bit part in *California Split*.

"He flew me out to California for the first time," Goldblum recalled to the *Los Angeles Times*. At their meeting, Altman told him, "'I have this other idea. You were wonderful in the play, and if you like me and I like you, we'd do this thing this summer—*Nashville*. I have this idea for you to be this silent kind of bike rider.' So, we did both things. This was at the height of his powers. He was feeling his oats. He was a brave and fantastic artist. Really what you look for is somebody who can make a good movie, and he was making good movies. And the way he worked was free and naturalistic."

One play, one meeting, and suddenly Goldblum found himself in something of a creative partnership with one of the most important directors in the history of cinema. Goldblum would eventually appear in *California Split, Nashville, Beyond Therapy*, and *The Player*, along with *Remember My Name*, which Rudolph directed. "He was Altman's kind of performer—unique, intelligent, funny, authentic, gets your attention without trying, physical, original, brings something new, up for anything, works well with others, all-around good guy," Rudolph told me. "Jeff stood out. Tall, young but with older sensibility and brainpower, shy and eager at once, mysterious in bearing and movement, deep eyes, wide-screen smile."

What really stands out is how little Goldblum stands out in

Altman's early movies. In *California Split*, he plays Lloyd Harris, a sort of bland, bespectacled, bow-tied, vest-wearing, well, nobody. He's the publisher of the magazine that George Segal's gambling-addict character both works for and blows off. All Goldblum does is walk out of an office, talk to his receptionist, and walk back into his office. The scene clocks in at under fifteen seconds. Adrian Danks, the editor of *A Companion to Robert Altman*, told me via email the role is likely "an intimation of the regard Altman held for him—giving him a credit, placing him front and centre at that moment, already leading towards his more substantive role in *Nashville*. . . . The limited use of Goldblum seems very deliberate, as if he is called onto the 'stage' to only realise that he'll have to wait a little longer for his opportunity. This is reinforced by Goldblum's bright, eager, and natural appearance from out of his office, to be informed that Segal's character has been told he wants to see him but has merely replied with a 'thank you.' . . . He only appears for around ten seconds, but the performance ends with a characteristic smile and a surprising credit at the end of the film (he appears on the list of key players, while others who make longer appearances do not). Plainly, Altman ha[d] ideas of how he wanted to use Goldblum in his next film—and he moved quickly between overlapping projects in this incredibly productive period in his career. So this seems to be holding Goldblum's full introduction in 'abeyance.'"

Plus Altman "obviously also felt that he was someone he would like being around (Altman would not return to an actor unless that was the case)," Danks added. "The fact that Goldblum appears in four Altman films across almost twenty years is a clear indication of the high regard Altman felt for him. Also, I have no idea whether Altman was aware of Goldblum's musical abilities (they certainly aren't used in *Nashville*), but they couldn't have hurt in terms of engaging with and participating in the musical 'forms' of his films (they often have the qualities of jazz and rely on actors keying into this sensibility in some way)."

He gets more screen time but fewer lines in 1975's *Nashville* as a silent biker. Wearing bug-eyed sunglasses and a wide-brimmed hat decorated with glittery palm trees (reminiscent of the one Bob Dylan wore during his Rolling Thunder Revue, which took place the same year), Goldblum's character rides around on a low-rider motorized tricycle, earning his character the name "Tricycle Man" in the credits. "Ever since that old *Easy Rider* movie, that's the kind of bike everyone's been driving . . . long, low, laid-back in the front," Lily Tomlin's character Linnea Reese remarks at one point.

"His character came from a grip on *Thieves Like Us,* who was always riding around on his bike," Altman wrote in his memoir *Altman on Altman,* describing the character as "connective tissue, whose main function was to ride around the city, giving the viewer something to follow as we traverse the city and come to understand the geography of Nashville."

Most of those scenes were shot under the radar, so to speak. Rudolph said, "On a day off just before actual production, Altman told me to sneak Jeff away with a whisper crew and shoot various cuts of him on his chopper which we might use later to tie things together—although Bob hadn't yet shot a frame of the ever-changing real film. There weren't resources or time to get these shots during production (*Nashville*'s total budget was $1.8 million—I know, I made it). So I took a few guys and camera car and shot whatever I thought we might need of Tricycle Man riding around Nashville. It was all used. Jeff as always was inventive and helpful, expertly controlling that cantankerous chopper."

His function "as an almost constantly moving figure," Danks said, "is to help join together the various strands of the narrative. *Nashville* works hard to keep its multi-stranded, networked narrative/form moving forward and Goldblum's character helps provide some of that connectivity (so he has a function such as giving other characters lifts from one place/location to another). He is essentially a linking device—though one that may leave us a little curious about his back-story, purpose, reason for being here—that frames the lack of deep connection at the heart of the film."

On instruction from Altman, Goldblum studied sleight of hand under a magician, a skill he employs throughout the film, such as when he's sitting in a diner and pours salt into his right hand before somehow making it disappear and reappear in his left. "We had Jeff doing all of these magic tricks, but you could just see them. He was not really very good at it, which was our plan," Altman said. He did master this one rope trick, but he didn't get the chance to use it . . . yet.

"Each time Goldblum appears he jumps off the screen—this is partly because of the goofy bits of costume that he wears (which, if true to much of Altman's practice, [Goldblum] may have selected him-self), such as those glasses and his mode of transport (which seems incongruous here), but also because he's probably the most difficult 'major' character in the film to pin down and place. What is he doing in Nashville?" Danks said. "He stands out, also, because his mode of performance is magic—performed casually and for whoever happens to be watching (in this way it is closer to the ubiquitous musical per-formances across the film).

"A key to the memorable nature of this character is its 'out-of-placeness' (though Nashville is a mix of the traditional and the mod-ern, even countercultural) but also the glee that Goldblum brings to his performance," Danks added.

While his fashion and his ride leap from the screen, now, some decades later, we've come to know Goldblum as a gregarious pres-ence, perhaps an enigmatic one but rarely silent—making the perfor-mance one of his odder ones. This could (and has) led critics and fans alike to claim Altman misused Goldblum, eschewing his inherent charisma by making him naught but a living piece of set decoration. And, sure, it's true that we see a character and not Goldblum, but— as reductive and obvious as this might be—that's, you know, the craft of acting. As the actor later said, "After *Nashville*, I saw *Buffalo Bill*. I loved it. The guy who played Sitting Bull hardly talked. Altman said, 'I learned something from him—he had the courage to be empty.'"

It does, though, highlight a paradox. By now, he's *such* a big, unique personality that when he plays against type, fans can be left disappointed. Which isn't fair, but that's part of the price of charisma, particularly now, in an age when the Internet offers tremendous access to the man's every interview/role/etc.

In truth, his roles in those two films—his other work with Altman came after he achieved fame—say more about Altman than about Goldblum. Casting was something of a religion to Altman, the foundation on which his movies were built, which is likely obvious when you consider that he flew our dude across the country for fifteen seconds in one movie and a silent role in another. In one interview, he said, "By the time a film is cast, about 85% of my creative work is finished, because the actors have to do it from then on." Keith Carradine, one of the stars of *Nashville*, added, "I've never auditioned well. It was never one of my strengths as an actor. Bob didn't require that of people. He didn't believe in that. He hired behavior; he hired essence. That's what he looked at."

And what's Goldblum if not essence?

An essence that stayed with the people he worked with, at that. After Rudolph worked with Goldblum a final time, directing him in his own movie *Remember My Name*, he said, "As actor, artist, human thing, Jeff was very special and seemed to me could go wherever he wanted. Guess I wasn't wrong. Because of blowing winds and roads taken, I had no further personal or professional connection with Jeff after that. But experiences and memories, especially the good ones, have their own calendar and occupy perpetual warmth in the heart. Although I personally never quite understood commercial success or standards, the fact that someone as genuinely gifted and terrific as Jeff Goldblum is a big box office star makes me privately proud and plenty pleased."

Most casual moviegoers probably first truly took note of Goldblum—at least enough to recognize his name—in 1978's *Invasion of the Body Snatchers* or 1983's *The Big Chill*, but he first wowed many industry insiders with parts in two small ensemble movies: Paul Mazursky's semiautobiographical *Next Stop, Greenwich Village** and Joan Micklin Silver's dramedy *Between the Lines*. Among those insiders was Woody Allen, thanks in no small part to his long-time casting director, Juliet Taylor, who led casting for those two films. "He was such a wonderfully full kind of character, even as a young actor," Taylor, who, like Altman, had seen a young Goldblum onstage in *El Grande de Coca-Cola*, told me. "He was so good at playing those characters who were out for themselves." Which is exactly what both movies needed.

In Mazursky's film, he plays an actor named Charlie Biletnikoff (but call him by his stage name, Clyde Baxter) who has studied under all the greats (Sandy! Stella! Lee!) yet still finds himself at a casting call for street toughs with a crew of other anonymous actors. Baxter both adores himself and is terrified that the receptionist will skip over him, so he keeps badgering her, trying to figure out when he'll be

---

* Also notable for being the first feature Bill Murray appeared in, though he was uncredited, has no lines, and is on-screen so briefly, you probably wouldn't notice him. A young Christopher Walken was also in the cast.

called. "I believe I was before that man!" he says repeatedly. The pay-off comes later when he makes it to the second step of the process, a screen test with the director, only to self-destruct and be kicked out for talking too loudly—and then arguing with the director.

"I think Goldblum was really wonderful," Mazursky said when revisiting the film to record commentary. "It's a brief part, but he captures a certain aspect of the actor's ego and the paranoia and the whole thing. It's really good."

His six-foot-four frame is on display in the scene, as he must lean over onto the receptionist's desk just to fit on the screen. When he straightens himself, he hulks over the other actors. Absent are the mannerisms we've come to know, the ones we call Goldblumy, the nervous hands and the truncated speech patterns. But he glows with a kinetic intensity that other directors noticed.

The first role in which he had both the screen time and the space to sink his teeth into comedy arrived in Joan Micklin Silver's *Between the Lines*, an ensemble dramedy about a Boston alt-weekly on the verge of being purchased by an "evil" conglomerate. Much of the movie revolves around wannabe Great American Writers Harry (John Heard) and Michael (Stephen Collins). But most charismatic is Goldblum's Max Arloft, a horny stoner music critic who seems fonder of his red satin jacket than meeting deadlines, though he loudly argues he's never filed a piece late. He spends his time hitting on women and selling the promotional LPs he receives to local record stores for petty cash.

Despite the cast's deep bench, Goldblum's hilarious performance stands out, something Silver predicted during casting. "He had one of the most sensational auditions I ever saw," she told *New York*. "He actually became the character."

Comedic performances often expose deep character traits, and this one was no different. Goldblum's love of language is on display when Max gives a lecture titled "Whither Rock and Roll" to a group of young women, potentially groupies. He's clearly winging it, saying things like, "What does the artist do? He does."

Eventually, Max says, "The answer is 'hither.' Some misguided people think that the answer is 'thither,' but they're wrong. Those theories are passé." Noting the potential groupies are writing down his every word, he continues, "They say that rock is here to stay. You've heard them say that: rock is here to stay. They never say where! Certainly not at my house. I don't have the room. My telephone number is 462-0702."

Scribble, scribble, scribble.

The moment that truly stands out comes later, when an overall-clad "artist" storms into the newsroom and breaks the secretary's typewriter by throwing it on the ground. He hands her a card reading, "You just witnessed an act of conceptual art by Herbert Fisk."

"I call it 'The End of Communication,'" the would-be artist says. "I want to be interviewed by Harry Lucas."

While he's talking, Goldblum's Max wanders over to a bulletin board on the wall and throws it to the ground, saying, "I call that 'Paper in Flight,'" thus beginning a conceptual art–off, including "Kicked Coffee Machine, with Punches," "Wall Removed, with Fist and Fingers," "Dead Coffee Machine," and "Stanley, Exposed" (which involves ripping off a confused editor's button-down shirt).

Goldblum mixes his physicality, these erratic movements, with a sly smirk and twinkling eye to puncture the seriousness and tension the would-be artist brings to the room, a skill the actor goes on to employ throughout his career.

The performance certainly caught the attention of critics. At the time, Gary Arnold, the *Washington Post*'s film critic from 1969 to 1984, dubbed Goldblum, along with Heard, the two "most impressive performers" in the film, adding that it would "be a dreadful waste if these two young actors do not get the starring opportunities their skills and personalities deserve."

"Goldblum, cast as a freeloading, slightly manic, wonderfully inventive rock critic called Max Arloff, takes brilliant advantage of the film's richest comic role. He has an unusually sexy, explosive humorous presence . . . there is a constant undercurrent of desperation in his joking and finagling that Goldblum seems peculiarly adept at expressing."

Plus, from the sounds of it, he was a delight on set. Ken Van Sickle, the movie's cinematographer, told me: "He was a pleasure to work with, not just to watch his fine acting but his consistent good mood and humor in the midst of a bevy of different temperaments." Unfortunately, he (and everyone else) declined to explain exactly what that means.

In both movies, he was a lot like a great guitar or piano solo—the thing you were waiting for without knowing you were waiting for it. His mere presence could relieve tension while adding something extra, something he would do throughout his career. Many critics compare him to Christopher Walken in this way. Adam Nayman, a film critic and author of multiple volumes on the medium, including *The Coen Brothers: This Book Really Ties the Films Together*, said, "He's kind of an actor who is almost designed to strike certain notes within ensembles. In that sense, he's a lot like Walken. . . . They're interesting on their own, and they would get to the point where they would carry movies, but you throw them into a hangout scene or a group scene, and they immediately dynamize it. Goldblum is someone who people bounce off, and who bounces off other people. He's a kind of flavoring agent or seasoning agent, and the movies really take on some of that flavor."

"There was something auspicious about him," Arnold told me years after praising his performance in those two films. "Clearly, you wanted to see more of [Goldblum]. He had this odd, sort of detached rapport with whoever he ran into" on-screen. At the time, Arnold thought he would go into comedy. "It's a little curious to me that he didn't become a part of the National Lampoon or the Lorne Michaels apparatus to any extent."

I t was Goldblum's forgetting his mantra in *Annie Hall*, however, that remains the role for which he is most remembered from his early days. Yet it was almost comically brief. Blink-and-you'll-miss-it brief.

This short cameo in a 1977 film became one of many clips to enjoy a second life with the rise of the Internet, and YouTube along with it. "Did you know Jeff Goldblum was in *Annie Hall*?" became one of those *whoa, that's weird* facts that get bandied around dinner parties and Reddit threads. At the time, Goldblum wasn't a household name, not even close, but Allen was taken by his role as Baxter in *Next Stop, Greenwich Village** and decided he wanted a meeting, one that was nearly as brief as Goldblum's role in the film.

"I went in and met him for *Annie Hall*. It lasted 45 seconds: 'Hi, thanks for coming in.' 'You're so welcome. Should I do anything?' 'No, we don't need you to do anything, Jeff.' I wore a workman's beige onesie, which I thought was great at the time. Like a cleaning person's polyester thing, zipped up to here. I'm an idiot in many ways . . . ," he told *GQ*.

Allen hired him to recite the single line, which is exactly what we

---

*Christopher Walken also made the walk in (God, I'm sorry) from Mazursky's film to Allen's. By 2006, the two had appeared in four movies together, but they had never actually met each other. Until, as Walken tells it, they found themselves driving: "I finally met him at a stoplight in Los Angeles. I was at the light, and there's a car next to me, and Jeff says, 'Hey, Chris.' That's how I met him."

see in the film. As Allen's Alvy Singer and Diane Keaton's Annie Hall are leaving a posh party in Beverly Hills, they walk by a young, besuited man (Goldblum) holding a telephone in one hand and running the other through a thick mane of black hair, distressed look on his face. "Hey, yeah, I . . . ," he stammers. "I forgot my mantra."

That's it, though there were other takes that didn't make the final cut.

"The cinematographer said, 'Do the line: "I forgot my mantra." Then you can improvise more if you want.' And I went on a little bit in the few takes we did, where I got into some kind of tiff with [the guy on the phone]. I said, 'Really? Well, you are a jackanapes!' because I'd read something from Shakespeare recently, and I liked the sound of that word." And though Allen didn't talk to the young actor, Goldblum said, "he turned to somebody and said, 'I think that's the first time I've ever heard "jackanapes" in a movie.'"

Of course, given Goldblum's adherence to the Meisner method, it tracks that he went so far as to create a mantra for his character. What that mantra was, though, is one of those great mysteries that make pop culture so engaging, like what Bill Murray whispered at the end of *Lost in Translation* or what that guy in the video for Radiohead's "Just" says that makes everyone lie on the pavement. At least, that's what we must tell ourselves, because he'll never spill the beans.

"I did have something specific in mind. My character was obviously supposed to be a California New Age spiritual type. In fact, I myself was not unfamiliar with transcendental meditation myself," Goldblum told Vulture. "I studied TM. When you're initiated and they give you your mantra, your initiator whispers in your ear. It's purposefully designed for you, and it must never be spoken aloud or told to anyone. So I adhered to that, even in the imaginary world. So I can't tell you."

Goddamn it, Goldblum.

I FORGOT MY MANTRA.

By 1978, after *Nashville* and *Annie Hall*, Goldblum had become something of a critical darling, but that doesn't mean the general public had received the memo. The first years of his career left a lasting impression on directors, critics, and cinephiles—but he hadn't yet received a role that a regular Joe bringing his girl to the pictures on a Friday night was likely to remember. Not until he was cast in Philip Kaufman's ambitious remake of Don Siegel's 1956 horror movie *Invasion of the Body Snatchers*. (They say horror movies are aphrodisiacs, so I guess our regular Joe knows what he's doing.)

In the wake of *Rosemary's Baby* and *The Exorcist*, the moviegoing public was more than ready to re-embrace the genre,* particularly smart remakes like *Invasion of the Body Snatchers*. The basic premise is alien plantlike things have invaded San Francisco and can create replicas of people as they sleep. The original bodies disintegrate, leaving the replicas to roam the world void of feeling and with only one mission—create more replicas. For the most part, though, they're indistinguishable from regular people at a glance. With these themes of surreptitious surveillance, the loss of individuality, and the potential extinction of humanity, the movie was perfect for a world still reeling from the Jonestown Massacre, Watergate, and the aftermath of the Vietnam War. As Kaufman said, "By the time we were making the film, paranoia had certainly gravitated to the big cities, where it probably lurks now more than ever."

Thus there was the perfect mixture of buzz around the movie and critical anticipation of Goldblum's career to earn a few brief profiles before the movie hit theaters, such as one in the *New York Times*

---

* Which, as luck would have it, is exactly where Goldblum tends to shine.

aptly titled "A Cinderella Story That Starts at the Castle and Gets Better"—which was one of the first pieces to mention his romantic life, something that would be a public fixation just a few years later.

At the time, he was seeing the actress Patricia Gaul, whom he met when he was cast opposite her in the play *Our Late Night* at La MaMa West. "I was playing her husband, that was it. We moved in with each other shortly thereafter," he told the newspaper. An innocuous quote, yes, but one that hints at his, erm, dating style. Though he and Gaul married at the turn of the decade and appeared in several of the same movies, including *The Big Chill* and *Into the Night*, they divorced in 1985. Barring some secret trysts we don't know about, it would be one of the final serious romantic outings of his life not written about ad nauseam.

The more prescient takeaway from those earliest interviews, however, was how you could see Goldblum's persona in the press shaping up. In 1977, he told the *Washington Post*, "I'd like to be like Robert De Niro, you know. Somebody asks him about his acting and he just sort of shrugs and walks away. Very low-key. But I can't do that. When someone wants to know about me, I spill my guts."*

Can we talk quickly about how amazing that quote is? What an incredible display of confidence! De Niro was batting an easy .950 in 1977, having just starred in these three films in this order: *Mean Streets*, *The Godfather: Part II*, and *Taxi Driver*. Yet when Goldblum invokes the revered actor's name, it's not to tell a national newspaper that he's envious of the man's acting ability. No, what he aspires to is *the way he answers interview questions*. To have the confidence . . .

ANYWAY, the movie essentially features four and a half main characters living in San Francisco when the invasion begins. The

---

* Well, someone other than *me*, I guess.

leads: Donald Sutherland as health inspector Matthew Bennell and Brooke Adams as Elizabeth Driscoll, a scientist who works in the same lab. The secondary characters: Goldblum as Jack Bellicec, a poet, and Veronica Cartwright as his wife, Nancy, who runs their Bellicec Mud Baths (their mud parlor, natch*). The half character: Leonard Nimoy's celebrity psychiatrist Dr. David Kibner, but it turns out he's one of *them*, hence his half status.

Sutherland and Adams carry a great deal of the film's suspense, with Cartwright adding emotional heft to the whole ordeal—particularly in the end, when she unceremoniously discovers she's the last non–pod person from the original cast (and, seemingly, in all of San Francisco).

Goldblum, meanwhile, flies in like a hurricane. We first meet him at a book party, where he's pissed that Nimoy's Kibner is getting any attention at all for his new tome. "His ideas are garbage. Kibner's ideas are garbage," he says, his words tumbling over one another. When a Kibner fan asks how he could say such a thing "about a man like Kibner," he responds, "I'm not saying it about a man *like* Kibner, I'm saying it about Kibner. He dashes one of these things out every six months. It takes me six months to write one line sometimes." When asked why, he says, "Because I pick each word individually, that's why!"

That scene encapsulates, to Kaufman, what makes the actor so special. It's funny, and he's being kind of a dick, but he's not incorrect. It's like that line from *The Big Lebowski*: "You're not wrong, Walter, you're just an asshole."

"The way Jeff delivers his lines, they could come right out of him," the director said. "His neuroses that he plays [have] a unique way of getting at something universal that's hidden inside of us. I don't know

---

*For the uninitiated, some people pay money that they earned by working to sit in a bathtub filled with mud as a therapeutic activity.

any other actor who does something like that. Most of them do it through anguish or broad comedy, but Jeff does it right there in the bookstore scene."

Jack Bellicec is also emblematic of the supporting roles Goldblum would continue to receive throughout his career. (And with a few key exceptions, most of his roles are supporting roles. As Arnold said, "he's an indispensable character actor.") Without the pressure of having to carry the entire film, he can be looser, more comedic, more of a spectacle. While Kaufman changed several things in his update of Siegel's movie, Goldblum's take on Jack Bellicec might be the most important. He punctures the self-seriousness of the original, but at the same time, he can betray an entire inner life the audience wants to learn more about.

"He always leaves you wanting more. It's like you're always invited in, but the party is a little bit beyond your grasp," Kaufman said, adding that such small character-actor roles are tricky. "Those are hard roles to play. If you don't do it right you become Ronald Reagan."

Kaufman, much like nearly everyone I spoke with, lights up when telling stories about Goldblum, saying, "The moment I met him, I just thought he was perfect. What a unique presence Jeff is. Witty and thoughtful." But he was giddiest when recalling the scene in which Goldblum's Jack risks his life, which he ends up losing, to save the others. Our quartet has discovered the invaders and begun piecing together that they've infiltrated the local public safety agencies, maybe even national ones. As mindless pod people chase them and helicopters hover overhead, Jack, after being self-centered throughout the film, finally performs a feat of heroism by breaking from the others to lead the creatures astray. In some ways, the scene beats as the movie's heart—in a film about inhumanity conquering us all, here's this previously selfish guy doing the most selfless thing a human can.

That's the kind of scene actors prepare for by digging into their past, finding some uncovered memory—maybe of hurt and anger, maybe of fear, maybe of personal sacrifice—and unleashing it on-screen.

So Kaufman asked him what he planned to mine for emotion.

"His motivation as he began to run with these helicopters and all this noise and commotion, I wondered what he as an actor relied upon for sense memory or something for the scene," Kaufman said, before bursting out laughing. "'Chicken Licken' is what he was thinking about. It wasn't like there was some deep childhood memory or anything."

"Chicken Licken," known overseas as "Henny Penny" and more colloquially known these days as "Chicken Little," is an old folk tale about a chicken who thinks the world is coming to an end after an acorn falls and bops him on the head. "The sky is falling" is repeated throughout the fable, which correctly posits that fearmongering is a bad thing. Of course, in the movie, the fear is real.

"It was perfectly appropriate. We didn't need to get any deeper than that, and that might have been his sense memory. As a child, maybe he was taken by the story," Kaufman said. "I remember just laughing with him in this dire moment in the film, before he went running off."

When he next appears on-screen, he's a mindless pod person, all humanity zapped out of him. And boy, is it effective. Because Jack's humanity was so thoroughly established, even if through his neuroses, his loss becomes more than a plot point. It's devastating. "However hurt and paranoid he was as a poet," Kaufman said, "you loved him."

"It's horrible," Nayman said. "Absolutely horrible. He's so irritating and funny and you can't guess what he's going to say or how he's going to say it." To see him as a pod is "really nightmarish."

Dark as the film is, there was a great deal of levity on the set—"If I can work with people like Jeff, that's what it's all about," Kaufman said. "We're making serious enterprises, but the moments in between are fun as hell"—particularly when Cartwright became his partner in shenanigans.

"Jeff Goldblum and Veronica Cartwright, they called themselves the Dancing Bellicecs,* they'd come dancing through our set doing a pas de deux," Kaufman said.

"This all started when we were in the showers," Cartwright said in an interview years later, referring to a scene in which the characters find a pod person in their mud baths, which are separated into several small rooms by shower curtains. Cartwright's Veronica walks into one to find what looks like a corpse covered in coarse white hairs. She throws up her hands, screams, and runs out, right into Jack. To make good use of the space, Kaufman shot the scene from various angles, prompting numerous takes.

"To get the angle, and the way the curtains were blowing, and to be able to pick the guy up who was in the bathtub . . . we hit the point we did it so many times we'd [*pantomimes dancing*]. So we became known as the Dancing Bellicecs," Cartwright said. "And we would sort of dance on [to set] together and dance off. It was hysterical."

Fun aside, however, the movie proved important to Goldblum's development as an actor. Namely, it was the first time he really felt he understood what he brought to the table.

"One day on the set, where I had this line to my wife Veronica Cartwright. She says, 'Why have we always thought they'd come in metal ships?' I said, 'Nancy, I never thought they were going to come in metal ships.' And Phil laughed at it. He said, 'Good. Cut. That's all

---

*If this book achieves anything, I hope it's that someone will be inspired to start a band named the Dancing Bellicecs.

we need. That's very good, let's move on.' And the way he appreciated me made me see myself, as I remember it, in a little different way, just a little different, and [I] realized that, gee, I don't have to do much, there's something in me that's a little my own," Goldblum remembered years later. "Sandy Meisner said, 'Don't copy anybody. Try to find your own voice in some way.' But there's something in me, even when playing a character, that maybe is special to me, that is right there, that I don't even have to kind of make a big effort for."

One quality Kaufman so admired was Goldblum's naturalistic characteristics, his ability to embody a character so deeply that he brings himself into it. That line is a perfect example. "It sounds like something that would come right out of Jeff Goldblum. He has this odd sense of bringing his neurosis and sharing it with the audience," Kaufman said. "It's such a great, truthful thing that really is the core of a movie. It's a science fiction movie that traditionally had invaders coming in metal ships. So that's what *Invasion of the Body Snatchers* is all about. And it takes this sort of neurotic poet that he plays to really get to the heart of that."

The small-budget film performed well, grossing nearly $25 million at the box office (about $96 million today, adjusted for inflation). That's especially impressive considering the low wages most of the actors made. According to producer Robert H. Solo in *"They're Here . . ." Invasion of the Body Snatchers: A Tribute*, Sutherland made "between $200,000 and $300,000" while Goldblum, Adams, and Nimoy made $25,000 each. (He wasn't sure about Cartwright.)

With a little cultural clout under his belt, Goldblum briefly stepped away from the silver screen and onto the small one, trading his secondary and tertiary film roles for a costarring slot on

ABC's detective series *Tenspeed and Brown Shoe*, featuring stage legend Ben Vereen as con man E. L. "Tenspeed" Turner and Goldblum as Lionel Whitney, the "brown shoe" (slang for "accountant"). Through some odd circumstances involving Nazi diamonds stolen from the Mob and hidden in the latter's wedding limousine, the unlikely duo forms a detective agency. Created by Stephen J. Cannell, who also created *The Rockford Files*, the series drew praise for imbuing the classic procedural format with comedy. For a sense of the show's general vibe, here are two excellent episode titles: "It's Easier to Pass an Elephant Through the Eye of a Needle Than a Bad Check in Bel Air" and "Loose Larry's List of Losers."

Goldblum never was much of a leading man, and though *Tenspeed and Brown Shoe* featured him in a starring role, the show belonged to the quick-talking, wisecracking Ben Vereen. That isn't to diminish the contribution of this book's protagonist. Goldblum, whom the *New York Times* described in this role as "a tall, somewhat goofy-looking young man who might easily be mistaken for a swarthy Carleton Carpenter in search of Debbie Reynolds," holds his own as a naïve daydreamer, a solid foil for Vereen's con man turned detective. "It came to this point where we just felt a vibration," Vereen told me, adding that to this day, it remains his favorite television show. Not just his favorite that he was part of, but his favorite in general. This is still before Goldblum bulked up, making it one of his last major roles before he became a sex symbol—which is significant in that it allowed him to be the butt of the joke occasionally, something that became much more difficult when everyone began lusting after his muscular frame and impeccable style. Though his character knew karate, which certainly came in handy, he was a talker first and foremost, using his intellect to get out of sticky situations.

Gary Arnold said when he first saw Goldblum on the silver screen, he wondered if the man's height would ever be a detriment, and it certainly presented a slight obstacle when it came to filming *Tenspeed and Brown Shoe*, though the problem was easily solved: "[Goldblum] stands on his own two feet, and I stand on a soap box," Vereen said at the time.

Though the first few episodes boasted high ratings, they quickly dropped off as the season went on. The show wasn't renewed, leaving the world with only fourteen episodes[*] (though Vereen would reprise his role as E. L. "Tenspeed" Turner almost a decade later in Stephen J. Cannell's *J.J. Starbuck*). It might not have left behind much of a cultural footprint, but it did amass a cult of dedicated fans, including President Bill Clinton. As the story goes, Goldblum met the president at the 1995 wedding of Ted Danson and Mary Steenburgen. "He came up to me and he said, 'Hi, Jeff. It's a real pleasure. I loved you in *Tenspeed and Brown Shoe*,'" Goldblum told the Associated Press. Supposedly, Clinton never missed an episode of the show, which he called his favorite series. I tried to uncover the truth, but strangely, the former president did not return my calls on this matter. Guess he's got "better things" to do.

With his true breakout role in 1983's *The Big Chill* looming, Goldblum continued to toil in television throughout the early eighties. He also popped up as Ichabod Crane in a comedic TV version of *The Legend of Sleepy Hollow*, along with a bit part in the TV movie *Rehearsal for Murder*[†] and guest spots in *Laverne & Shirley* and *The Devlin Connection*.

---

[*] Including a two-part pilot.

[†] Which also featured William Russ and William Daniels, actors whom children of the nineties might better remember as Alan Matthews and Mr. Feeny from *Boy Meets World*.

The only movie he appeared in between *Invasion of the Body Snatchers* and *The Big Chill* was director Richard Pearce's shockingly prescient medical semi–science fiction drama *Threshold*. The movie reunited Donald Sutherland and Goldblum, the former playing a brilliant heart surgeon and the latter a research scientist who has invented an artificial heart for usage in human beings. To call it methodical and/or rigorous would be an understatement. It feels like a documentary, even though its first theatrical run in 1981 occurred a year before Dr. William DeVries inserted the world's first permanent artificial heart into Dr. Barney Clark.

It's highly likely that even the biggest film buffs among you are scratching your heads and wondering how you've completely forgotten a movie with two enormous stars that literally predicted the future of cardiovascular surgery. But it's not you. It's the international boundary. A Canadian production, Pearce's movie didn't hit the States until 1983 and unfortunately didn't make much of a splash when it did.

Threshold is well worth seeking out, particularly for Goldblum fans. The characters feel as focused as actual medical professionals at the top of their field, doing world-changing work, meaning there isn't much room for romance, snark, humor, or the general frivolity with which Goldblum's characters normally concern themselves. What there is, though, is a severe intensity. "When you want to find somebody to play a humorless character, find the funniest person you know. Find a comic genius, and he is that. He just nails humorless and ego run rampant and all those things that make up his character in the movie," Pearce told me.

Despite the seriousness of his character, Goldblum remained "a joy" on set. On the first day of rehearsals, the actor was doing some dry runs of a scene that involved a live monkey—only the monkey hadn't yet arrived. "Finally, everything was ready for the shot," Pearce said. "Goldblum turned to me and he opened the door, and he said, 'Next time you see me, I will be *actiiiiing.*' And he just disappeared out the door. And I knew we were going to have fun.'"*

W hen *Threshold* finally reached the United States, Goldblum was on the precipice of fame. The movie didn't perform well, but it earned him a nomination at the Genie Awards—think: the Canadian Oscars, which have since merged with the Gemini Awards to become the Canadian Screen Awards†—for best performance by a foreign actor. Which is delightful in and of itself. The string of movies he then appeared in throughout the eighties raised his stature as an actor and earned him magazine covers, somewhat thrusting his personal life front and center. But even then, as his fame mounted, the tales told of the actor were few and far between—and never nasty. Which brings us to what is simultaneously the loveliest and most difficult part of writing a book about his life, perhaps one titled *Because He's Jeff Goldblum*, perhaps one that you are holding *right now*. Most

---

* Pearce's experience on set also offers some insight into working with a seasoned pro like Sutherland. "I'm a young director. This is my third film. I am absolutely in awe of Donald Sutherland [who had recently worked with the legendary Italian director Federico Fellini]. And we start work on a complicated scene for me, and I just wasn't satisfied. It just didn't work for me. We went through about eighteen takes, and it just wasn't working," Pearce said. "And I didn't know what to say. I was just intimidated. So I called a break, and the entire crew went off to get coffee, and I went and sat in this room alone to try to figure out what the fuck I was gonna do. And in the doorway appears Sutherland, and he walks over, and he sits down next to me and doesn't say anything for the longest time. I'm feeling like this is a complete failure. And he looks over at me, and he smiles, and he says, 'This is so great. I really hate when people settle when it's not right. This is just what it was like working with Fellini.' And he just made me feel, like, embraced almost . . . he knew exactly what I was going through."

† And you thought American awards shows were confusing.

stories feed off some sort of conflict, a central tension. That's the primary tenet of storytelling, after all. This book has none, a fact of which I'm well aware. Because, as Pearce summed it up perfectly, "he's not difficult. He's not someone that stories get told about. He's just a consummate professional, and he was then, as a young man."

And that's exactly why we love him.

INTERLUDE #4

Three Haikus Concerning Jeff Goldblum

Saved us from dinos
After becoming a fly
So who is this dude?!

He chilled Big, fought hard
Then he played jazz piano
The man, myth, legend

Jeffrey Lynn Goldblum
Five syllables can't be chance
Serendipity!

As a bonus, I thought it might be a nice idea for you to try your own hand at a haiku. So grab a pencil—or a pen, if you dare to be so bold—and fill in the blanks below! Remember, five syllables, then seven, then five. Feel free to email your best ones right to my real, actual email address that I definitely shouldn't be putting in a book: travis.m.andrews@gmail.com.

_____

_____

_____

Awards Season

There exists a generational dividing line when it comes to Jeff Goldblum. Namely, according to an informal poll I accidentally administered, your age is a fairly reliable indicator of which movie will spring to mind when the actor's name arises in casual conversation.

This is a good time to mention that at the time I wrote this sentence, my mother was thirty-two years and eight days removed from signing my birth certificate. It's also a good time to mention that said mother adhered to the MPAA guidelines, preventing yours truly from watching PG-13 movies until I was "of age." This is relevant because, as a young bookworm, I grew obsessed with the writing of Michael Crichton and couldn't wait to see what I thought of (and, even after all this research for the book you're reading, still think of) as his seminal work: *Jurassic Park*. For some reason, kids of my generation still think of that as Golblum's movie, even though he's on-screen for nearly the same amount of time as the T. rex. Some characters, such as Dr. Ian Malcolm, overcome the temporal boundaries of their medium and become, to employ a painfully overused word, *iconic.*

BUT! BUT BUT BUT! Ask anyone above the age of, say, sixty about his most iconic role (or, at least, about his most iconic film), and they will immediately respond with a lengthy diatribe on director Lawrence Kasdan's *The Big Chill.**

It's difficult to describe the magnitude of abstract concepts, so it's tough to put into words just how much *The Big Chill* captured, embodied, and spoke both to and about a generation in the bored grips of malaise. Did it get middling reviews? Oh, yeah. Did it seem like a big-budget, erm, *version* of John Sayles's little-seen indie drama *Return of the Secaucus 7*? Well, yeah. Does any of that really matter? Of course, and those are conversations better had in a book about the fidelity of film and all of that. What really matters here is that a lowish-budget ensemble film, one that most studios shied away from making after finding the concept of seven leads too confounding to market, became a breakout hit—launching (and buoying) the careers of several enormous movie stars, fading as they might be today.

The plotline is basic: Six college friends reunite about a decade after graduating from the University of Michigan for the funeral of their seventh friend, Alex, who has committed suicide. They, along with Alex's suddenly ex-girlfriend, end up spending the weekend at the South Carolina vacation home where Alex was staying. Their

---

* As I said, this was an extremely informal poll that went something like this: "Hi, I'm writing a book about Jeff Goldblum." Then, depending on the person's age: "Oh cool, I love *Jurassic Park.* 'Life, uhh, finds a way,' am I right?!" or "How neat! *The Big Chill* really changed my life. Would you like to listen to some Steely Dan with me?"

mourning and nostalgia (mixed with a good deal of booze, sexual tension, and drugs, of course) create a minefield of tricky topics, as everyone realizes how much they've changed—or, in some cases, remained the same—since their college days. The specter of the Vietnam War and the country's shifting politics hang over every interaction, but on the surface, the movie focuses on the interpersonal connections between the seven.

The title sprang right from Kasdan's own experience. When he was working on the first film he directed, *Body Heat*, he befriended some of the cast and crew. He grew close to one fellow in particular but said, "As we talked, every once in a while, he would say something I found so counter to my own beliefs, so repugnant in some ways, just awful and cynical, and I would feel a chill actually run down my body. Because here was a guy I got along with perfectly in every other way, but clearly we had a value split that was enormous. And that feeling, that big chill that I would get, was really the original impulse for this movie. Because it was about the fact that even though we had a certain kind of values, and held them dear when we were in school, they were put to a very severe test when we went out into the world."

It's the kind of title that could never exist today, one that doesn't immediately spoon-feed the audience a synopsis of the film. And if the title feels like a relic from the 1980s, just imagine compiling such an extraordinary (and extraordinarily famous) cast these days (unless, of course, we're talking about an Avengers movie). There are the owners of the house where Alex was shacking up, married couple Harold and Sarah Cooper (Kevin Kline and Glenn Close), dealing again with the affair Sarah had with Alex years ago while trying to remain gracious hosts; Nick Carlton (William Hurt), the impotent Vietnam War veteran who worked for a while as a radio psychologist but prefers ingesting (and, in fairness, sharing) a pharmacy's worth of various drugs; Karen Bowens (JoBeth Williams), a Detroit housewife bored with her marriage; Meg Jones (Mary Kay Place), a disillusioned lawyer worried about the ticking of her biological clock; Sam Weber (Tom Berenger), an actor embarrassed by his successful but campy *Magnum, P.I.*–esque cop show *J.T. Lancer*; and, of course, Michael Gold (Goldblum), a nihilistic, smarmy *People* magazine journalist who mostly just wants to nail Alex's grieving girlfriend, Chloe (Meg Tilly), even though he believes rationalizations are more important than sex.[*]

Drawing on what he called the "heyday of New York actors," Kasdan actually had to narrow the cast down to this astonishing list, though it wasn't easy. "I could have cast the movie twice over," he said before correcting himself. "No, probably twenty times over, there were so many good people around." Even so, "Larry always had Jeff in mind for the part, somebody who is always charming, who can make all these [cynical] points, and still be fun to watch," Michael Shamberg, the movie's producer, told me.

Kasdan had long admired Goldblum and originally considered casting him in Ted Danson's role in *Body Heat*—so when he began working on a new film, he gave the actor a call. "I had glimpsed him in a couple of things, like *Death Wish*," Kasdan told me, also singling out his performance in *Between the Lines*. "He's absolutely wonderful in it, just electrifying, jumps out of the movie. I was totally amused and delighted by him. His timing was so unusual. You have this

---

[*] Originally, the movie included an eighth primary actor: Kevin Costner, in one of his first roles, as the deceased in a flashback to their college days. Kasdan decided the film worked better set only in the present and cut the scene, leaving Costner's only appearance as a corpse. Disappointing as that probably was, things certainly worked out for Costner in the end. Kasdan felt terrible for cutting the scene but cast him as a lead in *Silverado* just a few years later.

enormous guy, who is very funny, whose timing is like no one you've ever talked to. . . . You don't learn that. You can't. You're sort of born with that and you have your whole history to make it stronger or weaker or more flexible. No one can do him, because no one would have thought of this being an acting approach. He's brand-new. He's original."

Once the cast was assembled, Kasdan had to figure out how to film the thing on a shoestring budget. Columbia Pictures, not wanting to pay for a long shoot, agreed to instead pay for a long rehearsal period, which was unusual even then (and unheard-of now). The actors would first gather in a windowless room—what Berenger called a "think tank"—in Burbank, California, and sit at a table around a tape recorder. "We would exchange parts, [and] we would improvise," remembered Close in the 1999 documentary *The Big Chill: A Reunion*.

Kasdan "did this real amazing thing," said Tilly. "He had the script, and then he had a whole 'nother script that we rehearsed, we memorized, and we worked, which were scenes that took place in between the scenes that we were actually going to shoot. So everybody had the same reference points as to where we were coming from."

Later, they moved briefly to Atlanta and continued the in-character rehearsal process, tackling some of the flashback scenes that were cut from the film. "We went in the house and we, literally in character, went for two or three days . . . creating these scenarios that were alluded to in the script. Maybe there were hints or clues in the script about certain backstory," said Place. The result, as Close put it, was the forging of a "communal language within our group."

Finally, they arrived in Beaufort, South Carolina, to film in the house, which had previously appeared in *The Great Santini*, where they followed Kasdan's primary rule. "He said, 'I just demand, I can't tell you how fervently I demand that you all . . . be kind to one another.' It was very important to him," Goldblum said. "So he set up an atmosphere that was actively, aggressively humane and communal."

It was also a blast. "It's the most fun I've ever had working on a movie, mainly because of Larry Kasdan but also because of the cast," Stephen P. Dunn, the second assistant director on the movie, told me.

The cast rented condos near the beach in Beaufort and began spending much of their free time together, becoming more than just on-screen friends. Kline and Goldblum rented a condo together, which everyone called the G-Spot,* and became particularly close. Kline had previously seen the actor, five years his junior, in *Between the Lines* and thought, "Who is this guy? He's brilliant." He told *New York* how he felt when he found out they'd be acting together: "I was thrilled. There's a reverse, a formality, when you first meet him. But when you get through that, he's viciously funny. He can be erudite and make fun of himself at the same time. He's so respected by other actors. All he needs is the exposure of the package, and I think this role will do it for him."

The duo's pad was party central, where the cast would gather for dinners and to play games like poker and Trivial Pursuit, which Close had brought down from Canada since it hadn't yet been released in the United States. "It was a fun set," Shamberg told me. "There were many highly competitive Trivial Pursuit games."

The cast's competitive streak didn't end there. "I remember I caught Jeff Goldblum cheating at charades, and I was incensed," Williams said.

"In those days, I thought it was cute to kind of cheat, and I was

---

* Talk about on-brand.

looking in the bowl of charades titles. JoBeth Williams saw me do it, but I didn't mind getting caught," Goldblum later told *GQ*. "She flushed red and went on a tirade. It humiliated me in such a way that it was a turning point: Cheating is not okay or fun."

Quickly the game nights and dinner parties morphed into weekly Saturday night shindigs.

"They would be playing the piano, taking turns and singing, and somehow it turned into 'We're going to have a party here every Saturday night.' And they did," Dunn remembered. "About half the crew and all of the cast would show up. And somewhere they'd turn into dance parties, and we just danced and played music and sang into the night. . . . It just kind of blew my mind. We had so much fun."

The hijinks ensued during the week too. Kline and Goldblum would put on Scottish accents and pretend to be brothers. They'd drive around South Carolina, fishtailing along the gravel roads crisscrossing the swampy beach town. The girls would roll up to the G-Spot while they were out to prank them, such as when Close, Williams, and Place hung oversized women's undergarments around the condo while they were out. "We hung them on the fan in their living room, and then when they arrived, we put the fan on slow and all of a sudden they noticed that these huge, huge pieces of underwear were circulating around the room," Close said. "And they would make the fan faster and faster until it was being flung all over the room, and we would laugh hysterically."

There were also kind gestures throughout the production. Shooting paused for a week during Christmas but much of the crew stuck around, so Hurt drove and "bought like 50 Christmas trees and gave them all to the crew," Dunn said.

All the while, the cast also learned each other's strange habits. "I remember [Goldblum] being so into health and pouring orange juice over his cornflakes. 'What the hell are you doing?' 'Oh, milk's bad for you.' And then I tried it. It's not bad!" Kline recalled to *GQ*.* "Every morning he would wake up two hours before the call, do vocal exercises. He read through the script every morning. It was inspiring."

"Kevin would kind of roll out of bed for the morning's shoot, have a little cold cereal, and he was ready to shoot," Goldblum said. "I'd do my exercises, and I'd have to put on my vanishing creams or whatever before I felt prepared to present myself."

The pair's repartee even spilled out into the press cycle after the movie. For a profile of Kline for *Rolling Stone*, Ross Wetzsteon watched Kline and Goldblum tape an interview for *Entertainment Tonight*. When the interviewers asked if there was any clashing of egos during filming, Kline joked that Goldblum idolized him. Wetzsteon wrote, "[Kline answered,] 'There's always a danger that when you spend a lot of time with someone'—he's now telling *Entertainment Tonight* about Jeff Goldblum—'that you'll unconsciously pick up a lot of his mannerisms.' He's scratching his neck as he talks, fondling his ears, massaging the nape of his neck—hey, that looks just like Jeff! 'I think I've avoided that,' Kevin says solemnly, and even Jeff is laughing."

All this closeness, both physical and emotional, led to a unique filming experience, which was "very intense," according to Kasdan. "They were amused by each other, and they were irritated by each other, occasionally. And what was challenging and wonderful for me is there were seven different ideas about acting, so you're trying to meld somebody like Kevin Kline and someone like Bill Hurt—not a

---

*In an interview with *Entertainment Weekly*, Goldblum even remembered "Bill Hurt eating, like, a whole onion with tons of mayonnaise," saying, "Unless I'm dreaming. He would take a whole onion, slice it up in quarters, eat it, and have like half a jar of Hellmann's mayonnaise." This was unverifiable and seems certifiably insane, and in the piece, neither Tilly nor Place could remember it, and I don't want to get sued, so let me repeat: this might be and probably is apocryphal. But it's not an image you'll soon forget.

natural combination—and people adjusted to each other and took enormous pleasure in it."

Plus, if any tension arose when it came to actually acting, Goldblum, ever the suave blade, could cut right on through by offering a variety of placating line readings. "You never knew how his lines would be read," Kasdan said. "When he had a variety of oddly timed or spaced readings, they always stimulated other people. And he could give you five others. I only had to say one or two words, and he could give you something completely different—that still had the unique Goldblum sound to it."

Through these rehearsals, the actors, in some sense, literally became their characters. Close, for example, wrote a letter to Alex as Sarah. Though their brief affair ended years earlier, the film makes it clear Sarah still has feelings for him. The letter wasn't used in the movie, however. Close merely gave it to Kasdan. At first glance, that might make it seem as if Close was going Method, but everyone was, to some degree. One night, Kasdan instructed the group to prepare dinner together, remaining in character, with no cameras rolling. Once they started, he just left. "And for five hours they remained in character without any authority figure, without any director to tell them if they were behaving or reacting in the correct way according to the writer's or director's ideas," Kasdan told TCM. "It became a very intense experience and they all came out of it exhausted and drained." But he credits it with turning the "actors into an ensemble." When they were shooting, Kasdan insisted everyone stay around the house to make it feel more lived-in. Characters might walk by in the background during scenes they weren't originally slated to be part of, but there they are, in reality probably looking for a sandwich at craft services, sure, but it's not like the audience is any the wiser.

To say the movie struck a chord would be an insult to understatements. "People of all ages would come up to me and say, 'That happened to me and my friends,' or they'd say, 'I wish I still had that group of friends,'" Kasdan told me. "I think one of the secrets of the movie and the reason it worked beyond my highest hopes is because that particular sound of conversation between the people had not really been represented in American movies. That particular group had not been dramatized. There were a lot of comedies about people that age, but what it sounds like when a group of friends from that era gets together—that had not really been on the screen. And it's a very powerful thing to hear something that sounds familiar."

Powerful, indeed. The movie performed well beyond expectations, eventually earning $56 million domestically ($158 million, when adjusted for inflation), even though it only cost an estimated $8 million ($20 million, when adjusted for inflation) to make. "We just all assumed, at least I did, that we were doing this nice arty little movie that probably not a lot of people would see," Williams said. "We certainly didn't get paid very much. Larry had a bunch of gross points* in the film, and when he realized that the movie was making money and that we were never going to see any of it, he gave each cast member half a gross point. So we all got some money out of the success of the movie."

Even the usually clueless Academy of Motion Picture Arts and Sciences (otherwise known as "the Academy" from here on out) had enough sense to recognize the movie, nominating it for Best Picture, where it lost to *Terms of Endearment*. Also nominated were Kasdan and his co-screenwriter Barbara Benedek for Best Screenplay (who lost to Horton Foote for *Tender Mercies*) and Glenn Close for Best Supporting Actress (who lost to Linda Hunt in *The Year of Living Dangerously*).

---

*Meaning he would make money if the movie proved profitable.

And the movie wasn't even the real success story. As J. Hoberman wrote in the *New York Times*, "The trade press found the success of the *Big Chill* soundtrack album an even bigger surprise than the movie's considerable popularity. (It was the year's 13th top-grossing movie and Columbia's biggest hit.) The most innovative aspect of the movie's marketing was a music video in which clips from the movie were scored to Marvin Gaye's 'I Heard It Through the Grapevine.'"

Both the movie and its soundtrack, though, might be cultural artifacts at this point in our current film culture, one both disrupted by the glut of streaming services and driven by intellectual property. "It really holds up for me," Dunn said. "They just don't make movies like it anymore. You can't even get the money to make that movie these days."

For our purposes, though, the movie and the soundtrack don't matter. What does is Goldblum, who had finally broken through to mainstream audiences, leaving a lasting impression on most anyone who saw the film. The key was how he still left people wanting to know more about his character, about him. It's a facet of "stardom in general. There's always just something you want more of. They just don't put it all out there," Shamberg observed.

Vic Ziegel profiled him in September 1983 for *New York*—an early signpost of stardom—in a piece subtitled "The Big Chill Makes Jeff Goldblum a Contender." "It's about time people learned the name that belongs to one of Hollywood's more interesting faces," Ziegel wrote. "Nobody can knit a brow like Goldblum. And the screen hasn't given us eyes as huge, as dark, as compelling since Bambi. Even more, his comic, stutter-step delivery and almost mimelike use of his rangy body make his performances jump off the screen—even in a crowd of contenders."

The profile also offered a brief glimpse into a thirty-one-year-old Goldblum's psyche, or at the very least, the way he dealt with the press, which was far less sophisticated than it is today. At the time he was still a tall, skinny guy—not the lothario who spends his free time pumping iron—and he definitely wasn't the fashionista we know him as today. Much of the piece focuses on his wandering his hotel room, fretting about whether he could wear a T-shirt for an on-camera interview. Gaul, his then wife, points out that Kline will probably be a bit more dolled up. Goldblum sticks with the T-shirt until the sound guy can't find a spot to clip his mic on, so he eventually leaves the room and settles on "a jacket, a shirt, a tie, a pained expression."

Never ceases to be intriguing, does it, how much we change over the decades?

What better way to follow appearing in your first Oscar-nominated movie than by appearing in your second? Maybe by first having a glass of champagne, but Goldblum has repeatedly insisted he's not, nor has he ever been, much of a drinker, so instead he teamed back up with Philip Kaufman for his epic Tom Wolfe adaptation *The Right Stuff*.

For a surprisingly lean-feeling three hours and thirteen minutes, the movie traces the origins of the US space program through our first astronauts, the Mercury Seven, who are portrayed by Scott Glenn (as Alan Shepard), Ed Harris (as John Glenn), Dennis Quaid (as Gordon Cooper), Fred Ward (as Gus Grissom), Scott Paulin (as Deke Slayton), Charles Frank (Scott Carpenter), and Lance Henriksen (as Wally Schirra)—with Sam Shepard as the god Chuck Yeager, the first pilot to officially break the sound barrier, along with litany of other records. In there are other great performances, such as Barbara Hershey as Glennis Yeager and Donald Moffat as President Lyndon B. Johnson.

Wedged toward the beginning of this massive historical beast are ten minutes of delightful comic relief, compliments of Goldblum and Harry Shearer. As you can guess, teaming up with Shearer, one of comedy's most lauded figures, from *This Is Spinal Tap* to *The Simpsons*, led to a good bit of frivolity, both on- and off-screen.

The two play a pair of besuited Washington recruiters, nothing but a pair of pencil-pushing pencil-necks to the rugged flyboys whom they're trying to convince to allow the government to shoot them into space. These two sure as shit don't have *the right stuff*. The proof is right there when the pair wanders into the Happy Bottom Riding Club, that dusty joint in the Mojave near Edwards Air Force Base where the boys gather to drink whiskey and talk shop. "I'd like a Coca-Cola," Shearer's recruiter tells the barkeep when he walks up with a bottle of the brown stuff. "In a *clean* glass." It's even more obvious later, when the two are vomiting over the side of an aircraft carrier in the middle of the sea.

"These were characters invented for the film," Shearer told me. "They did not appear in the book. There's a term in fiction writing called 'exposition' where some device must be used to give the viewer or writer information they need to know as the scene progresses. The trick in writing is to not make it sound like some device or character is there just to give you general information. And that was our job in the scenes we were in. So Phil [Kaufman, whom] I absolutely adore, said, 'You guys just figure something out.'"

Shearer, of course, is a master improviser, as evidenced by his work in *This Is Spinal Tap*, *Saturday Night Live*, and *The Jack Benny Program*, to name just a few. Even still, he felt slight trepidation.

"Jeff and I had never met before, and normally, in my experience, when you're just thrown into something with somebody that you don't know and told to improvise, it's not necessarily always the best way to go. Improvisation depends on listening, among other things, but it also depends upon chemistry and all of that," Shearer said. But the two hit it off. "We would just fart around and come up with stuff and then go back to the set and basically do it a few times. Phil was laughing, so it seemed to work out."

"The two of them were like a ballet together. They were just brilliant improvising together," Kaufman told me. And "most of it is them improvising."

"We just had an absolutely great time together," Shearer said.

Not that it was all gravy, of course. What set is? Though, normally, on-set issues aren't quite this ludicrous. Early in the movie is a scene in which the recruiters burst into a cabinet meeting in the White House to announce that the Soviets have launched Sputnik. Kaufman filmed the scene in an office building in downtown San Francisco. After running through the scene a few times with a crew of extras sitting around a long table, Kaufman told everyone to return to the hotel and that they'd be called back when the lighting was right— a wait that ended up taking like thirty-six hours.

"So we come back a day and a half later, and one of the guys at the table, one of the extras, is about eighty-five years old," Shearer said. "The first assistant director, who wrangles the extras, among other amazing jobs, says, 'When these guys come in and say they've just launched Sputnik, you just all turn around and look at them.'"

On the first go, the elderly gentleman does . . . nothing. Ditto the next and the next. "We go about fifteen takes, and he goes too soon, goes too late, doesn't do anything at all," Shearer said. "We're now at take fifteen or something, and everybody's like, 'Can we get this shot done? We got a lot of movie to do here.'" So the first AD walks over to the guy. "[He] puts the man's head in his hands, and he says, 'When these two guys come in, you just whip this old gourd around!' And he just twists the guy's neck so hard in one direction, I would have sworn he broke it. But that did the job. The next time he whipped that old gourd around."

Kaufman insisted on realism for *The Right Stuff*, so when it came time to film the scene in which our recruiters meet navy aviator Alan Shepard, he chose to film it on a real, active aircraft carrier. Which is all fine and dandy, save for the fact that no one mentioned to the pair that the ship would be sailing out to open water. More surprising, though, was the fact that, as Kaufman said, "to save money, the production manager, instead of putting them in a hotel, was going to have them sleep overnight, before the boat shipped out, sleep on the aircraft carrier."

Upon receiving the news, Shearer and Goldblum shared a look. "We get a little tour of the area where we might be sleeping, and we noticed that there's *unnamed liquid on the floor*," Shearer said. "And we look at each other and go, 'Should we say something to somebody?'"

"It was grimy, and they were sitting there, Harry eating bananas, and they were miserable," Kaufman said. "So I told them to come to my apartment in San Francisco.

"My TV was on a big wooden box that we picked up in Chinatown with all this Chinese writing on it, and on TV was *The Legend of Sleepy Hollow*" (the 1980 television movie in which Goldblum played Ichabod Crane). They watched it together. "Harry lit into Jeff's performance, and Jeff was backpedaling, in a funny way, trying to defend his performance. The two of them were amazingly hilarious. Then in the morning, I remember Harry doing yoga on the Persian carpet. He was all stretched out, maybe a few banana peels around him."

Another surprise rolled in the next day, after they'd all shipped out to sea. Goldblum and Shearer filmed their scene in which they mostly vomit off the side of the carrier and into the ocean and shake the hand of Glenn's Alan Shepard. Goldblum wipes speckles of vomit from his lips, the two explain how "haz-ard-ous" the mission is, and he accepts. The whole shebang lasts about a minute.

Of course, when they finished filming the brief scene, they were . . . you know . . . *still in the middle of the ocean*, and wondering how they'd get back. "And the AD says, 'You're choppering back,'" Shearer said. "Having just faked throwing up, now I'm thinking, 'Now we're gonna throw up for real.' I'm highly acrophobic, scared of heights. So we're in this helicopter with an open hatch just looking down at the Pacific beckoning us as we fly back to San Francisco." Luckily, they managed to make it back with their lunch firmly in their stomachs.

"Of course, I feel at home at sea because I was a whaler before I became an actor," Goldblum later jokingly told *Wired*, before adding, "No, that's not true. I'd hardly been at sea. I'm not really seafaring."

Throughout their stint in the film, Goldblum and Shearer constantly improvised not just dialogue but sight gags as well. Before the Coca-Cola line in the desert bar, for example, they get out of their car and accidentally put on each other's jackets, an easy laugh considering Goldblum towers a good ten inches over Shearer. "We hadn't really worked out the bit with the jackets until right as we got into the car to shoot it," the latter said. "We were kind of flailing for what could make this seem funny, and it made sense that we wouldn't have our jackets on in the car in the middle of the desert. So in the last minute and a half [before shooting] we thought, 'Let's try this.'"

"It was Jeff Goldblum and Harry Shearer at their best being with each other," Kaufman said. "They should be in a series of movies together. Now that we don't have Abbott and Costello, they could be a franchise. They could be a tentpole. Or Jeff could be a tentpole, and Harry could be the barker outside."

If you're one to measure movies through the awards they win (or almost win), then *The Right Stuff* blew *The Big Chill* out of the water, earning eight Academy Award nominations, including the mack daddy of them all, Best Picture. Commercially, though, their performances were starkly different. While Kasdan's indie flick became a surprise hit, Kaufman's epic didn't earn back its estimated $27 million budget—grossing only about $21 million ($59 million adjusted for inflation) in theaters.*

G oldblum rounded out this particular hot streak with a bit part in a movie that, if we're being honest, was mostly ignored at the time but has since earned a second life as a cult classic: 1984's *The Adventures of Buckaroo Banzai Across the 8th Dimension*. Once again, he found himself working with past collaborators, this time W. D. Richter, the screenwriter of *Invasion of the Body Snatchers*, who was taking a swing at directing. The sci-fi sendup's plot is too (purposely) weird and confusing for it to be worth explaining here,† but know that Goldblum plays a character named New Jersey who wears oversized furry chaps, a wide-brimmed white cowboy hat to match the white kerchief tied around his neck, and what Richter called a bright red "Gene Autry shirt." Like the rest of the movie, New Jersey (real name: Dr. Sidney Zweibel) is a slice of over-the-top zaniness dreamed up by Richter and Earl Mac Rauch, the film's writer, but he is also

---

*Those numbers aren't particularly shocking. People simply tend not to see movies that inch above the 180-minute mark.

† "One of the fun things when it came out was to read reviews, negative or positive, where the reviewer felt compelled to explain the narrative, the short form of the narrative," Richter told me. "I'd think, 'Oh, good luck.' It makes no sense on many levels."

required to explain the movie's kooky plot to the audience and make it sound at least half-believable.

Richter had noticed Goldblum's ability to "find stuff in the dialogue that I didn't quite see." "He finds inflections I didn't realize were possible," he said. "That's why you hire actors like that, because you can't direct them word-to-word, and you want them to startle you." Which is exactly why in this movie and many others with sci-fi or fantasy elements—such as *The Fly, Jurassic Park, Independence Day,* all the roles Goldblum is best known for—he's the scientist, professor, or journalist character who explains the scientific gobbledygook with such an easy confidence that we completely buy into it, no matter what it is.

In this movie, New Jersey figures out what's going on, which involves Orson Welles's 1938 radio broadcast *War of the Worlds.* Only, in this story, the aliens were actually real, and Welles had been forced to pretend otherwise. Here's the dialogue Goldblum delivers, which is completely ridiculous but, because he's the one saying it, utterly believable: "Wait a minute, wait a minute. November one, October, thirty days hath September, April, June, and November, the rest have thirty-one. October thirty-first. Halloween. Oh, don't you get it! Orson Welles. Halloween 1938. *War of the Worlds,* that fake radio news broadcast that got everybody scared thinking real-life Martians were landing in Grover's Mill, New Jersey. But then it all just turned out to be a hoax. So, maybe it wasn't a hoax, I mean maybe it isn't a hoax."

Yeah. It makes about as much sense in the movie as it does here on the page, sans context. Yet, if you pull up a YouTube clip of the scene, it'll *sound like* it makes perfect sense the first time you hear it. I don't know how to define that ability. He creates the suspension of disbelief *for you.* He does the work the viewer should be doing, though it comes off so effortlessly, it doesn't seem like work.

"When he explains the *War of the Worlds* thing, when you look at that on a page, it's just a lot of words to be said," Richter said. "That was my first directing job, and I probably kind of didn't pay a lot of attention to how it should be performed. . . . That could look really ludicrous. I mean, it's intentionally funny. But he also does it so beautifully, like it's the most important thought he's ever had, and it's just so compelling. He doesn't sound like an actor reading a line. . . . When he was telling everyone what was going on, I thought, 'He's doing this. He's actually solving the mystery right in front of me.' He's not thinking, 'This is how I should say these lines.' I know how to define [the trait]. You see it and you believe it, or you see it and you don't believe it."

Richter wasn't the only person in awe of Goldblum's performance. Later in the movie, he explains the whole thing again, and Lewis Smith's character, Perfect Tommy, is standing near him with a puzzled look on his face. In truth, Smith was doing everything he could not to burst out laughing.

"I was marveling at how he was getting all this crap out of his mouth," Lewis told me. "The dialogue is just insane. There's no sequence to it at all, and Jeff is totally making it logical. I have no idea how he got there, to make it logical."

Well, I have an idea: it's because he's Jeff Goldblum.

"The script for him is just a diving board. He can't wait to get into the water of the set. Where most actors, the script is their pool, because many actors don't have that Meisner training, so their listening isn't quite as acute as his," Lewis added. "When most people read and learn, they read it with the periods and commas. With Jeff, I think he marks out all the periods and commas. I'm sure he does. When he gets the script, he has someone mark out the periods and commas."

But Smith said there's more to it. "He's also as skilled as he is talented. Skill is something we acquire as human beings. It's not something given to us," Smith said. "And he's worked as hard on his skill as he has on his talent. He's tremendously versed in the history of cinema, the history of genres. He can keep up with anybody when it comes to quoting lines from movies, the top five or ten movies from every genre and so forth. His study is what makes him quite dangerous, in a good way."

In one scene, New Jersey and Perfect Tommy slink through an alien ship with their guns drawn. As they pass through a metallic room, New Jersey notices a green fruit that's completely out of place on-screen, the 1985 equivalent of that Starbucks cup in the final season of *Game of Thrones*, only, you know, it's an entire watermelon.

"Why is there a watermelon there?" New Jersey asks.

"I'll tell you later," Perfect Tommy replies.

The scene's sheer oddness could be synecdoche for the entire film. It makes no sense, but it's hilarious. It's funny, but it makes you ask a question. It's weird, but it seems purposefully weird. And, as it turns out, it was totally improvised.

J. Michael Riva, the production designer, and Richter "thought that what was missing from all science fiction movies was earthy stuff, and so he wanted organic material to be part of the movie. A lot of people, when they do these sci-fi movies, it's so sterile. Just metal and bright lights.

"[Riva, a] great production guy, a genius, he just started putting random stuff, like this watermelon, around the set. And Jeff was really the only actor to pick up on that stuff. So we're walking through that room, and he earnestly asked, 'What's a watermelon doing here?'" Smith said. "Acting with him is like working with an octopus. He's got his tentacles everywhere, and his tentacles are in each layer of the scene, and also in each layer on you. He's picking up on everything. Everything. He's like a sonar machine for the navy," Smith said. As an actor, "you can never relax around him. It's magical."

Plus, a repeating motif here, the guy was just a pleasure to be around.

"Jeff, you just let run. Jeff is a master class in scene stealing . . . ," Clancy Brown, who portrayed the delightfully named Rawhide, recalled. "He would come in with a joke every day. My favorite is when he decided to do the 'maha aha' routine from *The Three Stooges* and I would be stroked-out Curly, and he said, 'I say maha, you say yaha, and then say nonsense words.' And so we would do that all day on set, to the point of everybody [getting] tired of us."

He and Peter Weller even formed a band together, but we'll leave that as another bit of foreshadowing for now.

The film's most enduring image in the collective cultural consciousness is that outfit, designed by Aggie Rodgers. When Goldblum first put the costume on, "he had a great grin on his face, like he really got it. How could you not just see it and fall down laughing?" Richter said. Little did any of them know it would be a meme decades later, mostly because none of them knew what a meme was, mostly because the concept didn't yet exist.

Acting accolades from his colleagues aside, *Buckaroo Banzai* points to a path almost taken. The rest of the eighties would include a number of these purposely B movies. He could have—and almost did—become the King of Schlock. This is the same decade in which he would star in *Transylvania 6-5000*, *Vibes*, *Earth Girls Are Easy*, and *The Tall Guy*. You don't have to know what these movies are about to pick up on the vibe—their titles are proof enough.* This road filled with schlocky comedies is the exact path Gary Arnold predicted early in Goldblum's career that he would take.

And 1985 certainly didn't help dispel this notion.

---

*Important to note that *schlock* isn't meant in an insulting manner here. These movies range from good to great. Except for *Vibes*. Good God, *Vibes* is terrible. We'll get to it briefly, but both you and I will wish we hadn't.

I t should have been a very good year, after all. And for all I know, maybe it was for the tall dude. But things didn't go as (we must assume) he planned.

Goldblum finally nailed his first leading role in *Into the Night*, a movie by John Landis (known at the time for directing comedies such as *The Blues Brothers* and *Trading Places*, along with bro comedies such as *Animal House, Kentucky Fried Movie*, and other films with random extreme close-ups of bare breasts that eighties teenage boys would pause for, uhh . . . let's say personal purposes*).

The premise of *Into the Night*, which costarred a young Michelle Pfeiffer, hot off *Scarface* and *Grease 2*, contained promise. Goldblum's Ed Okin, a depressed aeronautical engineer, discovers his wife is having an affair and decides to take off, literally. So he drives to LAX, where Pfeiffer's Diana† jumps into his car and persuades him to drive . . . into the night. The reason, as it turns out, is she's a jewel thief who stole emeralds from the shah of Iran and is being chased by a bunch of Iranians (one of whom is portrayed by Landis himself, a decidedly non-Iranian fellow). Things get crazier and crazier, as you might imagine. David Bowie shows up as a British hit man for no apparent reason. Cringeworthy slapstick comedy mixes with realistic gun violence. Cheesetastic reverberating eighties guitar riffs soundtrack the whole thing.

Let's save some time: *Into the Night* is not a good movie. It possesses no idea of what it wants to be. The film attempts to capitalize

---

*Probably?

†Just "Diana." Perhaps because her character is somewhat shady, but this is also back when female characters often didn't get last names in movies. Perhaps not coincidentally, this is the same year the Bechdel Test first appeared.

on that feeling that our lives are broken and maybe one chance encounter could fix everything, a common trope that Landis runs into
the ground. In khakis pulled up just a little too high on his slender
waist and a button-down shirt a little too ironed, Goldblum must
play against type. He must play somewhat hapless—which is never a
good look for him—so by the end of the movie he can become the
enlightened hero.

"I would do it a little differently now," Goldblum said on the
Shout!Takes podcast, adding that if he were to film the movie now he
would further consider the character's backstory. He's a damn rocket
scientist, after all, but he's presented as just a dull, boring guy who
sort of bumbles through the evening. The character isn't presented as
a one-dimensional plot device, liked our beloved evildoer Unus, but
he lacks any sort of, well, spice. This is like a gumbo without the filé,
a jambalaya without the hot sauce, a holy trinity without the celery.
It's lacking. Goldblum would never throw a project or a director under the bus, but it's tough to hear the interview without thinking he
wasn't thrilled with the final product (even though he does say, "It's
such a rich movie that I love"). Perhaps I shouldn't ascribe feelings to
another person, but he spends most of the conversation describing
how much he would alter his performance, which certainly does make
you think . . . "I wish I could play that part now, for God's sake! I'd do
a different job."

"I think this piece of material, although gorgeously rendered,
could have withstood a *bit* of my newfound—in the last couple of decades, three decades—ability to take a line," Goldblum said in his
Goldblumy way. ". . . I think from moment to moment I could render
those lines in a way that came out of me more, that was more conver-
sational, more seemingly spontaneous and improvisational. Maybe I
could have even improvised a little here and there."

It's tough to know exactly what went wrong. Landis has made

some of America's finest comedies, and even notable directors don't hit a home run every time. The main issue is the tone, namely its lack of consistency. It likely didn't help that Landis briefly left production to stand trial for manslaughter. He, three other filmmakers, and a pilot were accused of acting with criminal negligence after a helicopter crash resulting from a special effects explosion killed actor Vic Morrow and two child actors, aged six and seven, while they were filming the big-screen adaptation of *Twilight Zone* in 1982. Everyone was eventually found innocent, but to have something so enormous hanging over your head while trying to direct a comedy certainly can't be easy.

Additionally, some of the film's racial politics don't exactly hold up, to put it mildly. Of course, many movies are products of their times and playing judge, jury, and executioner years later both ruins the fun and doesn't really change anything. Even so, *Into the Night* stands out as something that was almost outdated in its own time. Goldblum's Ed makes odd quips about "illegal aliens" that can't help but stand out today. The only thing that's really aged well is the stubble Goldblum sports in the final shootout.

Maybe the biggest issue is the cast. Few movies are striking once the credits roll, unless Nick Fury waits at the end of them to dole out information on a sequel, but perhaps the most interesting aspect of *Into the Night* is those scrolling names. Not many films so bluntly show what a microcosm Hollywood really is. Appearing in cameos are several directors who worked with Goldblum (or who soon would), including Kasdan, Mazursky, and David Cronenberg, along with about ten other notable screenwriters and directors. Even his then-wife Patricia Gaul makes an appearance as a flight attendant.

Cameos aren't bad if they have some purpose, but these feel self-indulgent and steal the spotlight away from the two leads. As Roger Ebert, who called the movie a "mindless, shapeless mess," wrote:

"What's the idea here? To make a home movie? If I had been the agent for one of the stars, like Goldblum, Michelle Pfeiffer, Richard Farnsworth or Kathryn Harrold, I think I would have protested to the front office that Landis was engaging in cinematic autoeroticism and that my clients were getting lost in the middle of the family reunion. . . . Maybe what the movie needed was more professional discipline and less geniality. As a rule, it's probably better to throw the party after the filming is finished."

Most critics agreed with Ebert. "*Into the Night* features cameo appearances by 11 directors, none of whom had the sense to get behind the camera and help the 12th, John Landis," wrote Paul Attanasio in the *Washington Post*, calling the movie "all cameos." Vincent Canby of the *New York Times* wrote, "All of it has the insidey manner of a movie made not for the rest of us but for moviemakers on the Bel Air circuit who watch each other's films in their own screening rooms."

The movie bombed, earning just $7.6 million ($19.1 million, adjusted for inflation) domestically. "[It] was my first box office failure, and that was quite surprising to me, because I hadn't done anything different," Landis, pretty much the only person surprised by the failure, told Collider in 2005. "It was dark. And that's another thing: critics don't like it when you fuck with genre. . . . When things get muddled, they're confused. I like *Into the Night*. It's got a wonderful cast."

He's right about exactly one thing here. The movie *does* have a wonderful cast. That their talents were so wasted should be the subject of a congressional hearing. "It's a really interesting movie to think about why it doesn't work. It's exactly the kind of movie that big filmmakers were making in the mideighties. It's like *After Hours*, a kooky, sort of genre-y film," Nayman told me. The thought path led him to speculate how history might have been different if Goldblum had appeared in Scorsese's *After Hours* instead of Landis's movie. "The question of could Jeff Goldblum be the lead of a big American movie would have been answered." As it stood, though, by mid-1985, it remained a question.

Luckily the rest of the year, and the decade, still had some nice surprises in store for Goldblum.

Sighted in the Wild

Given his dual hobbies of teaching acting and playing jazz music on a weekly basis when he isn't working, Goldblum is one of Hollywood's more accessible celebrities. That said, sometimes he's sighted in the wild under the strangest of circumstances. Much of this has to do with various projects, particularly his Disney+ show *The World According to Jeff Goldblum*, which he filmed in relative secrecy (at least, secret from the general public). That said, promotional stunt or not, here are my favorite three sightings.

ST. PANCRAS STATION

Just imagine wandering bleary-eyed into the train station for your morning commute, and you hear some jazzy riffs. Sure, Goldblum played in London's St. Pancras train station as a promo gag, but that didn't make it any less exciting for the passersby who caught the unexpected performance. Remember, all of life's a stage and all that. There's something inherently tickling about seeing a celebrity in the wild, but what a twist to see a famous actor wearing a slick black leather jacket and playing jazz piano—*before* he released an album, signaling his second act to the world.

CHEF GOLDBLUM'S JAZZY SNAGS

Though a notoriously picky eater himself—nearly every profile mentions his meticulous ordering, which feels reminiscent of that of Daniel Day-Lewis's Reynolds Woodcock in *Phantom Thread*—Goldblum doesn't attempt to dictate what other people should consume. Still, it must have been shocking for Sydney residents to find the actor not only on their continent but in a food truck named Chef Goldblum's Jazzy Snags, where he was handing out fancy sausage sandwiches and remaining coy on why. Only problem was, reportedly, the line moved a little slowly, as he took his time to chat at length with every guest. It was worth it, however, simply for the *Daily Telegraph*'s printing the following bizarre sentence: "Jeff Goldblum is a sneaky sausage."

NEW ORLEANS DECADENCE FESTIVAL

Admittedly, I revel in every opportunity to discuss my hometown of New Orleans, so this one excites me. Southern Decadence is an almost weeklong celebration of LGBTQ culture held in and around New

Orleans. The main event, natch, is a parade through the French Quarter. It was at this parade in 2019 that Goldblum appeared on a balcony like some DMT-inspired vision, dancing in his zebra-print pants and leopard-print shirt to Normani's "Motivation," before joining the parade.

A Star Is Blum-ed

The year of nineteen hundred and eighty-five included a few perks, or at least some events Goldblum probably recalls with fondness. *Into the Night* may have been a critical, box office, and—let's just say it—artistic failure, but it highlighted something more important: Hollywood's desire to transform Jeff Goldblum into a leading man, an A-list celebrity, and America's new crush. "People had a lot of hopes for *Into the Night*, and then it just died," Johanna Schneller, a culture journalist who has profiled him several times, told me. "People wanted to make him happen. There was a tremendous fondness for him."

The proof is in the pudding, if *Gentlemen's Quarterly*—i.e., *GQ*—happens to be a viscous chocolate substance rather than a glossy magazine. Goldblum first appeared on its cover in July 1985, which in retrospect was both a few years too late and about one year too early.

With all due respect to Jean Vallely, the profile is a demonstrative example of Goldblum's skill in navigating the press by giving what may feel like revealing quotes while saying nothing. Well, almost nothing. This is one of the only pieces of journalism I've stumbled across in which he betrays his desire to appear humble and almost confused by his success. It begins with his talking about a lamp, of all things, which sounds like a pedestrian lede for a story about a Hollywood up-and-comer until Vallely gets to his comments about it: "Look at it. Elegant, graceful, with some humor. Just like me."

Throughout the piece, he brags about partying with Kevin Kline and his sister, Pam (nicknamed, according to the piece, Whammo). The description of his pad, necessitated by print-magazine-profile law, includes references to that lamp, a couch (aqua green!), a dining table, chairs, an electric piano, and a drum kit.

Throughout the piece, Goldblum ducks and weaves his way out of saying anything of substance. He likes all the directors he's worked with, and he would work with them again. He's sad François Truffaut is dead. He thinks Robert De Niro is "very good." He's a fan of Humphrey Bogart's performance in *Casablanca* and Marlon Brando's in *On the Waterfront* and *A Streetcar Named Desire*. Stop the presses. This is some barn-burning stuff.

Of course, Vallely recognizes this, insightfully writing, "I feel like I'm interviewing Jeff Goldblum playing a Jeff Goldblum character—everything is just slightly off." But the mere fact that the profile appeared when it did is slightly off too, since it was hooked to Lawrence Kasdan's *Silverado*, a film in which of all the big names, he has by far the smallest (and, in a rare instance for him, most forgettable) role.*

---

*This is in no way meant to diminish the Western, a modern-day classic. It's merely that Goldblum portrays a gambling man named Slick who has about as much depth as that name. Toward the end of the movie, he's revealed to be a villain, but it's not a tremendous surprise since we never know all that much about him in the first place.

Every once in a while throughout the three-page piece, Goldblum slips up and lets out something that would seem unfathomable for him to utter today. "A good actor has to have an appetite to play and live truthfully under imaginary circumstance. And in that, a desire to reveal yourself in some way. A desire to find out who you really are and then let other people see it," he says, a refrain we've heard a thousand times since, a refrain I feel like I've written a thousand times in this book already. But then, in a momentary glimpse of something deeper, he finishes the quote with, "I'm not mainstream. I'm special."

Holy shit.

The quote is offset by Vallely's quoting an anonymous Hollywood insider in the very next paragraph who says he can never carry a movie by himself but that he'll be a character man until he dies. That's only half-true, since he essentially carries *The Fly* by himself a year later but never quite manages to capture that lightning in a bottle again.

The profile is littered with odd moments, such as when he tells the story of his and Gaul's meeting and says they're "relatively" happy, even though the couple is actually separated, a fact Vallely doesn't know and Goldblum doesn't mention.

He'd become a hot but confounding commodity everyone wanted to use, someone who appeared to be on the cusp of breaking out, leaving only the question of *how* in the wake of his failed attempt at (co)anchoring a movie. The answer would arrive soon enough, but first he flew out to Eastern Europe to film a little-remembered movie that helped launch him into stardom, thanks to whom he met there: Geena Davis.

With his marriage to Gaul teetering on the brink of collapse, he encountered Davis for the first time while in Yugoslavia to film *Transylvania 6-5000*, the final of three movies featuring him in 1985. They took to each other but played it too cool to let the sparks really fly, as they learned once back in Los Angeles. "We were just so weird,"

Davis told *GQ*. "For some reason I decided that Jeff liked me only because he thought I was cool, aloof, and he thought the same thing about me. Finally, he takes me out to dinner one night, all serious, and I'm thinking, Uh-oh, I knew this was coming, and he says, 'We can't see each other anymore. I really like you, and you don't like me.' So I say, 'No, I really like you, too,' and that was it. I have this idea about people in your life. I think you recognize them, that they're right for you. I recognized Jeff."

Goldblum felt the same, telling the magazine, "Geena made love, falling in love, so easy. She's purely loving, beguiling—irresistible. Steps would be taken gradually sometimes, and sometimes it swept along. And, of course, I'm wildly attracted to her. *Wildly* attracted. We'd talk about marriage, bring up the idea more and more over a period of months. We could, we should, wouldn't it be romantic? We would act out small scenes of life together: 'Hi, honey, you got some mail today.' It was very sexy."

The actual marriage happened quickly, creating a Hollywood love story they eagerly shared in magazine profiles and newspaper articles. And why not? It has all the strokes of a life-affirming romance. Much like "Young Goldblum and the Bathroom Mirror/Shower Door," it's impossible to say how true it is. Details seem to change from account to account, but the broad strokes remain the same. A fun story that makes you wish it were your story, that your romance burned so brightly, so spontaneously. But spontaneous combustion tends to be a bad thing, and those relationships generally don't last—this one included. Still, everyone loves a good story, so . . .

Things move quickly in the Goldblumverse. About a year after his divorce with Gaul, he and Davis were an item, the kind who appear in newsprint pages. And one particular vacation ended up everywhere from the *Washington Post* to *GQ*. Wanting to bring Goldblum somewhere he'd never visited before, she grabbed his good friend Ed Begley Jr. and Begley Jr.'s wife, Ingrid, and set out for Las Vegas. After having dinner, the foursome debated what to do next— maybe a show? Nah. Begley Jr. had a suggestion. How about instead you young lovebirds tie the knot, Vegas style?

At first it seemed like a joke, and everyone laughed as Goldblum began warming to the idea, saying maybe they *should* throw caution to the wind and get hitched.

"At first I was just laughing. And all of a sudden everybody seems to be heading out to the taxis or something, and I said, 'Wait a minute, wait a minute. You guys are kidding, right?'" Davis told the *Washington Post*. "Jeff goes, 'No, we were thinking about maybe doing it in the next year, and why do a whole big thing? Let's just do it. Maybe it will be romantic.' And I start crying, and I'm like, 'I don't know. I don't know.' And then I thought I'd wrecked it—even if I want to do it— because now I've been crying and ruined it. And he said, 'No. No, you didn't ruin it.' And so, at three in the morning we wind up in this chapel. And we did it."

The couple captivated Hollywood—and at least some of America. They presented together at the Academy Awards. They constantly did press as a pair. They even appeared together on the cover of *GQ* in 1989, an honor that hasn't been bestowed on many couples. Liz Smith, the grand dame of Dish, read that profile and wrote in her column that they "sound[ed] delightful!" Exclamation point hers, not mine.

"It was a bit of a fairy tale. They were so tall, and they were so beautiful together, and they were so funny," Schneller, who wrote the *GQ* profile, told me. "I don't think that they were ever fully mainstream, but they were a great couple for those in the know."

It helped that the two shared not only a romantic relationship but something of a creative partnership. Both were deeply serious about their craft. They even shared a private acting coach in the late Roy London, who also worked with Patrick Swayze and Michelle Pfeiffer.

When they met, Davis wasn't yet a household name despite having had a striking role in *Tootsie* and another in *Fletch*. Recognition would arrive for Davis in the next few years with *Beetlejuice* and *Thelma and Louise*. But by the mideighties, she still mostly worked in television, mainly run-of-the-mill sitcoms. So it's curious that the three movies she made with Goldblum all involved some element of sci-fi, fantasy, or horror—all in varying degrees and under varying circumstances. With that in mind, however, there isn't a tremendous amount of take-away, Goldblum-wise, from the first and the third.

Transylvania 6-5000, which came out in 1985, is a tremendously stupid, sometimes funny spoof on the classic monsters-in-a-castle film genre. That the title is derived from the Glenn Miller song "Pennsylvania 6-5000" should be all you need to know. Goldblum and his close friend Begley Jr. play reporters who head to Transylvania to get a scoop on Frankenstein. They meet some odd characters once they arrive, such as the creepy butler Fejos (a pre-*Seinfeld* Michael Richards, who is just *going for it*) and the sexy, scantily clad, and terribly horny vampire Odette (Davis), along with other classic horror film staples.

Probably the most interesting thing about it, other than the meeting of Goldblum and Davis or that it was filmed in Yugoslavia,* is that it was funded by Dow Chemical Company. The company needed to find a way to spend some funds that were frozen in the country, because Yugoslavian law disallowed the repatriation of money accumulated in the Yugoslavian currency, the dinar, which is a fancy way of saying if you had money in the currency in their country, you couldn't just pull it out and convert it to US dollars to spend on a bunch of Juicy Fruit or whatever at the corner store. The movie did

---

* Is that even interesting?

well enough considering the strange circumstances of its creation, making a little more than $7 million on a $3 million budget.

The final movie they filmed together was a similarly campy (but more interesting) picture, 1989's *Earth Girls Are Easy*. The movie is the kind of lambent bonkers batshit schlock that has become short-hand for the 1980s. Think of it as the film equivalent of a neon-green tank top with bright orange roller skates. If you haven't seen it, know that a written plot outline can never capture just how preposterous and outlandishly fun this relic is. Long story short: Davis plays Valerie Gail, a Valley-girl manicurist who works at Curl Up & Dye. She catches her doctor husband cheating on her, breaks everything in the house during a musical number—did I mention this was a *musical?*—puts on a minuscule red bikini, and sunbathes in her pool, only to have an alien spaceship crash in the water next to her. In it are three furry aliens, whom she and her boss Candy Pink (Julie Brown) later shave, only to discover they're a trio of hunky dudes named Mac, Wiploc, and Zeebo (played by Goldblum, Jim Carrey, and Damon Wayans, respectively). Our man, in particular, stood out after the removal of his blue fur. Deep in his metamorphosis into one of Hollywood's enduring sex symbols, Goldblum had become something of a hardbody, compliments of an on-set transformation in *The Fly* (more on this in a moment). The shearing of the character's protective coat to reveal what's underneath might as well be the definition of *metaphor*. As the girls take their alien friends out on the town, things get wacky. Hijinks ensue! Intergalactic sex is had! Mistakes are made! (Speaking of, the sex scene between Davis's and Goldblum's characters might be fun, but shooting it was anything but sexy. "We're lying on this plank, covered in gauze, and they're shining these rainbow lights all over us, we're sweating like crazy, and these two prop people are sprinkling us with these fake jewels," Davis told *GQ*. "It looks great now, but those rushes were the funniest I've ever seen. They're in slow motion, and these jewels keep hitting us in the face, we keep grimacing. At one point, I open my mouth in ecstasy, and this jewel goes right in. In slow motion, you see me gag, and *ptooey*, I spit it straight into the air.")

Earth Girls Are Easy is the movie equivalent of cotton candy, and not only due to its color palette. The movie goes down easy, fuss-free, and feels just satisfying enough to be worth the investment, even if it's all empty calories. Perhaps the best part of the film, however, has nothing to do with what's on-screen. Watching critics contort their arguments about it into bizarre shapes to avoid claiming they liked it is so entertaining that it should be an Olympic sport. In a clear instance of snobby critics' attempting to grapple with the fact that they enjoyed something so fluffy, many reviewers recommended the movie in the same breath as they insulted it.

In a generally positive review, *Rolling Stone*'s Peter Travers called it "an entertaining trifle" and "agreeably tacky" while encouraging his readers to "forgive the airhead plot." Ebert wrote that the movie is "silly and predictable and as permanent as a feather in the wind, but I had fun watching it." Kathi Maio wrote for *Sojourner*, "It's fluff. Is it ever. But at least it's female-oriented fluff, more or less."

Sandwiched in between the two, however, is the movie that arguably remains Goldblum's artistic pinnacle.

After my traumatic childhood experience, I didn't revisit *The Fly* until this project forced me to, and you know what? Given how masterfully crafted, designed, shot, directed, and acted the film is—and, as a result, how horrifying it is—my fear feels justified. Plus, I'm in good company. When revisiting the film decades after its release for Roger Ebert's blog, film critic Gerardo Valero wrote, "'The

Fly' . . . is among a very few movies that give me a sense of hesitation as soon as the credits appear. . . . [Aside from *The Exorcist*], I can't think of another horror film as intense as *The Fly*. They are both almost unbearable to watch and certain sections of the latter have the upper-hand when it comes to inciting a sense of disgust, and that's saying something." Valero rightly concluded it's "an amazingly effective movie, one that really gets under your skin, the kind you can't help but admire but feel no rush to come back to anytime soon and when you do, it's probably a good idea to skip the candy counter in advance."

It arrived at a vital moment in Goldblum's career. *Into the Night* made a convincing case against the actor as a leading man. Which was odd. The world liked him; critics loved him. He'd become a household name among people who care enough to discuss celebrities in their houses, a status only strengthened through his relationship with Davis. But at this point, he was still a great character actor, living comedic flair, and not much else. As Nayman said, he was more like a spice in a stew, an element that changes the general flavor profile but nothing you'd want on its own. Certainly not a name culture journalists would toss around when predicting the year's Oscar nominees. Director David Cronenberg, though, noticed something different in him.

At least, Cronenberg *eventually* noticed something different about him. When casting *The Fly*, he reportedly offered the film to actors such as Michael Keaton, John Lithgow, and Richard Dreyfuss. In the end, though, the right actor got the part. The movie could have so easily slid into the same category as the entertaining but schlocky parodic fare Goldblum had been pumping out (and, to some degree, would continue to) if it weren't for Cronenberg's brilliant direction and Goldblum's virtuoso performance.

Though deeply affecting, the plot's deceptively simple: A scientist named Seth Brundle (Goldblum) invents a teleportation device that he starts testing on more advanced creatures as he begins dating Veronica "Ronnie" Quaife (Davis). Eventually, he transports himself between the two pods he's set up in his scientific lair/pretty nice loft apartment. He doesn't notice the fly that snuck in with him, and their DNA intertwines. Quaife, who loves him until the end, watches his body slowly, then suddenly, disintegrate as he transforms into some human-fly hybrid. At first he loves the new superhuman powers the transformation bestows on him, but soon enough, he's literally falling apart. By the time he figures out what's happening, he's barely human—and unable to be saved.

"It's a grand movie and a grand part. I like the part because it's human. I thought there was charm and tension in the part and the circumstances were big and romantic, sad and horrible," Goldblum told the *Sun-Sentinel* when promoting the movie. "Isn't it tragic what happens? I love this girl more deeply than I've ever loved, perhaps it's the first time I've fallen in love. It causes a breakthrough in my work but then I start getting paranoid, having these awful jealous ideas that maybe she doesn't love me, it seems that I start getting nervous. Then the whole rest of the tragedy hinges on that one momentary failing."

As a result of the story's tragic nature, the filming was particularly antic-free, according to several folks who worked on it. Gillian Richardson, the script supervisor, said the set matched the feeling of the movie. While they were filming the scene when Brundle realizes his human body is disintegrating, and he begins peeling his fingernails off one by one, "you could hear a pin drop on the set. I'm just sitting there behind the camera, and the tears start rolling down my cheeks."

Instead of the parties of *The Big Chill* or the lurking romance of *Transylvania 6-5000*, Goldblum spent his time working out constantly on set, pumping himself up for the part, filling out his lanky frame. Remember, insects can lift several times their own weight. His routine proved infectious, as Cronenberg mentioned in the film's commentary. "We were very much into working out on this movie. As I say, when you fuse with your leading actor, and your leading actor is pumping up with weights, with dumbbells, before every shot where he doesn't have a lot of clothes on, then there's a trickle-down effect," he said. "So I was working out in my trailer, in my office, between shots, between takes. And of course, Jeff was doing the same thing. I actually ended up being in quite good shape after this movie, unlike most other movies, where I gained 15 or as much as 20 pounds."

To help with his research, Davis caught a fly and plopped it into a plastic baggie, which Goldblum kept in his trailer and studied. "We got a straight pin and a cork and put the Baggie up on the wall. We found a way to put some gravy in it and some food to feed this thing. I'd go up and watch it eat and move around for about a week," he told the *Sun-Sentinel* at the time. Years later, the story mutated into his carrying a fly in his pocket, a rumor he's always quick to squash. As he told the *Guardian*, he wouldn't do that, because he's "always been highly conscientious."

When he wasn't working out, acting, or watching his pet fly, Goldblum was having makeup applied. So much makeup.

Since the movie follows him in progressive stages of morphing into a flylike creature, Chris Walas and Stephan Dupuis had to create several stages of makeup, which included making body parts intended to rot. Your nightmares might remember Brundle's peeling off his fingernails and ears. Cronenberg "wanted to see someone falling apart," Dupuis said.

So "part of the challenge was getting Jeff's makeup to a point that would not be too restrictive for him, yet still be able to suggest something forming within. He had to look a bit swollen so that when the final creature emerged it would somehow look feasible," Walas told me. The process began, Dupuis said, with creating a full-body cast of Goldblum and molding the final fly suit.

Goldblum himself presented a slight hurdle. As Walas said, "When David was casting the part of Seth Brundle, he asked me if there were any makeup concerns he should be considering. Now, in doing prosthetics, it's possible to build out from the surface of the actor's face. But it's not really possible to go down from the actor's facial surface, so I told David if he could look to cast someone with a small nose and small ears, it would give us more leeway in making the makeup believable. Well, David called up one day and said, 'I think I have an actor I like, but I don't know if he will work for you. It's Jeff Goldblum.' So Jeff was pretty much what I had asked David to avoid. But I was a huge fan of Jeff's and I told David that he was a great choice and we would do whatever it took to make the makeup work. And it was a challenge. The worst was the ear-falling-off gag. Jeff has superhuman ear cartilage and we had to glue his ears down for the effect. Several bottles of our strongest adhesive later, we finally got them to hold down long enough for the shot!"

Of course, designing the Brundlefly was only the beginning. Then there was the actual application of the makeup, which forced Goldblum to sit in a chair for hours as Dupuis worked on him. "Most actors are just fine with the long process, but some are a pain, and some are a nightmare. Jeff seemed to be enjoying the process," Walas said. Davis would read aloud to him from the novels of Anne Tyler while he sat for hours having his makeup applied.*

In Brundlefly's final stage, there's basically no human aspect to

---

* Two years after *The Fly*, Lawrence Kasdan's adaptation of Tyler's novel *The Accidental Tourist* would hit theaters and earn Davis an Oscar for best supporting actress.

him left except the eyes, leaving Goldblum with little to work with. That led to what Walas called his "favorite moment."

"I stopped by to check on Jeff in the makeup room. I was busy prepping all the mechanical and puppet effects we were doing, but I'd stop by the makeup room to double-check every morning. I stopped in the doorway; Jeff was alone, waiting to be called to set. Usually this is a time when an actor is just sitting back relaxing or running lines, but Jeff was sitting in front of the mirror, practicing every move he could make in the makeup, seeing what worked and what didn't. He was making our makeup his makeup. I've never seen an actor so aware of what makeup could do for their performance. Honestly, I almost broke into tears. Having had all of us on my crew work so very hard on that show, to see what Jeff was doing with it was a huge reward."

If designing the makeup sounds like an ordeal, I cordially invite you to consider the baboon.

Oh, the baboon.

The thing to know about baboons is they don't give much of a shit about how we mere humans feel, so a relatively somber set doesn't mean a thing to them. And the thing about *The Fly* is one of the main characters is a baboon that Brundle sends through the transport pods. For the non-primatologists among us, baboons aren't the cuddliest of creatures. Some species can grow to around eighty pounds, and all baboons possess strong jaws and sharp canine teeth, i.e., fangs. They also tend to do whatever they want, particularly if something catches their eye.

Unfortunately for script supervisor Gillian Richardson, she caught the baboon's eye.

"Do you want me to be ladylike about it or very straightforward?" is how she prefaced her answers to my questions. I, of course, chose the latter option.

"When the baboon came on set, he spotted me out of the corner of his eye. I guess it was love at first sight, shall we say," Richardson said. "Apparently, his original owner was a small, petite blond lady. And I'm small, petite, and blond. So, apparently, he just got this massive erection. And it wouldn't go until he was off the set. It became a massive issue. And, of course, when we realized just how strong the baboon was, it was kind of scary, because this baboon has got fangs that are two or three inches long or something. When they placed the baboon in a pod, he was so strong that he just burst through the pod door, just broke down the door.

"Jeff, though, developed a really strong relationship with the baboon. He would hold him and what have you," she added. "Eventually, extra people were not to be on set with him. And you would hear him *screaming* in all the offices if he got 'agitated,' shall we say. . . . If it wasn't for Jeff developing that incredible relationship with this baboon and being really strong and holding him, it could have been a difficult situation for me. So I can honestly say Jeff probably saved me from physical assault from a baboon. So Jeff will always have a special place in my heart. The baboon, not so much."

Despite Goldblum's relationship with the baboon, the animal remained untrainable. "This is not an animal who will do tricks for you. We had to find ways to get him to perform," Cronenberg said in the film's commentary. So they got creative, particularly in the first scene in which a fly appears. It's buzzing around the baboon, who's seated in a bright red chair. "We actually attached a living fly to, in essence, a tiny fishing line made out of, I think it was, filaments from lightbulbs. So it was basically invisible. In those days, you couldn't remove a line or a wire by going into a computer. You would have to hand-paint it out every frame." So they waved the fly around in front of the baboon, using this contraption.

Then there's the issue of just how physically demanding the whole shoot was. One of the first hints that Seth Brundle might be mutating

into an insect-human hybrid is his sudden strength, which the film communicates by showing him doing what is essentially a gymnastics routine. Dressed in only a pair of khakis, Goldblum's character begins doing handstands while clutching the arms of a chair, as if they were parallel bars. "Jeff, who is about six foot five, could do the beginning of these gymnastic moves. He was very impressive to the gymnast we brought in to do the rest of the moves," Cronenberg said. "Gymnasts are not six foot five. The proportions of muscles to height and so on dictate that most gold-medal-winning gymnasts are five foot four, five foot five, five foot six at maximum. We found a couple of gymnasts who were five foot eight, and they were considered huge . . . they were nonetheless very impressed with the moves that Jeff could do. That helped me. The fact that he could do the beginnings of these moves on his own helped with the illusion with these [gymnasts] standing in for Jeff."

In one scene, to show off to a barfly (pun definitely intended) that he took home, he transports himself between pods. It's shot to look like he's completely naked, and Cronenberg hinted that Goldblum happily would have been, if asked. "Jeff is not shy. There was no false modesty or anything about Jeff. He would have done this scene completely naked if I'd asked him to. It wasn't a problem for him. I didn't want to distract from the movie by doing that, so we didn't do that."

Of course, for most of the movie he isn't naked, nor is he particularly, well, human.

The makeup could only transform Goldblum so much. The rest required a certain caliber of acting, to go from truly charming to ecstatic, like he's snorted four lines of coke, to increasingly angry, then despondent. At one point, the barfly spills alcohol on him, and he swings his wide palm out, slapping the glass out of her hand. He resembles a cornered animal lashing out much more so than a human—even though those five pounds of makeup have yet to be applied.

Not to mention Goldblum's physical acting, which had never been better. *The Fly* is "one of the great transformational body horror films ever made," film critic Sean Fennessey said. "And it doesn't really work without him and that sort of athletic, freakish, hyperintelligent physicality that he brings to it." At one point in his transformation, Seth learns he can climb up walls and on the ceiling. To achieve the effect, this being before the advent of today's CGI technology, Cronenberg and his team built a rotating room, what the director called a "Ferris wheel." It allowed Goldblum to crawl from wall to floor to ceiling all while being on the floor. We can't tell that the room is rotating, of course, but it rests an awful lot of responsibility on Goldblum's back. He shoulders it by crawling around on all fours, body outstretched and moving with a remarkably animalistic grace, the Fred Astaire of humans turning into insects.

Physical challenges abounded on the film, particularly when he wore the five pounds of full-body rubber makeup when the transformation reached its zenith. Goldblum not only had to act with this enormous suit on, he had to do so while wearing prosthetic teeth— one of the reasons those other actors passed on the opportunity. "Quite a few actors were approached about playing this role, and most of them who said no were afraid of the rubber," Cronenberg said. "They were afraid of the makeup. They were afraid that they would not be able to act through the rubber, that they would be lost. And Jeff was totally not afraid. On the contrary, he was looking forward to it. It was not even just a challenge. It was something he felt he could use."

It's often difficult to properly describe excellent acting, which is both severely physical and inherently abstract, so it's difficult to properly explain just how tremendous Goldblum is toward the end of the film. By that point, he's become mostly fly, which means he's been stripped of all his traditional tools as an actor. That's particularly true of Goldblum, whose primary tools are often his hand gestures and positioning his towering body in various ways. Here, though, he doesn't have access to his body, covered as it is by Walas and Dupuis's makeup. Instead, he's forced to act with only his eyes, which he'd been practicing so carefully. Yet he still manages to communicate the fact that he wants to die to the audience, using nothing but a pair of eyeballs surrounded by a pile of makeup.

Here's a fun game that can better explain how difficult this really is. Grab a romantic partner, a friend, a family member—whoever, just so long as this person knows you well. Then put on a mask, any mask. It can be a rubber Richard Nixon mask, a terrifying hockey mask, or just a piece of cardboard taped to your face with eyeholes cut out. Now pick an emotion and try to communicate that emotion through the mask, using only your eyes, and have the other person guess what it is.

Didn't go so well, did it?

So here's this dude acting through a five-pound rubber suit, sitting for hours on end for makeup, taking a role no one else feels up to, acting with only his eyes at one point, and audiences ate it up. The movie made $60.6 million at the box office, not bad for 1986 (about $142 million today). And what did the jamokes at the Academy do? They snubbed the ever-living hell out of Goldblum's performance, after rightly nominating and awarding Walas and Dupuis for Best Makeup. The actors who edged him out for nods? James Woods for *Salvador*, William Hurt for *Children of a Lesser God*, Bob Hoskins for *Mona Lisa*, Dexter Gordon for *'Round Midnight*, and the winner, Paul Newman for *The Color of Money*. Now, not to cast aspersions on any of these films, but none of them endured as *The Fly* has. The performances certainly haven't. Personally, I'm a huge fan of Scorsese's bold sequel to Robert Rossen's *The Hustler*, in which Newman reprises his role as "Fast Eddie" Felson and tutors Tom Cruise's young Vincent Lauria in the art of hustling through billiards. But to award Newman (especially to award Newman and not Cruise, who carries the movie) for the film remains a bizarre (and terrible) choice. It would be a head-scratcher if we didn't know the Academy often gives consolation awards to actors it has long ignored. In other words, the Academy often fucks up in profound ways to make up for former fuckups. *The Color of Money* marked Newman's tenth nomination. Previously, he'd lost for worthy, even iconic, performances in movies such as *The Verdict, Cool Hand Luke, Cat on a Hot Tin Roof,* and, yes, *The Hustler.*

All of which is to say, it's not unexpected that Goldblum didn't receive a nod. It would still be several decades before the Academy began taking horror, comedy, or supernatural (and superhero) films seriously—an ongoing struggle. But that doesn't make it right, as Gene Siskel made clear. "Goldblum got stiffed most likely because he was in a horror film and not a film with an obvious social conscience, the kind the academy traditionally honors," he wrote in a *Chicago Tribune* piece titled "Oscar Swats *The Fly.*"

Throughout the piece, which featured Goldblum accepting his snub with dignity, Siskel railed against the Academy, going so far as to say that the snub suggested "a lot of older academy voters, who dominate the Oscar ballot box, did not even see the film."

By Siskel's account, Goldblum initially pretended not to care much. At one point, he said he and Davis learned he hadn't gotten a nomination while lying in bed, and she started crying. That's what he really cared about. When asked who he would vote for, he replied, "I don't want to be namby-pamby, but I'd really like to mute the publicity value in all this and not aggravate someone's vanity. I really abhor that element in our profession."

Eventually, though, he told the critic that he had spoken with his therapist about the loss. "As much as I'm interested in the integrity of the work itself," he said, "there is a part of me that is sensitive to criticism, that delights to have any talent I may have acknowledged. I did hope that I would be nominated; I was excited about the possibility; there had been a lot of talk about it, and I was disappointed and hurt in a way. But I'm philosophical about it now, and I'm eager to act some more."

Unfortunately Goldblum would never again take on a role quite so rich—though he'd spend the next several years taking some admirable swings. His next movie *should* have been as rich, if not richer. *Beyond Therapy*, his follow-up to *The Fly*, once again finds him teaming up with Robert Altman, only this time in something of a leading role.

Goldblum made some tremendous missteps throughout his career in choosing which projects to tackle, but there's a good argument to be made that at least some of these missteps were somewhat unavoidable. Many of the movies in which he's a lead or co-lead sound good on paper, only to be mangled in the execution. In other cases, hindsight is 20/20. *Beyond Therapy* is not one of those cases. Yes, Altman had made a few stinkers in his career, particularly with material based on theatrical plays, but his last two movies (*Fool for Love* and *Secret Honor*, both adaptations from the stage) had been well received by critics if not a hit with audiences. There was good cause to think Altman was back on track.

Based on the Broadway play of the same name by Christopher Durang that had starred John Lithgow, Dianne Wiest, and David Hyde Pierce, the premise was promising enough: Two well-to-do Manhattanites, Bruce and Prudence (Goldblum and Julie Hagerty), looking to find love follow the advice of their terrible therapists (Glenda Jackson and Christopher Guest) and place personal ads in the newspaper, even though Goldblum's bisexual Bruce already has a jealous live-in male lover (Tom Conti). The main joke, of course, is that therapists are the ones with the real issues. It's a perfect setup for hilarity to ensue, especially since the material already made for a sardonically comical play.

And, in fact, according to the film's editor, Stephen Dunn,* the movie they filmed in Paris "*was* one of the funniest movies."

"Altman was a funny guy. He didn't want it to be *too* funny. So he took a lot of the humor out," Dunn told me. "I had huge fights with him when we were editing. I said, 'Why are you doing this?' Bob would rewrite the script. I've never seen someone rewrite the script in editing. He would just change it.

"Jeff was fantastic in it," Dunn was quick to say. He's right—the film clearly doesn't fail on the back of any of the actors, all of whom offer terrific performances. The issue is the script and the odd editing choices that led to a lack of momentum (and, often, humor).

Altman famously required most, if not all, cast members and crewmembers to gather each afternoon/evening to go over dailies (i.e., the footage shot that day). In Altman's world, these were parties, filled with pot, booze, and food. Normally, an editor might sit next to the director to discuss various takes. With Altman, though, nothing was ever normal. He didn't want to sit next to Dunn.

"He just didn't work that way," Dunn said. "But Jeff wanted to sit next to me. And it was so much fun. He would tell me, 'Oh, please don't use that. Oh, there, that's my best take!' And I actually took editing notes with an actor. Every day, we sat next to each other. Bob was down in the front row, and we were in the back, whispering to each other. And Jeff was just a smart, funny, and charming guy."

Lamentably, being a smart, funny, and charming guy—and even the two coming up with great editing notes—couldn't save the film from the man who created it. Though *Beyond Therapy* included Goldblum's most sizable role in an Altman film, it was a box office bomb, even by art-house standards. Critics hated it. Though this is

---

*The same who worked on *The Big Chill*.

an imperfect measure, it is Altman's lowest-rated film after *Quintet*, his baffling 1979 sophomoric stab at what he seemed to think was a profound postapocalyptic movie, according to Rotten Tomatoes, pleasing only a quarter of the critics who reviewed it.

Adrian Danks, the editor of *A Companion to Robert Altman*, told me via email the movie is "weak, rarely funny, and struggles for any sort of momentum," through no fault of Goldblum's.

Danks added, "[It's] curious that Altman gets to use Goldblum as the established (if surprising) leading man here—I guess it's a case of stars aligning at the wrong time. Plainly the 1980s is Altman's weakest period as a director, and his decision (though I'm not sure it was this) to make a series of works that are very contained and based on theatrical properties of one kind or another is a curious one. As was his decision to make some films—like this one—where he expressed little faith or even interest in the source material."

That very disinterest certainly bothered Christopher Durang, who wrote the play Altman's movie was based on. He later called the film "a very unhappy experience and outcome" and suggested that Altman didn't adhere to the original adaptation agreement.

"A friend of mine who knew my play *Beyond Therapy* from Broadway saw the movie version and said, 'Well, it's not much like the play. It's sort of a jazz variation on the play.' Which is the nicest way of looking at it," Durang wrote. "Altman wrote his own adaptation of the play before I even started to write mine—which certainly wasn't the agreement. Then I wrote mine, which he pretty much ignored. And he was hurt I didn't like his version. Eventually I requested that we have a shared credit (since his version still had chunks of the original play in it), and I secretly hoped that the actors would improvise a lot, as was known to happen in Altman films. However, the finished film is pretty close to what Altman wrote. His version, in my opinion, throws the psychological underpinnings out the window, and people just run around acting 'crazy.'

"I think the play would have made a good commercial comic film if the track-able psychology from the play had been kept. As well as more of the play's dialogue," he added. "Plus the movie lost me when Jeff Goldblum started sucking Julie Hagerty's toes in the restaurant in the first five minutes. Unpleasant, unlikely to do in a restaurant, and the action told you that you were in a fake world."

Danks bemoaned the fact that Goldblum wasn't a star earlier or later in Altman's career. The eighties were, as discussed, arguably the director's worst decade, though it's tough to pin down exactly *why*. I suppose every artistic genius must fail sometime in the pursuit of pushing the boundaries of a specific medium. That Altman's lows were as low as his highs were high[*] might simply be the price of brilliance.

"In some ways, although Goldblum becomes a star in this decade it is the period least suited to Altman's sensibility and approach. The film itself highlights the conflict between a mediocre source (the play) and Altman's attempts to pull this out of shape and create something closer to his earlier films (so it manically moves from one character/actor to the next while building up little momentum)," Danks wrote. "I guess, at some level, it does draw Goldblum back to the theatrical environment in which they first encountered each other—but that is the problem here, the film can't decide whether it is a filmed play or something else. Once again, Goldblum wears particularly expressive costumes, uses props dexterously, and is probably the only truly Altmanesque performance in the film. [*New York Times* film reviewer]

---

[*] And, obviously, Altman produced far more highs than lows.

Vincent Canby did provide a nice description of Goldblum here: 'He comes in with the eagerness of a lapdog that doesn't know it's the size of a Great Dane.' That does indeed say much of the quality of Goldblum's (too) eager performance, but the film itself most certainly can't contain it. But there is a physicality, lightness and groundedness to his performance here that certainly isn't matched by the others. But boy is the film (& Goldblum too, unfortunately) tiresome."

The always (sometimes over-) confident Altman had his own, erm, far-fetched theory for the movie's failure, as he shared in his memoir: "The unfortunate part of *Beyond Therapy* was that when I came to release the film in America, the day it opened *Time* and *Newsweek* magazines came out with AIDS as their cover story. So AIDS opened too, and that finished the film because of the bisexual attitude in the play. It was about a bisexual guy in love with the guy he lives with and a girl who comes into his life."

There is a particular irony to his reasoning. This is meant in no way to make light of the AIDS epidemic, but the tragedy arguably helped *The Fly*. Cronenberg has repeatedly insisted his movie is not an allegory for the AIDS epidemic, but artistic intention and audience reception often have little in common. *The Fly* is one of the starkest examples of that phenomenon. Valero noted it "was released at the dawn of the AIDS epidemic and was seen by many as a metaphor for the disease." Though Valero ultimately disagrees with this assessment, he conceded that "the shoe certainly can fit." In truth, the movie is about several things, including aging, disease (abstractly), and the sense of losing one's humanity. Hence Brundle's asking Quaife if she's ever heard of "insect politics." He's no longer human.

But let's pretend Cronenberg *did* intend for the movie to mirror the AIDS epidemic in some way. Since people thought that was what it was about then, for all intents and purposes, that's what it was about. The movie made $60.1 million worldwide ($141 million, adjusted for inflation), two-thirds of that coming from domestic markets. *Beyond Therapy* made $790,000 ($1.8 million, adjusted). Clearly the idea of seeing a movie that *might* bring to mind the AIDS crisis didn't drive audiences away from theaters. If anything, it might have drawn them *toward* theaters.

Beyond Therapy simply wasn't very good. And Goldblum simply isn't *really* a leading man, a point that can't help but come up again and again, particularly as we enter the 1990s, when he really made a go of it. There's something just a little too eclectic about him, a little too tall, a little too out of place for him to be the type of movie star that opens films. He's like caviar: delicious in small portions but overwhelming as an entire meal.

Every good theory, of course, needs an exception to prove the rule. For this one, we have his last film of the decade: *The Tall Guy*, the debut of screenwriter Richard Curtis. To this day, the rom-com stands out in Goldblum's oeuvre, partly because of the sheer *Britishness* of it all. He plays Dexter King, a frustrated American stage actor who has spent years as the punchline in a two-person comedy revue called *The Tall Guy* with Ron Anderson (Rowan Atkinson). He's got hay fever, though, so he goes to a doctor and falls in love with a nurse named Kate (Emma Thompson). A series of increasingly strange events lands him in *Elephant!*, a musical based on *The Elephant Man*. (Yes, the one you're thinking of.) One of his costars comes on to him, and things spiral out of control from there.

With a smart script and a trio of actors giving wonderfully off-kilter performances, it's one of the best offerings in his filmography. Doesn't hurt that the movie also involved a lot of, erm, *shagging*—to use the queen's English. But it was so tastefully done that some of the folks who don't like that sort of thing didn't mind it. Thompson told the story of one of the sex scenes (her first) on the podcast *My Dad Wrote a Porno*, saying, "Because it was a comedy sex scene, we were shagging on the piano, we were shagging in the breakfast things. There were shots of my ass with bits of toast stuck to it. Two fucking days of being nude on set. And when the campaign came out, the Campaign Against Pornography, which used to exist, I know that's a hilarious idea now . . . Anyway, they said that if they were to show their children a sex scene, they would show that one, because it was fun and funny, and it was full of humor. Because I noticed at the time that all sex scenes, everyone was so angry. They're angry! You look at people's faces, you look at *Basic Instinct*. Sharon Stone and whatsherface . . . livid! So livid! So cross!"

Sounds great, right?

Well, that's because it is. It still stands out in Gary Arnold's mind. "It seemed like he could be the leader in a fresh approach to contemporary comedy," he said, calling *The Tall Guy* "a potential turning point. . . . There he was, about to turn 40, and suddenly it seemed like he was going to be part of a British comedy apparatus, oddly enough, that flattered him a great deal. But there was never any follow-up to the satisfying parts of that film, which still plays very well. But it didn't set off a new kind of sex comedy, unfortunately. I wish it had, and I wish he and Emma Thompson had been paired up again."

One reason for the lack of follow-up might be that when a movie pulls in only $510,700 (a little more than a million, adjusted), it doesn't exactly launch its actor into leading-man status. Curtis fared well in the long term, delighting audiences with similar scripts years later. In fact, one DVD version of *The Tall Guy* touts that the movie is "from the writer of *Four Weddings and a Funeral* and *Notting Hill*," both of which came later. History has a funny way of rewriting itself. Thompson, of course, shot into the stratosphere of the Hollywood elite. Just four years later, she'd be polishing an Oscar statue for her work in *Howards End*.

Goldblum, though, still hadn't found his place. Was he a leading man? An A-list star? A character actor? An actor who made a great celebrity or a celebrity who happened to be a great actor? His singularity both helped and hindered him. No one could really figure him out. "When people see something original, they recognize it. When they see something singular, they recognize it. And I think that Jeff's career might have been a series of people trying to stuff a square peg into round holes. Everyone's like, 'Where does this guy fit, because we like him, and we want to use him and see him?' But they never quite found the place he fit," Schneller said, adding, "The fact that he eventually broke out to the extent that he did is kind of a miracle." So after *The Tall Guy*, he found himself filming *Framed*, an HBO movie. Not that he minded. "I'm not snobby about mediums, because I see bad movies—movies that I wouldn't want to be in," Goldblum told the *Los Angeles Times*. "And I see television things that are sometimes interesting and OK. So I'd rather be in the interesting and OK things, no matter what they are."

Such a strange left turn might prompt some to ask, why on earth would this guy who was so recently touted as a strong Oscar contender, one who was justified in the use of the word *snub* when referring to the fact that he didn't get a nod, one who had just appeared on the cover of *GQ* for a *second* time, why would he take a role in a TV movie, careerist or not? I suspect you know the answer, so, please, everyone repeat after me.

Because he's *Jeff Goldblum*.

A Brief Yet Thorough List of Everything That Happens When You Are Foolish Enough to Write a Book About Jeff Goldblum

10. You see the movie *Vibes*, which, if you don't remember, for some reason costars Cyndi Lauper.

9. You purchase a DVD player, to play all the $2 DVDs you ended up buying in the course of "reporting."

8. You scour the Internet to find tonics to make you tall and thin and muscular like Goldblum, only to learn it takes awful things like *work* and *discipline*.

7. You buy a new phone and don't understand how it works. (This might not involve Goldblum but is a thing that happened during this time period.)

6. You begin using the phrase "Jeffy boy," and not in the context of like your creepy uncle or the guy who owns the company you work for.

5. You think about *Vibes* far more often than you should, to the point of telling everyone about it so much that your friends and family and coworkers just presume it's your favorite movie.

4. Your Google alerts get . . . interesting.

3. Everyone asks you if you hung out with Goldblum and then you have to do that weird thing where you're like, "Look, no, it's not that kinda book." And they ask why. And you're like, "I guess he had better things going on?" And they're like, "Hrmph!" And you're like, "Dude was in the highest-grossing movie of all time (at the time) so buy the damn book, please." And they're like, "Sure, but only because I feel socially obligated."

2. A life-sized cutout of Goldblum is hidden in your kitchen, so when you get home one day and are talking to Stevie Nix the doggie for ten minutes, then turn around, you naturally scream and throw your phone (see above) at the handsome intruder.

1. You learn where to donate $2 DVDs.

Hold On to Your Butts!

hree years after leading a Robert Altman film, Goldblum voiced a character named Verminous Skumm in *Captain Planet and the Planeteers*. If you aren't a child of the nineties—and if you didn't have a child in the nineties—the show was an incredibly cheesy, desperately tree-huggy cartoon that was all about saving the planet.* It follows five international superheroes whose powers sound like names Gwyneth Paltrow and/or Chris Martin would give to their children: Earth, Fire, Water, Wind, and

---

*To give you a sense of how environmentally focused, often to the point of parody, the show could be, here's a snippet of dialogue from that episode:

GI: *Did you know whales might be as smart as humans?*
WHEELER: *Then why haven't they invented anything?*
GAIA: *You mean like weapons that could end all life on Earth?*
. . . Sick burn, Gaia . . .

~*groan*~ Heart. The five occasionally combine their powers to summon Captain Planet, a super-superhero who possesses much stronger versions of all those powers. Verminous Skumm, a gargantuan humanoid rat, is one of the—wait for it—*Eco-Villains*, who loves trying to destroy cities with infestations, such as when he contaminated a South American water supply with "rat rot," a brew that transformed people into human-rat hybrids. Goldblum only voiced him for five episodes, so Maurice LaMarche had taken over by the time the character tried to get the Catholics and Protestants of Northern Ireland, the Israelis and Palestinians, and the blacks and whites of apartheid Africa *to nuke each other*, respectively. Yeah, it's one wild-ass show.

Goldblum wasn't the only Famous Person to appear on the show for a short run. Maybe its co-creator Ted Turner was cashing in favors with everyone; maybe everyone really cared about saving the planet. Whatever the reason, Meg Ryan, Tim Curry, Whoopi Goldberg, Martin Sheen, and even Sting all appeared in it at some point.

Still, it points to something we'll see throughout his career, particularly since the early nineties. The man's a workhorse, generally appearing in about three major projects a year, plus a smattering of guest roles, voice-overs, and the like. He always insists that he follows his muse, only working on what interests him. There's bound to be some flukes when taking that approach, and boy, are there some flukes in this chapter, which covers the nineties. For the most part, there's no need to discuss them. For the sake of Goldblum and other great actors like, say, Eddie Murphy, and our own sanity, we can just let movies like *Holy Man* die that second death when one's name is mentioned for the last time.

Perhaps it's ironic or perhaps it's merely logical that the decade that represents Goldblum's highest-grossing movies is also littered with projects best left forgotten. "He had a little bit of a dry spell right before *Jurassic Park*. He was kind of in the Judge Reinhold zone at that point. Everyone knew who he was. He'd be on talk shows. He had a *Larry Sanders* moment. But his career was a little indistinct. You knew exactly who he was, but you may not have been able to name a bunch of movies he was in," Bryan Curtis, the editor at large of the pop culture and sports website the Ringer and noted *Jurassic Park* enthusiast (obsessive?), told me. Thing is, his career remains a little indistinct after it, as well. When's the last time you thought about 1996's *Mad Dog Time*, the mobster comedy with Ellen Barkin, Richard Dreyfuss, and Diane Lane, or that same year's *The Great White Hype*, the star-studded boxing farce with Samuel L. Jackson, Damon Wayans, Peter Berg, and Jamie Foxx that riffed on Larry Holmes's 1982 fight with Gerry Cooney and Mike Tyson's 1995 fight with Peter McNeeley (both hyped for their racial components)?

The decade kicked off sadly, with the dissolution of Davis and Goldblum's marriage. They played it coy. The year after the divorce, Davis insisted to *People* that they were still "on the phone all the time" and that they "[saw] each other occasionally," before adding a hint as to why things may have petered out: "I always think of that episode of the *Dick Van Dyke Show*. Laura was mad at Rob, and some neighbor just then said, 'You're so lucky you're married to Rob, you guys just laugh all day long, have nothing but fun.' And Laura said [gritting teeth, rolling eyes, seething], 'Oh, yeah, it's just a barrel of laughs.' You knew she was pissed about this thing, but other people's perceptions are that it's just perfect, he's the funniest guy. This is not a reflection on Jeff. I mean, it can apply equally to me. We were a normal couple and had all kinds of experiences. We weren't sitting around just laughing all day, putting on shows for each other." A year after that, Goldblum said slyly to the same magazine, which was predicting a romantic reunion of the two, "We're both independent types, unconventional and free-spirited. I think we were lucky to get together, and we both had a great time."

According to Johanna Schneller, who had just written about their marriage in *GQ* the year before, the news shocked everyone. "People were surprised. 'What, them? Really?'" she said, comparing the culture's collective disappointed sigh to the one we all let out when Kenneth Branagh and Emma Thompson's marriage dissolved. "Because they were likable, they were genuinely likable. They weren't like anybody else. They were funny, and they made each other laugh, and you had the sense that it was the real deal, as much as anything can be."

The breakup might have disappointed fans who looked to them as proof that romance wasn't dead, but it arguably also dramatically altered their artistic paths. Maybe it's coincidence that they immediately stopped appearing in films together and that films weren't being made *for them*, but that seems unlikely. "There could have been an alternate Katharine Hepburn/Spencer Tracy universe for them. I think if either of them had had a couple of hits following up on *The Fly*, it would have led them in that direction," Schneller said. "But also people weren't writing those movies, which is too bad because they would have been a hilarious Nick and Nora Charles, for example. They really were both quite glamorous but kind of unconventionally glamorous."

Instead, Goldblum stumbled through a few movies you've probably never heard of, much less watched, such as *Fathers & Sons* and *Shooting Elizabeth*. Worse than the fact that no one saw these movies is just how bland they were.

The issue with both is, basically . . . the movies themselves. *Shooting Elizabeth* is a comedy that follows Goldblum as a businessman who wants to kill his wife (Mimi Rogers) but ends up acting so strangely, she runs away—which results in his being accused of killing her. Its tagline was "When divorce just isn't final enough." Funny stuff, right?! To say this movie doesn't hold up now would be to ignore the fact that it didn't hold up then. I'm all for black comedy, but

So I Married an Axe Murderer, this is not. *Fathers & Sons*, meanwhile, finds Goldblum as a widower trying to connect with his son, when he meets a psychic who tells him a serial killer will one day attack said son. *Yeah.*

This pair of essentially ignored films once again hammered home the point (to anyone who deigned to see them) that there is such a thing as too much Goldblum. Those same eccentricities that nourish his work as a character actor become too much as a leading man. At the same time, though, audiences don't want him to tone it down. Cake and icing are two different things. Proportions are key.

For proof, consider the bright light during this brief rough patch* that arrived in Bill Duke's extremely dark *Deep Cover*. It features Laurence Fishburne as undercover cop Russell Stevens Jr., who descends deeper and deeper into the world of drug trafficking. Goldblum plays his corrupt lawyer David Jason,† a white man obsessed with black culture who just happens to be a member of the very drug-trafficking network Stevens is investigating. As Stevens begins losing himself— and faith in the system in the process—Jason falls prey to the very white stuff they're selling and the money that comes with it, leading a lavish cocaine-fueled lifestyle destined to collapse upon itself.

If the plot sounds cliché, that's because it is. Without question.

---

*If being a multimillionaire actor who gets to pop up in Robert Altman's *The Player* as an absurd version of himself really qualifies as being in a "rough patch." And while the satirical takedown of Hollywood is brilliant, Goldblum doesn't have an awful lot to do in his small cameo. As Danks put it, "Goldblum here mainly plays in the background . . . as with pretty much all the other celebrities playing 'themselves' here (which includes Jack Lemmon, Harry Belafonte & various others in this scene alone) he works as part of the ensemble deepening the realistic or naturalistic texture of the environment. In some ways, and although he is a very human figure here, he appears as a kind of Hollywood 'prop' (though he's hardly alone in that here)."

†How this name makes me laugh. Has anything ever been *whiter*? This is the artisanal tea shop of names.

But it doesn't matter, thanks to Fishburne's and Goldblum's arresting, lived-in performances. The former's all steely eyes and remorseful reserve while the latter grows wilder and wilder, finding himself saying jarringly un-Goldblumy things like "Why do I love balling black chicks so much?" after doing just that, and murdering defenseless people in cold blood as he coolly explains to Stevens that he knows the undercover cop's "dick gets hard for money, power, and women" and instructs him to "forget this Judeo-Christian bullshit. The same people that taught us virtue are the very ones who enslaved us, baby."

Jack Bellicec, this is not. But Duke's direction finds a humanity in the character, enough humanity that Stevens feels a certain fondness for Jason, a fondness that puts his life in danger on multiple occasions. The movie teeters on the edge of being another crime B-picture, and with another pair of actors it might have been. But "Goldblum and Laurence Fishburne had great chemistry, and they felt believable," Duke told me of the casting. "Jeff is a wonderful actor, and when we talked, we didn't talk about him as a bad guy but about being a human being who was desperate . . . sometimes people make choices out of desperation. People make mistakes. He agreed with that, so we went from there."

While *Deep Cover* showcases Goldblum's best acting of the 1990s, I know you've been waiting to read about a particular movie, the one that forever altered Goldblum's career in ways that probably seemed unfathomable at the time, one of the most popular movies ever made. Yes, of course, I'm talking about *Jurassic Park*.

Deep Cover is probably the kind of role Goldblum *wishes* he was known for, considering his dedication to the craft of acting, et cetera, et cetera. Instead, the movies most people remember him from were spectacles to the nth degree. Not long after *Jurassic Park*, he made *Independence Day* (and, of course, a sequel to *Jurassic Park*). He's best known for two movies that could have easily worked without him* but from which (with a boost from nostalgia) he feels inseparable. And the fact that his character isn't necessary in either—at least, it's not necessary for them to be portrayed in the manner in which he chooses to portray them—is the very reason he's able to stand out so mightily.

"They're the kind of movies that are not dependent on his performance at all. The star of *Jurassic Park* is the dinosaurs. He's in these massive movies that everyone has seen, young people have probably seen multiple times when they were on television, because they're the kind of films that when you're eight or nine or ten, if it's being replayed on television, you just kinda watch," Chuck Klosterman said. "His imprint is huge, because he's in these massive movies, even though nothing is at stake in these movies. Nobody watches *Jurassic Park* and says, 'That movie would have been better if they would have cast someone other than Jeff Goldblum in it.' That's not how it works. It's completely secondary. So anything he does that's memorable almost counts extra, because he's adding value to something where the human element doesn't matter at all."

If you're curious just how popular Steven Spielberg's adaptation of Michael Crichton's dino-epic really is, then I suggest you put this book down immediately, head to Google, and set up an alert for "Jeff Goldblum."† I have one such alert set up. Every single day—this is no exaggeration; this happened *every single day* for nearly a year—Google

---

* Here's anecdotal proof, at least for *Independence Day*. What's his character's name? I'd bet my bottom dollar you can't remember. Now what's his name in *Jurassic Park*?

† Yes, I realize the second half of this sentence should be "then continue reading," since that's arguably why you purchased this thing in the first place.

alerted me to a story in which a journalist has written, "As Jeff Gold-blum's Dr. Ian Malcolm says in *Jurassic Park*, _____." Filling that space is "Life, uhh, finds a way" if the story is whimsical, nice, or news of the weird; "Your scientists were so preoccupied with whether or not they could, they didn't stop to think if they should" if the piece is about either a wild scientific discovery, something to do with climate change, or the announcement of a strange food item; or "Must go faster" if it's a sports story.

It's difficult to overstate how popular it was at the time. The movie crushed records faster than a T. rex can crush a Jeep. It earned more than a billion dollars at the box office, back when doing so was earth-shattering news. It quickly became the highest-grossing movie ever released to date. "I was eleven when that was released, and it was a cataclysmic movie," said Sean Fennessey. "Every single living human I knew went to see that movie."

As Klosterman alluded to, the thing to realize about *Jurassic Park* is Goldblum isn't the star. "He's such a significant part of it and has the most memorable lines in the movie," Fennessey said, but he isn't the *star*. Nor is Sam Neill or Laura Dern or Richard Attenborough or Samuel L. Jackson or . . . well, you get where I'm going with this. All the actors are mere window dressing. As Klosterman said, the real attraction, much as in the actual park, is the dinosaurs. He's not the only one who thought so. That remains the case now, and it certainly was back when it came out in 1993.

"The dinosaurs were the stars of the movie. One hundred percent. I remember picking up *Newsweek* and the picture [on the cover] was of the Tyrannosaurus chasing the car. . . . There is no way for me to overstate how shocking those dinosaurs were in 1993," said Bryan Curtis. And that was no accident. Spielberg insisted on creating "real" dinos, with Stan Winston building life-sized animatronic dinos to later animate over, so the production could use as little CGI as possible. "This movie is not *Alien*, where they can take whatever form your imagination suggests and be anything you want *them* to be because they don't exist in history or physiology. These are dinosaurs that every kid in the world knows," Spielberg told *Empire* magazine at the time. "Most of our dinosaurs were shot full size. Stan Winston built them for us in his creature shop—which we refuse to call it, we call it his 'animal shop.'"

With such lifelike puppets, Curtis (like Klosterman/anyone who has seen the movie and thought about it) said, "the [human] characters merely had to be acceptable. And Goldblum was better than acceptable; he was really good. So in a way, he was a bonus. . . . [But] Goldblum got carried along by the dinosaurs."

And to think there is a world in which he didn't get the part, some parallel universe where Jim Carrey put his own manic spin on Malcolm. "I read the book and I thought of Jeff Goldblum right away," casting director Janet Hirshenson told *Entertainment Weekly*. "There were several other people we taped for the part, though. Jim Carrey had come in and he was terrific, too, but I think pretty quickly we all loved the idea of Jeff."

Spielberg clearly felt the same, saying, "There's no epiphany for Malcolm. He has a line in the movie where he says, 'I hate being right all the time.' He's kind of that useful character in a movie that stands around telling everybody that their best laid plans are going afoul, the '90s equivalent of the soothsayer of doom standing around the streets of New York with a sign saying, 'Doomsday is near.' He's the mathematical equivalent of that. Jeff was tremendous typecasting for this part, and he will not be a surprise to anybody 'cause he's perfect for it."

"Malcolm is really the single memorable performance in that movie and really the only character that, even by the standards of pulp, has three dimensions. . . . In the book, he's this pretty naked vehicle to smuggle in all this chaos theory and scientific mumbo jumbo. And what Goldblum did is turn him into a comic character," Curtis said. "He does for *Jurassic Park* roughly what Han Solo does for *Star Wars*. He's the character who's winking at the camera, and if you're not a nerd, he makes this crazy dinosaur fantasy palatable to you. He's the way to smuggle in all the people who were not fifteen-year-old me. He is the guy they related to on-screen."

Schneller added, "*Jurassic Park* was the perfect amount of Jeff. He's sort of just there, he can do the eye roll, he can do the pause. He gets the good lines, and he sells the good lines. When he's afraid, you're afraid." The trick, as Schneller pointed out, is "calibrating the right amount of Jeff per movie."

While credit for Malcolm primarily belongs to both Spielberg and screenwriter David Koepp, Goldblum played an unprecedented role in shaping the character. First, there's the look. Around this time, paparazzi photos often featured Goldblum in a black leather jacket, black button-down open at the chest, and squarish-framed black semi-tinted glasses. You know, the same damn thing he wore in the movie. Turns out, that's no accident. Spielberg "was actually very trustful and very collaborative," according to Goldblum. "So I remember when I went into the costume, saw the costumier, I had my own ideas and had already done a lot of shopping and said, 'How about this and this?' And I think they took everything [I suggested]," he said on Marc Maron's podcast. He knew Malcolm was "a science-y, kind of geeky guy, but I wanted to make him as cool as I could. Sex it up. Scientists are cool!"

Fennessey theorized that the character worked so well, the cool scientist character became an archetype. It helped that, as Curtis put it, "the nineties were the *let's make science cool for the kids* era of American culture," as seen in shows like *Bill Nye the Science Guy* and the aforementioned *Captain Planet*. The cool scientist quickly became an archetype, but an archetype that only Goldblum could play perfectly. "The fact that somebody was the smartest person in the room, had foresight, and could also credibly wear a leather jacket and denim and speak about the power of evolution in a meaningful way, and you thought that he was cool," Fennessey said, "it feels rare. It feels like he has strict ownership over that archetype in a lot of ways. Can you think of anyone else who has been able to pull that off?"

That's no accident. Said coolness was hyper-important to Goldblum and a deeply specific choice. "It's fun to play the smart guy who gets to figure something out before everybody else," he told the Associated Press in 1996, while promoting *Independence Day*. But when the interviewer mentioned that the actor had become an inspiration to "nerds," he replied, "Easy now, that nerd thing, I don't think that's me. Super-smart, yeah, maybe. Misunderstood, yeah, sometimes, but also cool. None of the science types I've played are the kind who've ever been bullied, probably the opposite, and none of them run scared, not even from a T. rex. . . . I'm not a follower. Science doesn't have to mean mindless regimentation. I'm reading Carl Sagan now and he makes science feel human and cool, even romantic, and wondrous, spiritual and sexy and virile."

Goldblum suggested an important tweak to the original script, which found Malcolm running away from the T. rex when he sustains the injury that leaves him propped up on his elbow, wearing an unbuttoned shirt. "It was written in the script that my character did exactly what the lawyer did. I was another scared person who didn't know what they were doing but ran away from [the dinosaur.] And then the T-Rex chased after me and poked me, and I had this bad leg which led me to take my shirt off and suffer for the rest of the movie, and that was it," he recalled. "I said to Steven, 'I have an idea. What if my character didn't just get so scared but was kind of heroic and brave? It's going to result in the same blocking and the same idea.'" That idea was that Malcolm would run *toward* the dinosaur to distract him, shooting off a flare as he went, giving Neill's Dr. Alan Grant enough time to save the children. Spielberg thought on it for a day and agreed, which led to one of the more iconic scenes in the movie, while helping solidify Malcolm as heroic (in addition to snarky (in addition to cool)).

People certainly took notice. Though he's arguably the third lead in the movie, he's the one who hosted *Saturday Night Live.*[*] And in his monologue he announces, "Last week, *Jurassic Park* surpassed *E.T.* to become the highest-grossing movie of all time. I guess the guy who made *E.T.* must be kind of bummed out right now. I heard E.T. phoned home and didn't get an answer because everyone was out watching *Jurassic Park.*" But even in his tangential appearances *around* the movie, he isn't the star. The rest of the monologue involves fake audience members asking him what it was like to work with dinosaurs. When he hosted again in 1997 in support of *The Lost World*, the monologue revolved around the dinos, this time with Jim Breuer interrupting to impersonate raptors and T. rexes and the like for a full three minutes.

By then, Goldblum was a star. How big of a star? Big enough that Aerosmith's fame junkie of a front man, Steven Tyler, took a shine to the actor. In a story that feels like a Mad Libs in which every prompt is "famous nineties celebrity," Goldblum met the band when he first hosted *SNL* and they were the musical guest. During the week, he became friendly with Tyler, the two even dining at Peter Luger at one point. About a year later, he and Tom Arnold[†] costarred in the Hugh Grant–Julianne Moore rom-com *Nine Months*. One day, as Gold-

---

[*] Though Laura Dern *does* appear in the monologue. After several "audience members" ask questions and make it clear they don't know that the dinosaurs are fake, Dern pops up and asks, "Do you remember when we were in the Jeep and the T. rex attacked us? God, weren't you scared it was going to eat us?!"

[†] Yep, *that* Tom Arnold.

blum relayed to *NME*, Arnold said, "Hey, my pals Aerosmith are playing out at this stadium. We're taking a helicopter."

With Grant in tow, the three did just that. "I knew Steve Tyler and Joe Perry, so I was showing off a little bit—we went backstage," Arnold told *GQ*. "I saw Jeff talking to the keyboard guy, asking about his equipment, and I thought, That's cute."

Goldblum said, "I found myself backstage and stood in the wings watching the whole show. Towards the end of the show, Steven Tyler says: 'Hey, Jeff Goldblum! Are you going to play with us or not?' The keyboard player moved aside and told me the chords. Steven Tyler came up to me singing in my face. It was great, but that was enough for a lifetime."

"And the concert was going on, and Hugh came up and he goes, 'Where's Goldblum?'" Arnold remembered. "And I said, 'I don't know. Fuck him.'"

So maybe he wasn't a dinosaur-level star, but by virtue of everyone's seeing him (and some people's seeing him again and again), he'd become what could comfortably be described as an A-lister.

His relationship with Laura Dern, which began after filming concluded, certainly didn't hurt. It quickly became media fodder, already being trotted out in press for the movie. One *Jurassic Park*–pegged profile of Dern, for example, found her waxing philosophically about their relationship. "They make it sound a lot more fabulous in print than it probably ever would be in person. Because once all these preconceived ideas about how glamorous it is go away, there's a man and a woman. And you have to figure out how to have a relationship. To me, that's very hard work," she said in the profile. "I think the hardest challenge we have as people is to be honest—in our relationships but most importantly to ourselves. . . . I think the pursuit of that in my field is fascinating."

For years, the two enjoyed a very public on-again/off-again rela-

tionship. When she appeared during Goldblum's first *SNL* monologue, he called her "honey," and when he appeared on *The Larry
Sanders Show*, one of the characters asked him about her.

Then things became murky, mysterious, and downright mystify-
ing, qualities they seemed to champion by being willfully obtuse when
discussing their pairing.

Goldblum proposed on Christmas Day in 1994. Fast-forward two
years, and the couple no longer lived together, nor were they engaged.
But in a profile in *Redbook*, when a writer suggested they had gone
splitsville, Dern replied, "Who said we broke up? No we're not engaged anymore, but Jeff and I love each other, and we're trying to figure it out. . . . I know in my heart that Jeff is going to be in my life
forever, and I've never said that about any other man. If he's not my
husband, he'll be my best friend. We've worked diligently at making
sure we understand why it can work and why it can't work, based on
our choices. So there's no resentment here. I really love this man. But
I analyze everything endlessly, and unfortunately for Jeff, that means
relationships, too."

Umm, *what*?

The pair clearly enjoyed fiddling with the press. Dern famously
appeared as Ellen DeGeneres's love interest in the historic "coming
out" episode of *Ellen*. In the run-up to that episode, the pair kick off
the bluntly and unfortunately headlined *Entertainment Weekly* story
"Laura Dern Is Not a Lesbian" by Tim Appelo by reveling in the
mysterious nature of their relationship. Wrote Appelo: "'You smell
like sandalwood,' murmurs Jeff Goldblum as he sniffs Laura Dern's
hair in the rather restrained restaurant of L.A.'s Four Seasons Hotel.
Dern—her leopard-spotted Dolce & Gabbana pants pressed against
his lanky frame—responds softly: 'Do you like my manicure? I did it
with my teeth.' The former lovers and *Jurassic Park* costars smooch
noisily, hamming it up. 'I love Jeff,' says the 30-year-old Dern after he

exits. Does this mean their on-again, off-again wedding is back on? 'You never know,' she teases. 'That's where he's going now, to get his tux, but don't tell him I told you. Doesn't that pique your curiosity?'"

By 1997, Goldblum spoke of their relationship in his typical non-definitive definitive way: "We're not traditionally together right now. I respect her, adore her acting, adore her as a person."

Right.

O n-screen, he continued carving out his cool scientist niche in *Powder*, a movie that should have been bigger but ended up being to Blockbuster what R.E.M.'s *Monster* was to used-record stores. It follows the story of the titular Powder (Sean Patrick Flanery), an albino teenager whose mother was fatally struck by lightning when he was in the womb. The boy lived, only to be disowned by his father and raised by his grandparents, who kept him in a basement, away from other people. As a result, the brilliant young man, who, as it turns out, is an empath with paranormal abilities stemming from the electromagnetic charge his brain and body carried, learned everything about the world from books instead of in the classroom— despite possessing the highest IQ in human history. A child services psychologist (Mary Steenburgen) rescues him, which lands the boy in high school—not a welcoming place for someone so different. Only his physics teacher, Donald Ripley (Goldblum), sees him as more than a freak.

The movie presents yet another example of Goldblum's playing a role in which he must explain some pseudo–sci-fi amphigory and make it believable, something that had become his calling card of sorts—because of the way he can hypnotize with his line readings, turning the mundane, or the otherworldly, into something lyrical. One of the reasons Goldblum is so good at believably delivering such dialogue, according to Curtis, is "he's kind of self-mocking in a way. He's explaining something that is a real and complicated idea, but he's so self-mocking about it and so funny that you're kind of listening to him. Like, I don't think Sam Neill could have explained chaos theory [in *Jurassic Park*]. It has to be somebody who kind of finds the idea that he's a scientist kind of ridiculous."

"He's great at exposition, because it becomes music. And he had a lot of that in *Powder*," Bradford Tatum, who also appeared in the movie, told me. "Those were the only dailies I went to see, because I wanted to see what he had done that day."

Despite the subject matter, Goldblum took his acting on the movie as seriously as he did when working with Altman or Kasdan.

"In my career, I've had the pleasure of working with some of the giants, like Paul Newman, Robert Duvall, and Clint Eastwood, blah blah blah, the kind that when you're around them, you take the cotton out of your ears and put it in your mouth—just listen, don't talk," Brandon Smith, who also appeared in *Powder*, told me. "Jeff Goldblum is among the giants."

He remembered sitting in a semicircle with the cast between shoots. Mary Steenburgen "always knitted. She must have completed two or three different projects in the six weeks of shooting." Smith would shoot the shit with Lance Henriksen about anything and everything—except acting. Then there was Goldblum, "the type who was totally absorbed with acting all the time, even when he was relaxing in his chair."

Smith, the son of a Broadway actress and a rodeo cowboy, began acting as a child. Though his general demeanor and South Texas twang might cause the stereotyping kind to assume otherwise, he's a classically trained actor. But he's still a Texan, and he'd be flipping through the sports pages on set, catching up on his doomed Houston Astros. "[Goldblum] would sit down with some book, a biography of

Olivier, or something, and he'd start reading to me out of the book," Smith said. "'Listen to this! Listen to this!' I'd put my paper down and politely listen, and finally after about three or four times, when I got to know him better, I'd look at him and say, 'Jeff, I'm reading the sports page here.' And he'd go, 'Oh, oh!' and then go pull a chair up next to Mary."

Different people on the set remember Goldblum's reading different-ent books, but everyone I spoke with recalls how excited he was to share anecdotes from them. "My earliest memory of Jeff is walking into the makeup trailer every morning, and he was obsessed with this Brando biography, to the point where he'd read it out loud in that sort of hipster haiku way he speaks," Tatum said. "It would come just to-tally non-solicited. He would just start reading from the book when he was doing his makeup. And this was a daily thing."

"He was totally absorbed in his art, to the point where he'd be so excited when reading a paragraph that he'd have to share it," Smith added. "I appreciated that."

What most struck Smith is how his excitement bled into his work: "He always tried to find something fresh and something spontaneous for each take. Every new take with Jeff Goldblum, he came up with a newly minted, beautiful penny—right off the mint. And it was just always so spot-on. He really does feel the moment. A lot of actors say they do, and it's horseshit. Jeff Goldblum is one who really does."

The movie might have been another major hit for the actor, but horrific details emerged about its director, Victor Salva, a previously convicted pedophile who sexually assaulted a twelve-year-old actor he worked with on his first film, to whom Disney handed this project a few years after his release from prison. As Salva's past came to light, his victim, Nathan Winters, launched a boycott campaign against the movie.

"It was kind of like that movie never happened," Tatum said.

"They absolutely refused to promote it, because to promote it would mean people would learn about Victor's past, and they just couldn't have that. I mean, it was Disney. They couldn't have that."

Even so, it did well enough. Wrote the *Los Angeles Times*, "Despite potentially damaging disclosures that its writer/director is a convicted child molester, the new Walt Disney film 'Powder' placed second at the nation's box office over the weekend. The $10-million film grossed a higher-than-expected $7.1 million despite protests from the now-20-year-old victim, who urged the public to boycott the PG-13 movie."

By the time *Independence Day* came out in 1996, his cool-scientist schtick may have been growing tired. At the very least, it felt uninspired. "I don't know if you know this but in Hollywood, there's a law that says when you do a sci-fi movie you have to have Jeff Goldblum," Dean Devlin, who cowrote the movie, told the *Guardian* at the time. "But, in all seriousness, Jeff Goldblum is to this kind of movie what Arnold Schwarzenegger is to action movies. There are so few actors who can take relatively technical gobbledy-gook expository dialogue and make it engaging. He has this unique gift."

Years later, film critic Adam Nayman put a finer point on it. "He's in *Independence Day* because there's nothing sincere about *Independence Day*. You have him there because he's been in *The Fly* and *Jurassic Park*. Nothing in that movie's real," he said. "So instead of saying, 'Hey, I bet the scientists in an alien invasion would be like some guy from *Jurassic Park*,' you just cast the guy from *Jurassic Park*. And he's essentially just playing himself."

But on this go-round, for one of the first times, he's among the more forgettable characters in an ensemble, with Bill Pullman's POTUS and Will Smith's hotshot fighter pilot really owning the screen. Hell, even Judd Hirsch, who plays his father, feels more compelling. Not that it matters. Much like the stars of *Jurassic Park* are the dinosaurs, the aliens are the true stars here. Goldblum, Pullman, Smith—they're just a little flavor. Plus Goldblum had greater things in store: expanding the biggest brand in movies at the time. *The Lost World*, one of Spielberg's most forgettable movies, opened in 1997. And, much like *Independence Day*, it tells us basically nothing about Goldblum. "*The Lost World* really is the closest a movie ever came to being put solely on [his shoulders] as like a two-hundred-million-dollar movie, but the *Jurassic Park* brand is what made it a huge hit," Nayman said.

It's difficult to overstate how little he matters to the movie, even while being its supposed centerpiece. "He doesn't really do much in that movie, except run around and be chased. I think it probably proved Jeff Goldblum is not an action hero. He's better as a talker than a runner and a fighter," Curtis said. "That movie is such a mess. I remember at the time being very personally disappointed. I just thought, 'Oh, my God. This sucks. It has no resonance at all.' It wasn't like *The Phantom Menace*, where everybody's talking about how bad it was. It just kind of made a ton of money and vanished like a ton of sequels do."

Amid his run of pale but popular movies in the latter half of the nineties, he received his only Oscar nomination, in 1996—for directing a short film titled *Little Surprises*, which these days requires a trip to the Library of Congress for a viewing. He had been teaching several times a week at Playhouse West, a drama school he founded with his fellow Meisner student Robert Carnegie, admittedly an unusual hobby for a famous actor. When the opportunity to direct a project of his own devising came about, he turned to his students. "He came to a group of us in the theater company and said, 'Look, there's no guarantee that you guys are going to be in the final version of the film, but would you guys be interested in fleshing out a story?'" Mark Pellegrino, who indeed ended up in the final version, told me. "He asked about five of us, and we jumped at the opportunity."

That wasn't particularly unusual. Goldblum often invited students to his house to help him rehearse various roles. So the small group gathered at his home. "We improvised for a few days, just playing with this story while cameras followed us around the house. It was fun, a great experience," Pellegrino added, saying those days of improvising eventually became the basis for the script.

"He devoted so much time to that film, over a year," said Robert Carnegie, director of Playhouse West. "He is extraordinarily dedicated and does all this out of the goodness of his heart. The students adore him."

Yes, the short is mostly forgotten now. And, no, he didn't win the Oscar. But this project better represents what his career would become after his span of blockbusters: a series of increasingly head-scratching (but often lovely) projects, culminating in a public jazz career. As he told the *New York Times* in 1997, "I'm enjoying this time period right now, but who knows what will happen?" There's a certain prescience to that. Because probably the most unpredictable possible thing would happen: he would essentially disappear into these strange, generally unpopular projects. But it wouldn't matter because by that point, he could do anything and be forever remembered. "In a way, his immortality is assured. Just because he's in a movie that makes a billion dollars," Curtis said. "I don't want to dress up *Jurassic Park* too much, but that's like what happens to the people in *The Wizard of Oz*, right? You're just in a movie that has been seen so many times by so many people and then becomes part of people's nostalgia with memes and that stuff. You can never be forgotten."

Not only that, some writer might even scribble out a whole book about you. Who knows what will happen?

A Seemingly Random Batch of Paragraphs
About Bill Murray and Christopher Walken
(and Sort of Warren Zevon and Randy Newman
but Not Really) as a Means of Understanding
Jeff Goldblum Slightly Better

Consider, if you will, Warren Zevon and Randy Newman. That, suggested Gavin Edwards, a culture critic and the author of several books, including *The Tao of Bill Murray*, is a good lens through which to compare and contrast Goldblum, Bill Murray, and Christopher Walken. Necessitating such a comparison is the fact that many of the critics I spoke with about Goldblum while reporting this book mentioned one of those two men a second after reciting the phrase "You know who Goldblum kinda reminds me of?"

It's a stunningly common thought among people who think seriously about actors and fame and movies, but why? To understand why these actors might feel interconnected, Edwards first considers those iconic, idiosyncratic Los Angeles singer-songwriters. "They were like the *weird* version" of rock musicians, "but they were in the industry enough that they could both do things like get the Eagles to appear on their records. They were in that world and knew how to play by the rules and made a choice not to."

These three actors—Goldblum, Walken, and Murray—are also the *weird* versions of famous movie stars. All immediately recognizable and arguably beloved, the three boast IMDb pages that zig where they should zag and vice versa. But each is both like the others and different in his own way.

The parallels between Goldblum and Walken are clear enough. Both speak in specific, unique, inimitable patterns. Both came up around the same time, even appearing in several of the same early films in the late seventies, including *Next Stop, Greenwich Village*; *The Sentinel*; and *Annie Hall*. That they would end up in the same bin in our collective minds seems only natural.

Murray and Goldblum feel more apart. They're both strange Internet darlings who work in both drama and comedy, but they share no physical similarities, no speech tics, nothing like that. Maybe what links them is that they both seem up for everything. Consider that Wes Anderson cast them as rival oceanographers in *The Life Aquatic with Steve Zissou*. Oceanographers! At one point, Murray's Zissou literally says of Goldblum's Alistair Hennessey, "Don't be nice to Ali. He's my nemesis."

"In all these cases, you're hiring the X factor," Edwards said. "You want someone who isn't going to just come in and hit their marks, but maybe someone who will shake it up and give a line reading that feels unexpected. . . . All three have kind of mastered the art of walking right up to the point where you almost wink in the camera, and that can be a really powerful tool."

And that's the tie that binds. All of them, to again go back to Nayman's analogy, are like a spice in the stew. Only all three are different kinds of spice.

"There's so much Hollywood entertainment in which you can lie back in a warm bath because you've seen versions of it five hundred times before. But if you have anything that's sand in the Vaseline, as the Talking Heads once put, it gets your attention," Edwards said. With Walken, it's the speech patterns. With Goldblum, it's the eccentricities. And with Murray, well, he "creates that effect by not reading the script, showing up, giving it a quick glance, and then saying like, 'Okay, let's throw this out and get to something that gets the idea across but we're going to improvise our way through it.'"

But Walken and Murray also represent different extremes in where that X factor can land you. Over time and numerous *Saturday Night Live* appearances, Walken grew to be more and more parodic of himself. Just consider the famous sketch in which he played music producer Bruce Dickinson, who continuously interrupts the Blue Öyster Cult while they record "(Don't Fear) The Reaper" to insist on "more cowbell." Will Ferrell acquiesces, growing more manic with every take. Years later, Ferrell said on *The Tonight Show* that Walken told him, "'You know, you've ruined my life. People during the curtain calls bring cowbells and they ring them. The other day I went for Italian food lunch, and the waiter asked me if I wanted more cowbell with my pasta Bolognese.'" Added Ferrell, "I think he was really mad at me. . . . From *The Deer Hunter* to *Pulp Fiction* to 'more cowbell.' That's all he gets now." In fairness, while Walken has continued to act consistently since the sketch, nothing he's been in has done particularly well. So this random flashpoint has come to define him. Anyway, he surely embellished the story for late-night television, but the fact that Walken is known more for these bits than his previously famous roles rings true.

Murray, on the other hand, intentionally pivoted away from anything that would make him seem like a parody. "Points at which Bill [could have become self-parody], whenever people have clamored for him to make a sequel or make the next obvious movies, he sometimes, literally, fully leaves the country. I think he abhors the idea to such a degree that he's really succeeded in not becoming a parody of himself. He put a lot of work in that. And he succeeds to such an extent that it's hard for us to imagine where those potential pitfalls were."

Goldblum split the difference, only leaning into his Goldbluminess in his later years (such as the exaggerated version of himself he plays in *Thor: Ragnarok*) but never quite making himself the punch line.

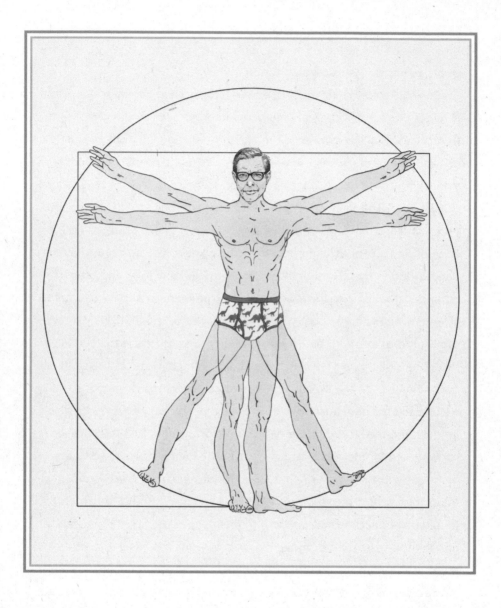

said, "I love when I'm not sure where the guest is going. And his refusal to do a conventional interview? I loved it. It was great. It kept me on my toes the whole time."

For the most part, it's a standard Goldblum interview, meaning it's easygoing and agreeable. Goldblum lays on the charm, as he always does. Goldblum interviews can be many things, but they're never contentious. They're never tense. Except with this one.

Early on, he lavishes compliments on Simmons, saying he possesses "the hair of a young Steve McQueen and the piercing blue eyes of Peter O'Toole in *Lawrence of Arabia*." When Simmons mentions he began his career as a writer, Goldblum flips the interview (as is his wont) and says, "Tell me all about that." Then when Simmons says, "I like how you flipped this podcast on me," Goldblum says, "I'm not flipping anything!" Again, standard fare.

Things get interesting when they begin playing the IMDb Game, a Simmons go-to in which he runs down an actor's filmography, mining it for conversation. The rules as Simmons explains them to Goldblum: "We go through some of the movies you did, and just the trigger of the names prompts you into some sort of memory from the past."

The conversation begins sounding somewhat contentious with the first movie, *Death Wish*. Goldblum uses the prompt to say he hopes one day we'll live in a world without guns, to which Simmons (probably jokingly) says, "So you're saying *Death Wish* isn't gonna age well?"

"Hey, I'm talking about something else entirely besides the commercial legs of a movie, of a stupid little movie," Goldblum responds. "Who cares?"

Things don't get much better when Simmons doesn't know his famous line from *Annie Hall*. ("Maybe you researched it?" suggests Goldblum.) Then the actor does what he often does in interviews and avoids any self-praise. In doing so, he sometimes seems unaware of his cultural status, such as here, when he refuses to acknowledge *The*

The Lost Chapter

Goldblum long insisted he is not and has never been careerist. It's one of those phrases he employs so often it begins to feel (and probably is) rehearsed. The thing about Goldblum, though, is that he truly is not a careerist. The proof, oddly enough, hides in plain sight, right there in the middle of an episode of *The BS Report*, the podcast helmed by Bill Simmons.

For those who aren't obsessed with Boston sports or pop culture/sports crossovers, Simmons was an influential columnist for ESPN who later founded Grantland and then the Ringer. He often applies sports thought to culture, such as ranking movies, performances, etc., and discussing moments when cultural figures are on the upswing or downswing or whatnot. All of which is to say, he thinks about culture and acting vastly differently than Goldblum, which quickly became apparent on the podcast. When introducing the segment, Simmons

Big Chill was his big break, arguing that saying such a thing would be "careerist."* Instead, he says (as he always does) that he's on the brink of his best work yet. The interview gets downright strange when this exchange occurs:

BILL SIMMONS: *Silverado*, people feel like, is one of the lost, really good eighties movies.

JEFF GOLDBLUM: Really?

BS: I dunno. That's what people say.

JG: Well, you said it. Are you just running this up the flagpole to see what I say? Yeah, I think a lot of people do like that movie of course.

BS: We're doing word association with your movies. I'm trying to set you up.

JG: Oh, yeah. Well, you're starting the association. You're throwing me off, because you're starting me on the association. You're like, "Drive the car away, and I'll drive for the first block. Take my wheel whenever you want." Let me drive it!

[The two then briefly discuss Silverado.*]*

BS: So, Costner's in that. And he's about to become a mammoth star. Could you see that? Like, when you're doing a movie like that, are you looking around, going, "Oh, that guy's somebody. Something's happening to this guy?"

---

*If he truly feels this way, then *woooooo boy* is he gonna hate this book.

JG: So you're asking questions that have the sensibility of careerism to them, and I'm telling you . . .

BS: So you don't like the careerism stuff?

JG: It's not that I don't like it. I've never been focused on it. So the answer to the last question is no.

His tone isn't exactly antagonistic, but it's bumping against that border. And considering how effusively kind and agreeable Goldblum normally is, it might as well be hostile. I'm near positive that neither man would characterize the conversation this way, but it's difficult not to believe the actor after hearing his deep insistence that the craft (and nothing else) has always driven him.

And yeah, yeah, yeah, talk is cheap, but there's really no other explanation for the twists and turns his career took after *The Lost World*. To call it a roller coaster* wouldn't be precise, because that would suggest ups and downs. Instead, it's more like a tilt-a-whirl, simply a series of odd diversions that don't necessarily lead anywhere, but ones that collectively showcase a rare and admirable quality: passion.† Goldblum clearly did whatever he wanted to do, taking roles that interested him. There's simply no other explanation for a career this nonsensical, especially after reaching A-list status. After all, this was the same period in which he made a half-mockumentary titled *Pittsburgh* and took a role in a local production of *The Music Man*. Clearly, the guy had experimentation on his mind.

"From the very start of getting into this, I did it for the sheer joy

---

* Oh, hey, look. A callback!

† From this point on, to honor Goldblum's lack of careerism and my lack of a stronger outline, the book will only be in semi-chronological order.

and fun and adventure and romantic excitement, the creative excitement of doing it," he insists to Simmons. Let's hope it was fun, because this mindset resulted in several peculiar projects, some bad, some terrible, some good, some great, some forgettable, but most of which haven't survived in the annals of time. So, with chronology thrown out the window, let's take a gander, shall we?

Once upon a time, television was a dirty word, at least to the film actors who viewed the medium as *less than*. This was during the dark ages of modern times, before the days of Netflix, HBO, and whatever streaming service hasn't yet been invented. Goldblum never showed much of an ego regarding the boob tube, though. Long after those early days, he popped up in random comedies, be it as an exuberant acting teacher upon whom Joey Tribbiani (Matt LeBlanc) accidentally urinates during an audition in *Friends*, as himself on *The Larry Sanders Show* asking out a woman for Larry (Garry Shandling) because the talk show host is too scared to do it himself,[*] or as the predatory psychology professor Ira Fermstein on *Crank Yankers*, who calls coeds and says creepy things like, "If I tuck it between my legs, will you slap my bottom with a dead fish? I'm just asking!"[†]

Will & Grace, King of the Hill, The Simpsons, The League, Mr. Show with Bob and David. If you can name a famous sitcom from the pre-streaming era, there's a solid chance Goldblum made a guest appearance. Even late in the new millennium, hell, even *now*, he's still appearing on TV. The man did a stint on *Glee*. *Glee*! And clearly he's

---

[*] "Next time he's having a fucking nervous breakdown, maybe book David Viscott," he tells Rip Torn's Arthur, the producer of Larry's show, in a truly all-time-great line.

[†] If you haven't guessed, the *Crank Yankers* bits have aged about as well as Bill Cosby.

up for anything, as evidenced by the 2006 sketch on *Late Night with Conan O'Brien* in which the host sets up a giant salt lick to lure celebrities, the way hunters do with deer. Goldblum sneaks onto the set, sashaying over to the huge white block; sniffs it; and, indeed, rubs his tongue over the rough surface while Conan shouts, "It's a Goldblum, ladies and gentlemen!" Naturally things don't end there. Goldblum then saunters over to the stage, climbs over the chairs (sniffing the place Bruce Willis marked last week), and smells Conan's hair before licking his forehead. The sketch ends with Goldblum, still in deer mode, making out with Rachel Dratch, another celeb who always seems up for anything, who is also in deer mode.

While comedy seemed his forte, he also took some big stabs at hour-long dramas, including teaming up with Graham Yost early in Yost's television career.* Yost had already earned clout for writing *Speed* and would go on to create the celebrated modern Western series *Justified*, based on Elmore Leonard novels. But in the mid-aughts, he found himself fresh off his ambitious show *Boomtown*, the Peabody-winning procedural following criminal investigations in Los Angeles that was neutered by NBC and eventually canceled. At the same time, he was nurturing a high-concept idea to push the limits of the detective genre even further.

Yost often thought about the fact that, technically, in any murder investigation, the deceased is essentially a client on whose behalf the detective works. Without the victim, there would be no need for the police. "How do you do a show where the victim is the client of the episode?" Yost wondered. "*Raines* was the answer."

That answer was a police procedural in which the main character,

---

*But still after his work writing on *Hey Dude*. I'm sorry for mentioning this, Graham, but it is one of my favorite facts in the world.

the unmatched Detective Michael Raines, possesses what is either a unique power or a mental illness. He hallucinates the murder victims, usually against his will, as if they're still alive. It isn't a supernatural thing. Though he speaks to them, they're more like imaginary friends, or partners, if you will. They only know things that he knows, even if he only knows them subconsciously.

It was a strange premise, requiring an actor quirky but serious enough to sell it. Yost told me he first considered Matthew Perry, someone who was "funny, younger, a little sort of manic, a little wild, trying to deal with this shit because it makes him feel he's going crazy." But Kevin Reilly, then the president of NBC's entertainment division, suggested Goldblum. And Yost said, "Look, Kevin, I love Jeff Goldblum. I just don't see him in this part. He's one of my favorite actors, so that's hard for me to say."

Yost surprised even himself when he said that. "I was a huge fan of Jeff's. I'd seen *Between the Lines* back in the day, and I just thought, 'Who's *that* guy?' And he was someone I just followed through the years, and I'd get excited and see a movie if he was in it," he said. "He was one of those actors you just root for, who you're hoping will have a good and long career." After auditioning a few others, Yost realized Reilly might be onto something. It would just require a bit of rewriting, something he was happy to do.

Eventually, not only did Goldblum sign on to the project but Frank Darabont, the director of a little film called *The Shawshank Redemption*, agreed to shoot the pilot.

In the end, Yost was thrilled to work with Goldblum. The character of Raines is so obsessed with the old Los Angeles noir writers that he moved to the city because of them, which came from Yost's own experience. "I'm the guy in the narration. I came to LA and I loved [Raymond] Chandler and I love [Dashiell] Hammett, but specifically Chandler because of his LA. That's one of the reasons I got into the business, one of the reasons I moved to Los Angeles. That's one of the reasons I love Los Angeles. Where other people were complaining about it, I was like, 'Are you kidding me?! We're in Los Angeles!'"

Yost's enthusiasm for Chandler didn't only bleed into the character but bled into Goldblum as well. "On the pilot, he really got into the noir thing. And he'd be reading Hammett or Chandler or other hard-boiled noir-ish writers, and he'd read from the book out loud, just above a mutter. He's an idiosyncratic guy, and he'd be walking around reading this stuff just before a scene," Yost said. "And he'd be right at the door, you know, he's gonna do a little knock and talk to someone. So he'd be standing there, reading this stuff, and [someone yells,] 'Rolling! Speed! Action!' And he would just throw the book away and go in and do the scene. But he was reading aloud from the book right up to the moment that he was going to do the scene. And it was funny. With a different actor, it might have been annoying, but with Jeff it was just endearing. . . . He wasn't doing it to create an atmosphere. He was doing it to keep himself in the world of this noir thing. I think it was just enjoyable for him and maybe it was good for him to be thinking of something else so when he comes into the scene, he's not treating the scene like a scene. He's just behaving and being the character in that moment."

Yost lived in Monterey and was only in Los Angeles for half the week, having reluctantly taken on the job of showrunner after enthusiastically writing it. (Another showrunner came and went very quickly early on.) Goldblum, though, lived in the area and used his proximity to maximum effect. "What Jeff liked to do when we were heading into a new episode is, he liked to get together with the writer and go through the script, maybe with other cast members, and they'd get together at his house," Yost said. "He would have the writer to his house, and basically they'd just spend like three hours going through the script. 'What's this line mean? What's the relationship here?' And he wasn't being critical, just making sure he understood it."

The show debuted in 2007, though NBC cut its feet off before it ever had a chance, allowing a mere seven episodes, something Yost attributes to the show's high concept. "It was a hard show to figure out. I remember being at the upfronts for the show, and it was the same year that NBC launched *Heroes, Studio 60 on the Sunset Strip,* and *Friday Night Lights.* And I remember being at the upfronts and thinking, 'I understand those shows. I know what they are. I don't know what the fuck *Raines* is.' It was hard to describe in one sentence. It was a complicated conceit. I still think it's an interesting idea. I think it had emotional moments that were spectacular, and it was funny and all that. But just too complex for an audience just flipping channels to land on and say, 'I wanna watch this.'

"Any of the blame for *Raines* not working is all mine. Nothing in terms of the casting, directing, the music—all of that worked, except, I think, the central premise," Yost continued. "But what worked best was Jeff. He was compelling, lovable, interesting." While he's right about the latter, I'm inclined to disagree with the former. I firmly believe Yost is something of a genius. For my money, *Justified* is one of the top five shows of all time, and the first season of *Boomtown* is unforgettable. *Raines* should have been a hit. It had all the trappings of a traditional procedural with just enough of a spin to entice so-called prestige TV viewers. *Raines,* like so many other outstanding shows (*Wonderfalls, Freaks and Geeks, Veronica Mars, Firefly*—we all know this list by now), simply arrived before its time. "The thing that bothered me the most was not giving Jeff a hit show that would run as long as he wanted," Yost said.

"My biggest concern about the show [failing was] it might put Jeff off television, and it might put television off Jeff. And I just thought he was somebody who might work great in a show," he added.

The experience of *Raines*, however, did not put Goldblum off television. If anything, it appears to have increased his interest in the medium. After its failure to capture the attention of America's home viewers, Goldblum accepted a relatively more guaranteed role as Detective Zack Nichols on *Law & Order: Criminal Intent*, appearing on a detective series as a regular for a third time (the first being the Clinton-endorsed *Tenspeed and Brown Shoe*). As you've likely come to expect by this point, he threw himself into the character while imbuing it with his special sense. The brainiac detective was always chock-full of Goldblum-esque quips, such as "I try to avoid transferential relationships with dead people. It's always so one-sided." As Dick Wolf told me, Goldblum "played his role as a detective with the perfect mix of gravitas and humor. A difficult combination, but he pulled it off."

"He came into what some people might think of as an uphill battle, because it's a show that's already been on for a long time. And there's obviously the pedigree of Dick Wolf, which is its own stamp, and having to find yourself in relation to that stamp," executive producer John David Coles told me. "And he just did a fantastic job of sussing out what needed to be done while also bringing himself to it, and that's a really hard thing to do—to combine those things, to understand the situation and figure out how you fit into it without losing your own sensibilities."

Added Coles, because of course: "Jeff is one of the most charming, smart, funny, committed, talented people I've ever met. I'm sure you've heard that echoed from a lot of people in a lot of different ways, but I would like to add my voice to the chorus of huge fans."

Unsurprisingly, Goldblum took the role as seriously as any other. He and Vincent D'Onofrio, one of the show's other leads at the time, followed a checkerboard shooting schedule, meaning they would be prepping D'Onofrio's episodes while shooting Goldblum's and vice versa. "On the weeks when Goldblum wasn't in front of the camera, he would come to the production meetings, and the script meetings and the this and that—he would just throw himself at it," Coles said. At one point, "he went down to One Police Plaza and met the actual major crimes squad these detectives had been fashioned after. He was all eyes and ears, listening to these people and their stories and how they worked. He'd ask these questions that were additive to his process in ways you could never expect. Like, he was really interested in how they got to work. 'Do you take a car? Do you take the subway?' It was, like, every little detail, how they dressed, what they were interested in, how they work together, how's it work with the old-timers vs. the newcomers."

The role required Goldblum to spend large swaths of time in New York, and producer John Roman said his requirements were simple enough. "He just wanted a big loft, because he likes to walk around not so clothed, and he needed a grand piano. Just a place to do his exercises, and a fucking piano," he said with a laugh. "He's so excited to come to work each day. That's a man who lives totally in the present."

Goldblum's on-set behavior awed Roman, namely the fact that he remembered the name of not only every member of the cast and crew but also the employees of the craft services crew. Plus, procedural shows like the *Law & Order* series tend to have the same couple dozen extras throughout a whole season, and Goldblum made sure not only to know their names but to engage them. "During the last two months of filming of that last season, he's got the script with him. He had his lines highlighted and he made a point" to read lines with all twenty-five of the extras who had been on the show all season, Roman said. "Can you imagine, you get to run lines with Goldblum? It was really sweet. He's something else."

"He's just a regular Joe, yet he rises above the rest of humanity," Roman concluded. If anyone said something half as nice about any of us, we could probably go ahead and die happily.

His twenty-four-episode run for the show was . . . fine. He certainly added a bit of spice, to use Nayman's term, to the *Law & Order* universe and was more than exciting to watch, but it mostly represents yet another strange turn in the career of a man who doesn't consider such pedestrian matters as *careers*.

Some might wonder why a film actor would choose television projects, particularly back in the late aughts, before that was the thing to do. Coles pointed out the upside. "In my experience, film actors who come to work in television kind of love it, because they get to work all the time. When you work on a $150 million film, and you're doing four shots a day, it's kinda boring. You have to get yourself up and going every four hours to do this moment. But if you're in a television show that's doing seven pages a day, you're out there working. It's very invigorating. They're not worrying about the schedule, or the number of shots for each scene, or this and that. They're just out there working," he said. "If you were a rock musician, and someone asked if you wanted to perform once a month or every day, you'd say 'every day' if you really loved to play."

So it logically follows, then, that he would also want to continue dabbling in theater. After all, what better place to, as Michael Winner told him so long ago, *aaaaaaaaccccccccctttttt*. Some of the plays he appeared in, such as *Seminar*, fit well with his personality. But the one that fully captured my obsession, mostly because I admittedly didn't get the chance to see it and cannot fathom the combination of people involved even though I know this is a thing that really happened, is *The Pillowman* by Martin McDonagh. You've probably heard of him. He's the man who wrote and directed *In Bruges*, *Seven Psychopaths*, and *Three Billboards Outside Ebbing, Missouri*. *Divisive* doesn't begin to describe him. His humor trends darker than licorice, brilliant but bordering on cruel. His characters act like absolute monsters, though ones who keep your eyes glued to the screen.

In other words, they aren't particularly Goldblum-esque.

The Pillowman follows the story of Katurian, a short-story writer living in an unnamed totalitarian police state who pens gruesome tales that often involve things like child abuse and pedicide. Oh, and he murdered his parents for abusing his younger brother Michael. The play takes place in an interrogation room, where Tupolski (the "good cop") and Ariel (the "bad cop," who does things like stab people in the ears with pens) are questioning Katurian and his mentally slow brother Michael about a string of actual child murders that have taken place, which they think could be connected to his dark stories. The play includes such pleasantries as severed body parts, premature burial, sexual abuse, physical abuse, verbal abuse, mental abuse, you name it! If you're familiar with McDonagh's work, this shouldn't be particularly surprising.

In this iteration of the play, which ran in New York City's Booth Theatre in the spring of 2005, Billy Crudup played Katurian, Michael Stuhlbarg played Michael, Goldblum played Tupolski, and Zeljko Ivanek played Ariel.

Obviously, this is much, much darker material than Goldblum normally futzed with. As we've discussed, ever since *Death Wish*, he never went quite so dark again. And even here, he plays the nominally "good" cop, but still—it seems slightly incongruous with his persona.

So, uh, *why Jeff Goldblum* for the blackest of black comedies to hit Broadway?

"The character is very complicated. Everything you see is not what you get, as it were. The character is capable of being charming and cruel, turning on the dime, manipulative. Which is not to say that's what I think Jeff is as a person. He also has to make the audience really laugh but in a quite dark way, and I feel that Jeff has all of those qualities," producer Robert Fox told me. "A kind of wonderful eccentricity, where you're never sure what's quite going to happen next with him, which works really well for Martin's writing and Martin's style."

McDonagh can't quite remember, but he *thinks* casting Goldblum was his idea. "We needed a great actor who had a tremendous dexterity with comedy, but who could also be quite dark and dangerous and sinister," he said via email. "It's actually quite hard to find an actor who can do both those things at the same time, but that's why Jeff was perfect for it . . . because people just like Jeff, it was kind of good to use that to allow an audience in, and maybe have them be surprised at how much his character turns out to be the villain of the piece."

The actors, meanwhile, were enticed by McDonagh's sensibility. Billy Crudup told me that after reading a page and a half of the play, he thought, "I don't know what the fuck this is about, but it's incredible writing." He said, "There was not a single piece of familiar language or theater in what I was reading, and that's a pretty remarkable thing to come across. . . . It was certainly one of the most difficult pieces I've ever performed."

Excitement buzzed around Goldblum's casting. He'd enraptured McDonagh back in his 1978 turn in *Invasion of the Body Snatchers*, partially because of his peculiar line readings. McDonagh said he likes "the way he breaks up sentences and has peculiar emphases on certain words (often for no fathomable reason!). Christopher Walken has a similar methodology. . . . But, weirdly, no matter how they break a sentence up, or choose a weird emphasis, because there's always a *truth* to what they're doing, it always seems to work." Crudup, meanwhile, had long been dazzled by "the daring of *The Fly*": "Such a virtuosic attack on lunacy! The film is absolute lunacy, and he has the most incredible attack on it. I had an attachment to him even before I wanted to be an actor." Though he hadn't worked with Goldblum, the actor was on Crudup's "artistic conscience." "He's such an incredible figure in pop culture. . . . The opportunity to get to work with him and to get to see such an incredible mind at work was something I was really looking forward to."

As is his wont, Goldblum didn't disappoint. "Jeff is just the loveliest guy; tremendously open, very funny, very sweet, very smart. Just a joy, really. And it's lovely when you've been a fan of someone for such a long time and they turn out to be such a decent guy," McDonagh said. Fox called him "quite an exceptional character in the most delightful way. . . . He could not have been a more delightful person to work with."

"When he arrived, he had been preparing as he does for a role in L.A., and he came with very specific ideas," Fox continued. Not all of them fit the play. Some actors might grow angry, lash out, make a scene. Not our boy. "He was very good-natured and amenable when they said, 'No, we don't want that. We see the character differently.' And he adapted to what they wanted."

Crudup agreed. "He was so incredibly well prepared from day one, and that was thrilling to watch," he said. "And in some ways, you might regard that as incredibly serious minded, and to defy that, I can remember that during rehearsal, he kept pulling out this rope, and in the middle of one of the interrogations, [he'd] tie this rope into a knot and then magically make it disappear. This must have happened two or three times, then he would self-deprecatingly say, 'No, it's too much. The rope is too much.' And then it would come back again.

"Martin is incredibly protective of his words and his work, and nowhere in the script is there stage direction that says, 'He takes out a rope and does a magic trick.' At one point, I think John, the director, or Martin said, 'Jeff, sorry, what is with the rope?' And Jeff said, 'You know, I thought it might work. The fact of the matter is I learned this rope trick years ago, and I've been trying to put it into something ever since then.' It was so charming and self-effacing, and I remember that from rehearsal in the most enjoyable way."

As with most of McDonagh's work, reactions to the play varied wildly. There were several accounts of audience members' walking out, while others seemed ecstatically into it, and still others seemed bored. Goldblum told the *New York Times* that during one show, he caught two women asleep in the front row. "I couldn't believe it," he said. "We thought we were doing a show that was just cooking, and there they were sound asleep. But there was also a guy who was so into the show that he was actually pounding on the stage. It was like he thought he was at the Blue Man Group."

But, as Crudup told me, it didn't really matter how the audience reacted on any given night. The quartet knew they were performing something special, and their six weeks of rehearsal prepared them for anything, as "one of the virtues of doing a play is the rigor that goes into rehearsal. So in the same way that athletes can perform again and again under pressure, you build yourself a good muscle memory for how to communicate on what you all collaborated is the story you're going to tell.

"You feel as though you're a part of a team that you can understand," he said. "And if you start each show at the beginning, it will, with its own inertia, lead you to the end. Whether or not you give a great performance or whether or not the audiences like it—or in this case, whether or not somebody has a heart attack in the middle of the play and needs to be removed from the theater so that they can be revived, which happened in this play—there is always that capacity based upon the rigor of your rehearsal to produce some version of it each and every night."

I wonder what the play would have been like, though, with that rope trick.

The answer to the question I cleverly set myself up to answer came between Goldblum's detective television shows in what might be his most Oscar-hungry performance since *The Fly*: *Adam Resurrected*, a Paul Schrader–directed adaptation of Yoram Kaniuk's novel of the same name, which follows the story of a former circus clown who is spared during the Holocaust by despicable means.

Goldblum and Schrader seem like an odd couple at first glance. Schrader is best known for penning dark, brooding, and (often) intellectually simple characters in movies carried by the lead, such as *Taxi Driver*, *Raging Bull*, or *First Reformed*. Adam Stein, the concentration camp survivor in a mental institution some fifteen years after the war, certainly sounds like one of those characters at first glance. He's the Jewish version of Randle McMurphy from *One Flew Over the Cuckoo's Nest*, a smooth-talking patient with the run of the place, even carrying on a sexual affair with the head nurse. But he's also a raging drunk haunted by trauma, a deeply broken survivor on the verge of shattering beyond repair, who still manages to befriend and help cure a boy who thinks he's a dog.

But that's only half the film. The other half explains the reasons for his kinship with the boy, showing Stein before and during the war as a circus performer, a fine entertainer who carefully throws knives around his volunteers, performs magic tricks, dresses as animals, dances, and generally brings glee to everyone around him. In fact, it's very much his charisma as an entertainer that saves his life once he's in the concentration camp, albeit in the most horrid of ways. Upon his arrival, an SS commander named Klein (Willem Dafoe) recognizes him from his old stage show and essentially forces a deal upon him, one requiring Stein to humiliate himself at all times for Klein's amusement. Stein can live in relative safety and comfort in

Klein's quarters if—and only if—he always acts like a dog, a deal he accepts in hopes of saving his family. But the Nazis also force him to entertain Jews as they're marched to the gas chambers.

Schrader needed someone who could be both flashy entertainer and guilt-wracked survivor. An actor so deeply in love with the craft, he'd be willing to degrade himself for the part. Immediately upon reading Noah Stollman's script, Schrader said, "Jeff Goldblum was born to play this role. This is him." He was 100 percent right.

It's easy to see why the project appealed to an actor like Goldblum and why, despite generally disliking the film, several critics suggested this was his Oscar performance. He openly said at the time it was the "most challenging part [he'd] ever had," adding, "I don't think there's been as emotionally demanding a part as this." Plus, the script calls for all manner of capital-A Acting. He gets to do so damn much. For one, he tackles an accent, a rarity for him. While imprisoned by Klein, he crawls around on all fours, barks, pants, and even uses his mouth to wrestle meat from the teeth of a German shepherd, whom he befriends. In the institution, he also must get blind drunk, have surreptitious sex (with a barking woman portrayed by Ayelet Zurer), walk a boy as if he's a dog, and act charming and terrifying and broken and hysterical. Finally, in the flashbacks, he must be an utterly irresistible circus entertainer.

He prepared for a year and a half for the film, learning to play the violin, visiting Israel for the first time, and speaking with concentration camp survivors.

And yes, midway through the movie, he performs that damned rope trick as part of a metaphor to the young boy.

Here's how much actorly stuff he must do: Know that old phrase about a dramatic actor getting to "chew the scenery"? Well, in this case, that phrase could be used literally. Toward the end of the movie, the man literally eats dirt.* And apparently, it wasn't some stage con-coction. As Goldblum told *LA Weekly*: "Toward the end of the movie, we come to that scene where I visit the grave of my daughter, and I flip out. That had been written in several different ways; we'd talked about different approaches. So we're shooting the scene and I'm on the ground by the grave, crying, and Paul says, 'I think you eat the flowers.' So I ate the flowers. And then he says, 'I think you should pick up some dirt and put that in your mouth. Eat the dirt.' And I said, 'Okay, okay, that sounds great, really great, really crazy. Do we have some edible dirt?' And he says, 'Jeff, just eat it, eat it.' I say, 'No, no, that's horrible. That's bad for you.' And he says, 'Jeff, Jeff, look,' and he leans down and scoops up some dirt, and he eats it. So what could I do? I ate the dirt. That's a partnership. That's collaboration."

As you've probably picked up on, the movie is batshit insane. And they knew it. Goldblum said in that same interview, "We were on the high wire and could have fallen off in a million different ways, but we'd have done so together." Some people, though, did think they fell off—though most critics put the failure on Schrader's shoulders for not turn-ing the movie into a more coherent, emotional narrative. Goldblum's performance is truly astonishing, though whether that astonishment has positive or negative undertones depends on personal taste. The movie, unfortunately, feels structureless and flat, a series of strangely memorable scenes that add up to nothing. As Stephen Holden wrote in the *New York Times*, it "feels so detached that there is not a laugh, nor even a wicked smirk of nihilistic glee, to be gleaned." If you asked someone what happened in it, they'd probably say, "Oh, Jeff Gold-blum barked and crawled around on all fours and then there was this

---

*The film is not what you'd call *subtle* with its metaphors.

burning bush and, oh, some little kid also thought he was a dog and then Goldblum was a clown and, I dunno, a whole bunch happened." If someone asked what it was *about*, they'd probably clam up and say something like, "I dunno, the Holocaust, sort of, but also sort of the power of entertainment I think?"

My main takeaway from the film? You probably shouldn't watch it with your dog.*

B oy, it must have felt good to perform the rope trick in Schrader's film, because he'd been trying like a fiend to get it into *something*. Just ask Nick Guthe, the director of the 2006 film *Mini's First Time*. It's another one of those odd projects Goldblum found himself involved with during this decade-long creative wandering period. This is his one project that maybe aged worse than the *Crank Yankers* sketches. It follows Mini, a young teenager (Nikki Reed) who begins having an affair with her stepfather (Alec Baldwin) and decides to slowly and secretly drug her mother (Carrie-Anne Moss) to make her think she's going insane. Eventually, they decide to murder her, which leads a detective (Luke Wilson) to investigate, while a nosy neighbor (Goldblum) who is obsessed with Mini may or may not begin piecing things together. That might sound dark, but it's not quite *Pillowman* level, partly because it's generally played for laughs.†

---

*I made the mistake of watching the movie with my then-thirteen-week-old border collie/Lab puppy Stevie Nix. She was wigged out by the whole movie. Interestingly, she responded most strongly when Zurer barked, more so than Goldblum or even the actual dogs. Which makes me wonder, if Stevie Nix were a member of the Academy, would she have nominated Zurer for Best Supporting Actress? I mean, technically, us humans really don't know which actors barked the best, when you think about it.

† You may remember the movie from a kerfuffle that took place in 2017 when Baldwin wrote in his memoir that he didn't know Reed, with whom he had several sexual scenes, was sixteen years

The part was small, but Guthe said, "If I asked him to rehearse seventeen hours a day, he would do it. He loves acting, he really does. He loves the process. He loves rehearsals. He wants directors to download him on as much backstory of a character as possible. He actually asked me to write a very long description of Mike Rudell's life, outside of what was on the page." Guthe happily acquiesced, and Goldblum surprised him throughout the movie by drawing from that background.

Some of the film's best moments come when Goldblum's improvising, such as the scene in which strange circus animals arrive at the house, thanks to the fact that Mini has used her mom's credit card in an attempt to make her drugged mother feel like she's losing her mind. Watching the animals arrive from his balcony with his lover, Goldblum's Mike Rudell comments, "The giraffe can clean its own ears with its tongue, because the tongue is approximately twenty-one inches long. Is that true or false?"

"We thought, 'How can we make the scene crazier?'" Guthe told me. "Let's place him on the balcony, and I told him, 'Just go. The giraffe has arrived, so just comment.'" Later in the movie, Rudell plays piano, something else that wasn't in the script. A piano happened to be in the house where they were shooting, and like a moth to flame, he gravitated toward it while in the middle of shooting a scene.

Perhaps most important, though, in one of the outtakes for the movie, can you guess what Goldblum's doing at one point as his non-magician character? "He brought, like, a rope, and he was doing magic tricks," Guthe said. That damn rope.

---

old at the time. Guthe and the other producers on the movie claim this is blatantly false. Dana Brunetti, a producer on the film, told the *Hollywood Reporter* at the time, "It's a lie. I read it and was like, 'What the f—. Of course he totally knew how old she was. That's why there's no nudity in the movie. He knew before we even cast the movie. I think he's been method acting Trump too much and he doesn't know the difference between fake news anymore."

Guthe was a young director at the time, and his main takeaway from working with Goldblum might sound like something you'd learn from a fourth-grade teacher, something that's incredibly useful but requires a complete lack of ego to come up with. "So Jeff shows up to set and says to me, 'You know, it's a little bit frustrating not knowing who everyone is.'" Guthe agreed. Goldblum suggested everyone in the cast and crew wear name tags for three days. "I literally gave everyone name tags to wear, actors would take them off when they were in the scene, and by day three we all knew each other's name. You wanna talk about building cohesion on a set? After that, I wondered why we didn't do that on every movie. But it took Jeff's simple desire to connect with people, to understand the importance of if you connect with people, they will work hard on a project because they feel invested, they feel seen, and they feel appreciated."

The theory that Goldblum only tackles projects he finds artistically interesting and never falls into the trap of careerism falters a bit when considering some of his more commercial work. Specifically speaking, there's just no real way to square some of his video game voice work. That is *not* to disparage video games as an art form. Instead, it's to disparage the 1996 video game *Goosebumps: Escape from Horrorland*. That's probably unfair—it might be a great game. But boy does it sound like Goldblum, who voiced Dracula, probably had better things to do from an artistic perspective.

"I'm disappointed to report that Jeff's portrayal as the Prince of Darkness is understated to the point of being inaudible," Matt Elliott wrote for *PC Gamer* after somehow finding this game and a system that will still run it. "Maybe it's the fake teeth he has to wear, which make him talk like he has a mouthful of biscuits. Or maybe it's the ignominy of playing a cartoon vampire in a forgotten CD-ROM game. Either way, it's like you can feel him firing his agent as he urges out every reluctant line."

Some of his video game work makes sense. He voiced his characters in the *Jurassic Park* and *Independence Day* games, which likely came from some contractual obligation. But then his work in 2015's *Call of Duty: Black Ops III*? That certainly *seems* like a paycheck, but maybe he was excited to experiment in a new medium.

After all, some of the more surprisingly delightful work he's done happened in advertising, as commercial a medium as exists.[*] Goldblum became a spokesperson for Apple in the 1990s, representing the recently resuscitated brand in a series of commercials. Steve Jobs apparently considered himself a fan of the actor. "Jobs called me up a few decades ago to be the voice of Apple," Goldblum said, according to CNET. "That was early on, and I did not know it was Steve Jobs." It's unclear if he meant that Jobs wanted him for those commercials or to eventually become the literal voice, as in Goldblumi instead of Siri, but it's clear titans of industry noticed Goldblum's advertising potential early on.

Ever since debuting the Macintosh during the 1984 Super Bowl in a Ridley Scott–directed, *1984*-inspired ad featuring a dystopia upended by a spunky Anya Major wearing a vaguely Hooters-esque outfit and wielding a hammer, Apple has been known for inventive ads. These often starred celebrities, such as one from 1995 featuring this eclectic bunch: George Clinton, Hunter S. Thompson, Spike Lee, Oliver Stone, Marlee Matlin, and Dave Stewart. The next year, the

---

[*] This seems as good a place as any to remind everyone that Bob Dylan was in a Victoria's Secret ad, so it's not that crazy for capital-A Artists to make a few bucks in advertising.

company paid for product placement in the original *Mission: Impossible* movie, then took all the footage of Tom Cruise and co. using Apple products and strung it together into a standalone TV spot.

It was certainly no shock to see Goldblum in the ads at the end of the nineties, though he isn't given a tremendous amount to do in them. Some feature images of iMacs with ridiculous voice-overs such as this one in which Goldblum channels his inner capitalistic Robert Frost: "Two roads diverted on the way to the Internet, and I took the faster, simpler, less expensive, and far more colorful one. And that made all the difference." Others feature him in nineties casual wear (e.g., a white T-shirt and unbuttoned flannel) saying things like "So, you know, it seems like there's a big party going on these days. Everybody says, 'What's your email address? What's your email address? Hey, everybody, I'll email you.' . . . 'I don't have an email. What's this?' . . . Well now, good news. There's a computer so easy, ten minutes out of the box, you're emailing everybody, you're part of the party. It's as easy as licking a stamp." My personal favorite is the one where he just ruminates about beige, which he calls "one of the worst colors, it's not even a color, it's like oatmeal or sand, bland," and wonders if the people who made computers beige have been "in thinking jail."

He shines even brighter in a series of 2015 European ads for Currys PC World, a British electronic retailer. All of these two-to-three-minute spots begin with a family in the midst of a holiday crisis, generally someone receiving a gift that they hate. Goldblum then pops in, introduces himself as Jeff Goldblum, and teaches the unhappy person the basic tenets of acting by assuming the role and giving a demonstration.

"I'm delighted to be involved in this clever and timely campaign that will hopefully help people find the perfect holiday gifts for the people they care about most—without all the risky guesswork," Goldblum said of the ads. "It's so disheartening to put your heart and soul into a gift choice for a loved one only to discover they have three of them already—and don't use any of them ever."

In one, a husband gives his wife a jigsaw puzzle, though she wanted a computer. Goldblum appears, switches glasses with her, and plays the part of pretending to be happy. The punch line can be seen from miles away: the husband then passionately kisses Goldblum, who has to say, "That's the scene, Martin, that's the scene. I'm glad you do what moves you." But it's still genuinely, laugh-out-loud funny.

In all of these, the character he's playing is himself. That's often the case the further we get from 1999 and certainly was by 2015, when these ran, but rarely is it quite so blatant. It makes a bit more sense when you realize these were created for big screens. They played in movie theaters and on ad-supported video-on-demand services.

But what he's really known for here in the US is his work with Apartments.com. Just consider *that* for a moment. America's offbeat, brainy sex symbol being an exaggerated version of himself with the intention of convincing people to visit a website that helps them rent apartments.

They position Goldblum as Brad Bellflower, a self-important Silicon Valley tech type who suggests Steve Jobs and who calls himself the inventor of the "Apartminternet."* Appearing in smart suits while graphics straight out of movies like *The Matrix* swirl around behind him, he compares the website to such enormous concepts as fusion.

"They already existed, but there was real opportunity in that space, and they wanted to make a smash," Pat Mendelson, senior VP and executive creative director of RPA, the advertising agency responsible for the ads, told me. "We created this campaign where Jeff plays this larger-than-life, kind of audacious, modern entrepreneur. There

---

*Say that out loud. It'll tickle your mouth in a lovely and unexpected way.

are a lot of those these days. A lot of times, celebrities don't want to be a spokesperson. They want to play a part, which is what he's doing."

Yeah, sure, he's playing a part, but that part feels awfully close to the real guy.

"They were going for the loony futurist kind of thing. They were trying to glom onto that sense of technological wonder, and short of getting somebody from *The Big Bang Theory*, it made a lot of sense to put somebody like him in," Doug Zanger, an editor for *Adweek* who has written about Goldblum's campaigns in the past, told me. "You look at Goldblum [in the Apartments.com campaign] and you go, 'That makes sense. That makes absolute sense.' And he is being nothing other than himself. The idea of classifying him is impossible. He has his own category, the Goldblum category, [because] Jeff Goldblum can really go either way. You can't necessarily classify him as a comedic actor. You can't classify him as a dramatic actor. He is unclassifiable, and I think that's part of his appeal."

And, of course, everyone who worked with him on the spots seemed to love him. Seriously, is anyone more well liked than this dude?

"He is an absolute gem to work with, such a pleasure. I can't say enough about who he is. He's not just putting it on; he's a very generous, curious, intelligent person. When we're doing a spot, there's an area called the video village, where agency and client people will sit. And some actors don't go into that area quite as much or whatever. Jeff loves it. He gets to know everybody's name. He gets to know people all over the set. It doesn't matter what they do, who they are. And he's curious. He remembers who they are and asks them questions. He's such a unique person in that way. He just seems to love life and love people," Mendelson said, adding (as have so many others), "Sometimes when you actually meet people and work with people, you're disappointed. With him, it's the opposite. You go in thinking it's going to be really fun and interesting, and it's even more than that."

It's tough not to consider these anything other than a cash grab, but Zanger waylaid that notion. The money is obviously part of the equation, but he said actors enjoy shooting commercials because it "keeps them sharp, and, I'm not going to lie, it's profitable." A little more work honing their craft while taking home a nice paycheck. What's not to love?

My reaction to that thought can be described as cynical at least and incredulous at best. Though this response is based on the faulty assumption that a blockbuster movie and a commercial aren't essentially the same thing, even if they're presented as different. *Thor: Ragnarok* sells tickets while being a vehicle to later convince us to buy merchandise, and a commercial blatantly sells whatever product it happens to be peddling. How different are they really? After working with Goldblum in the aforementioned Marvel movie, Taika Waititi directed an Apartments.com commercial. What's the difference? And if that's what it takes to work together again, why not do it in a commercial? I'm pretty sure some people (Martin Scorsese, at least) would argue there isn't much difference between the two. "I think Jeff just wants to do interesting things with interesting people in interesting ways," Zanger said. "And the form and function that it takes can be unique."

All these projects, of course, kept him somewhat in the public eye—particularly his television and film work. But if you were to make one of those stock market graphs with the jagged red and green lines showing the trend of one's career, the actor seemed to be slipping out of the supposed A-list. Which, again, is something he has repeatedly insisted he doesn't care about, an assertion we have no reason not to take at face value. Still, it certainly seemed that without some sort of purposeful change in course, Goldblum might slip away from our collective consciousness.

But that was before the Internet.

Jeff on Jeff:
A (Tony Award–Worthy) One-Act Play

It's a common fantasy, wondering what you'd say to your younger self if ever given the chance. So, as a natural extension of that, my editor Jill Schwartzman got to thinking: What would an older Goldblum say to a younger Goldblum? What wisdom would he impart to a version of himself that was still years removed from all the tough trials and tribulations that earned him the very wisdom he had to impart? Such a good question deserves a thoughtful, almost meditative consideration, one that might reveal deep truths about celebrity, film, and perhaps humanity itself. Instead, probably to her chagrin, I wrote this. Please enjoy my exceedingly brief one-act play in which a sixty-seven-year-old Goldblum meets himself a half century earlier.

ACT 1, THE ONLY ACT

Scene 1, The Only Scene: A Jazz Club

Enter YOUNG JEFF GOLDBLUM (17 years old), munching on a BLT, and OLDER JEFF GOLDBLUM (67 years old), sipping on a green smoothie. The two immediately begin fighting over the piano.

YOUNG JEFF GOLDBLUM

Whoa, whoa, whoa! What are you doing, old man? I called this place and asked if they needed a piano player and they said yes, so I came right here after eating this BLT, which I eat every single day! Anyway, as you can tell from my Buddy Holly glasses, I'm the piano player tonight.

OLDER JEFF GOLDBLUM

Ahh, you mean *pianist,* simultaneously one of the most beautiful and erotic words in the English language. *[Purrs]* I'm here, dear boy, because you are me and I am you. We are one and the same, and not in the way all of us share the same bountiful energy, no. We are one and the same because I am you, later in this great cosmic journey. *[Purrs for seven and a half minutes]*

Each pulls out a bag of lozenges and offers one to the other at the same moment. They begin to laugh.

YOUNG JEFF GOLDBLUM

Ahh, I enjoy a good lozenge, I'll tell you that. Good on the ol' throat. But the Halls aside, I'm so excited to meet you. I mean me. I mean you. How delightful! I don't even know what I mean! Tell me this: are there BLTs in the future?

OLDER JEFF GOLDBLUM

Well, yes, but I tend to stick to the leaner cuts of meat these days, if I indulge at all. Say, do you still do that thing in the bathroom?

YOUNG JEFF GOLDBLUM

You mean, uhh . . .

OLDER JEFF GOLDBLUM

No, no, no! The other thing, with the bathroom mirror!

YOUNG JEFF GOLDBLUM

Ummm, what?

OLDER JEFF GOLDBLUM

Look, do me a favor, will you? If you could just start writing "God, make me an actor" in the steam on the mirror every day with your finger after taking a hot shower and then wipe it off really quickly before anyone sees, that'd be really just terrific.

YOUNG JEFF GOLDBLUM

Uhh, sure. To be honest, I'm still a little taken aback that I won't still be eating the sandwich I eat *every single day* in the future. Oh, boy. Can't quite say I'm thrilled about that. Do I at least make it out of Pittsburgh? What else do I need to know?

OLDER JEFF GOLDBLUM

You make it out almost immediately! So quickly, it isn't even that good of a story! Oh, also, know how you have that thing for other people's hands? Soon enough, you won't have to hide it! In fact, you'll mention it in an interview every few years, and it'll take over the Internet nearly every time.

YOUNG JEFF GOLDBLUM

The Internet? Is that a jazz club? Because it certainly sounds exotic.

OLDER JEFF GOLDBLUM

Oh, yes! Sure, why not. Oh, golly yes!

YOUNGER JEFF GOLDBLUM

Well, what is it? Oh, never mind! I have so many other questions for you! You're so strikingly handsome, and look at your clothes! Do we ever get to sleep with a lady? How did we do? Do I still play piano? What does the world think of us, if anything? Am I married? Do I have kids? Most important, am I, uhh, I mean are *we*, an actor? Or *actors*? I don't really know how the grammar works in this situation, but it's the only thing in this darn world I want to do!

OLDER JEFF GOLDBLUM

Oh, oh, oh. I don't know. Sandy Meisner said it takes twenty years to become an actor . . .

YOUNG JEFF GOLDBLUM

Who?

OLDER JEFF GOLDBLUM

Why, the acting teacher in New York who—oh, never mind. Do you like games? What am I saying? I know you do! Let's play a little game, shall we? I'm going to name some movies I, err, we've been in, or will be in—gee, the grammar really is tricky here, isn't it?—and you guess what they are. How's that sound?

YOUNG JEFF GOLDBLUM

(blurting it out and cutting off his older self)
Oh, wow! Movies, plural! Sure, let's play.

OLDER JEFF GOLDBLUM

Let's start with *The Big Chill*, *The Fly*, and *Jurassic Park*. What do you think those three movies are about?

YOUNG JEFF GOLDBLUM

Well . . . hmmm, I'm guessing an extremely air-conditioned prison, an airline pilot, and a really old parking lot? Kidding about that last one, of course. I'm kind of a funny guy. It's about a national park, probably.

OLDER JEFF GOLDBLUM

Ehh, close enough. To be honest, I'm stalling a bit here, because I've put us in a metaphysical pickle, so to speak, all for the chance to gallivant a wee bit with my younger self. Gee, golly, see, the thing is, I'm not sure there's space in the universe for both of us to *be*, if you catch my drift. I've been reading a lot of Stephen Hawking and Christopher Hitchens lately, and while they don't so much directly address this conundrum, I do believe I can draw out the conclusion that, well, one of us may need to cease for the other to be.

YOUNG JEFF GOLDBLUM

(who, during this long speech, has grabbed a pair of piano wire cutters, which he plunges into the older version of himself)
Way ahead of you, old man! This is like one of those Philip Roth novels I'm always reading. Kind of. Now get back to the future, you rich coconut!

OLDER JEFF GOLDBLUM

(as he lies dying)
Honestly, I'm brimming with pride. And blood. Yep, that's blood.

Fin.

Pittsburgh/*Pittsburgh*

Pinpointing the moment someone becomes himself is tricky business. Most of us, after all, spend our lives becoming ourselves. It's different for Famous People. Casual fans, the kind who don't read books about them, consider them in phases. What comes to mind, for example, when you think about Lindsay Lohan? The child actress? The troubled young adult? The person trying to put her life back together? Those are all snapshots of a life.

Goldblum is no different. Now he's a domestic dude, married to a woman named Emilie Livingston, with whom he shares two children. He's nerdy, seemingly kind, pretty weird, and no longer an A-list star. He's a lovable oddball. But that wasn't always the case, right? When you think about the actor from *The Fly* or *Jurassic Park*, you probably think of someone seemingly more serious, seemingly hungrier. There was that whole Lost Chapter period, in which he slowly became who we think of today. But when exactly did it happen?

Pinpointing that moment is a slightly ridiculous exercise, but this is an exceedingly ridiculous book, so I'm going to go ahead and do just that and say it happened during his first extremely public return to Pittsburgh in 2004 under the strangest of circumstances, ones that would muddle fact and fiction, truth and Truth. The box office giant stepped away from the silver screen to perform alongside his brand-new fiancée (half his age, natch) in a local production of *The Music Man*. Oh, yeah, and he brought a camera crew along to make a documentary, or maybe a mockumentary, of the whole thing. Naturally, its title is *Pittsburgh*.

"I still can't tell if he was goofing on us or not," *Pittsburgh Post-Gazette* reporter Sharon Eberson said of the whole thing. No one can. And that's why I've chosen this moment as the moment Jeff Goldblum became Jeff Goldblum. It's the moment he mythologized himself.

"There are many people, like Andy Warhol, who denied their Pittsburgh roots. But Goldblum has embraced them," Eberson said, remembering the circus that was Goldblum's return to the city in 2004. And that's partially true, but he also had a lot more in mind that had little to do with the city of Pittsburgh or *The Music Man*. Instead, he was in the clutches of newfound love and artistic restlessness, a combination that can be either toxic or fruitful. Which it ended up being in this case is in the eye of the beholder.

Months earlier, Goldblum was waiting at the Seattle airport for his flight back to Los Angeles when he noticed a young dancer named Catherine Wreford, a young twentysomething touring with the Broadway production of *42nd Street*, in which she played the lead Peggy Sawyer, killing time with the rest of the cast before boarding a plane to Costa Mesa. Armed with experience from his two marriages to Patricia Gaul and Geena Davis, not to mention a cavalcade of girlfriends, he decided to approach her.

"I guess he'd seen me or something and asked who I was. Somebody came over to me and said, 'Jeff wants to meet you.' I said, 'Okay, well tell him to come over here,'" Wreford said. Thus began a whirlwind courting process that found Goldblum sending her flowers in Costa Mesa, before appearing at the opening night of *42nd Street* when it hit L.A. Though Wreford was reticent, she finally agreed to a lunch date with the man, who was nearly thirty years her senior.

At the time, she didn't know much about him aside from having seen his Dr. Ian Malcolm in *Jurassic Park*. Her family, from rural Canada, paid so little attention to pop culture that her parents needed to look him up. (To understand just *how* removed Wreford was, consider this: She went with Goldblum to a dinner party at Sharon Stone's house, where she sat between him and Jane Fonda. "I only recognized her because my mom had those records of her doing workouts. I said, 'Oh my gosh, you're the person on my mom's records! You're the workout lady!' She gave me the dirtiest look and said, 'That is *not* what I'm best known for.' And then she wouldn't speak to me the rest of the time, and Jeff had to tell me, 'No, actually she's really famous.'")

"I found him incredibly interesting, and I wanted to know more about him [after that lunch date]," she said. "Then we went out on a date one time and ended up back at his house. He had a grand piano in the middle of the living room, and he just started playing jazz music. And I was like, 'You play the piano?!'

"Then he started playing Broadway tunes, and I was singing. We just sat there singing and playing piano until late in the evening, and then he drove me home. That was sort of our first date. It was beautiful."

Things sped up from there. "After two or three weeks in L.A., I moved into his house," Wreford said. "We spent two months there, then spent two months in San Francisco." She flew to Italy while he filmed Wes Anderson's *The Life Aquatic with Steve Zissou*, before heading to Pittsburgh. Soon, they were engaged.

Meanwhile, a twin narrative had begun unfolding when unortho-dox documentary filmmakers Chris Bradley and Kyle LaBrache screened their first feature together, 2003's *Jon E. Edwards Is in Love*, at the home of Keith Addis, who happens to be Goldblum's longtime manager. The black-and-white movie, which scooped up awards on the festival circuit, follows a somewhat delusional, entirely overconfi-dent soul singer. To wit: "When James Brown dies," Edwards says, "I'm the fuckin' king. I'm the only man for that throne. There's some other motherfucker in Cleveland, but he's not wearing Gucci." The problem—and the thing that makes it so compulsively watchable—is that he's not that good of a singer. Not at all.

Joe Leydon wrote of it in *Variety*, "For the first 30 minutes, *Jon E. Edwards Is in Love* plays like a *Spinal Tap*–style put-on about a bel-ligerently confident but marginally talented entertainer. Only gradu-ally does it become clear . . . [Edwards, the] titular subject, isn't joking—whether he's proclaiming himself 'Soul Brother No. 1' or listing Johnny Rotten and Harry Belafonte among his musical influ-ences."

Taken by the movie, Addis mentioned to the documentarians that he worked with Goldblum and sensed a potential collaboration. "We met with Jeff at that time, and he was really interested in doing some-thing that had the Meisner message in it,* which would be actors act-ing and improvising but amongst real people," Bradley said.

They began kicking around ideas, such as creating some sort of background plot to *The Life Aquatic*, something to tease a second, stranger movie out of it. Nothing was quite clicking, though, until they considered bringing Wreford into the fold.

"He met Catherine, and as he's prone to do, it was a whirlwind. It

---

*Does everything make sense now?!

was a very fast-moving relationship. They got engaged very quickly, and his advisors and friends said, 'Whoa, hold on. Slow down. Pump the brakes on this,'" Bradley said.

Naturally, they didn't listen. One day, Wreford learned that the Pittsburgh Civic Light Opera (CLO) planned to stage *The Music Man*, and the idea that they should perform in it together was born—but things didn't go as planned.

The musical follows con man Harold Hill, who plans to trick the people of a small Midwest town into buying a variety of instruments from him by posing as the leader of a boys' marching band, despite not having any actual talent or experience. "It's a beast to stage," Ronald Allan-Lindblom, the former artistic director of the Pittsburgh Playhouse and Point Park University's Conservatory of Performing Arts, said. On its face, the role isn't an obvious fit for Goldblum, who is often all kinetic energy and moving limbs. As a trickster, Hill is often portrayed as charismatic but somewhat still, someone who both stands out and blends in. To the shock of Goldblum and co., those staging the play were hesitant.

"Keith called the Pittsburgh CLO and said, 'Jeff Goldblum wants to play Harold Hill,' and thought the response would be, 'Great! That's awesome! How do we make this happen?'" Bradley said. "But it wasn't at all. They actually were hesitant and said, 'We're going to have to have them audition.'"

As it turns out, *hesitant* is a hell of an understatement. "Everybody was completely against it," said Richard Sabellico, the Broadway veteran who directed this iteration of *The Music Man* and can be found yelling at Goldblum throughout *Pittsburgh*. "Everyone except for Van [Kaplan], the producer. This is not a disparaging remark about him, but Van saw dollar signs. Jeff was a big movie star. They don't get big movie stars. They get television stars on their way out, or they get Broadway stars nobody gives a shit about."

It wasn't that any of them had a problem with Goldblum himself, at least not yet. Sabellico told them, "I'd love to work with Jeff, but *The Music Man*? I don't think so."

Though that might seem like a deterrent, to say the least, the mixture of a relationship not everyone approved of, an adversarial director, and a potentially career-derailing role created a much-needed narrative for the semi-real, semi-fictional "documentary." "We thought, 'Now let's start filming. This is great,'" Bradley said. "This is what we wanted: something bizarre, something [that played with] Jeff's life as a celebrity and all the things he goes through."

So that's exactly what they did. They shot a documentary in which Goldblum inhabited the acting adage he always did—living truthfully under imaginary circumstances—but taking it to the next level by layering real circumstances on top of imaginary ones. In other words, he was playing the character "Jeff Goldblum" in the real world, where everyone thought he was actually Jeff Goldblum and not a character "Jeff Goldblum." Yeah, it makes the head spin.

It begins with his visiting Ed Begley Jr. and his wife, Rachelle Carson, who politely question his relationship with such a young woman. Throughout the movie, Goldblum gets a work visa for his fiancée (former councilman Doug Shields, who said he helped "grease the wheels," claimed this part is true but Wreford confirmed it was entirely fabricated), auditions for the play (true), is essentially told he's terrible in the role by director Richard Sabellico (very true), turns down a movie offer from Michael Bay (maybe true), is hounded by Begley to be a spokesperson for solar panels (kind of true), and hangs out with his friend Illeana Douglas and her then-boyfriend Moby (let's not even try to fact-check Moby's dating history). So much more occurs, but you get the general idea here. Not knowing what is fact or fiction is half the fun. Did he really turn down a Michael Bay movie to star in the play? Did Craig Kilborn know the whole thing was

something of a put-on when Goldblum appeared on his show and began talking about regional theater?* Was Moby aware of what was
going on, like, at all? The joy lies in not quite knowing, because the
whole point was watching Goldblum react to things that may or may
not have been actually happening.

"We weren't pranking anyone. It's not something making fun of
people. It's meant to be realistic, and the people who are real are real.
But then the actors are real but also have story lines they're aware of,"
Bradley said. Still, there were a few setups. Conan O'Brien was partially in on the idea when he had Goldblum on his show and chided
him for doing the play. "You're going second. Guests who open big
Hollywood films go first!" he says. At other times, for the purpose of
having a "scene," they'd sometimes build in an interruption, something to give sequences narrative cohesion.

At times, the setups led to more behind-the-scenes absurdity. In
one instance that didn't make the final cut, Goldblum was running
lines with a costar named Joanne at his house. Eventually, she stood
up to leave but couldn't find her car keys. Goldblum, thinking it was
a setup, kept pushing her to look for the keys. But, in reality, she simply couldn't find them. "And it goes on and on and on and on. We
didn't have a traditional set where we could yell 'cut,' so we just kept
filming," LaBrache said.

"Her car was actually stolen. She had left the keys in the car, and
she finally went out, and the car was gone," Bradley added.

But, for the most part and by all accounts, what we see in the
movie is what actually happened, "one hundred percent honest," as
Sabellico put it.

Speaking of the devil, much of that Truth follows Sabellico's scold-

---

* For what it's worth, Kilborn told me he didn't remember the interview.

ing, admonishing, and even insulting Goldblum in a variety of ways. The director was quick to say, "I adore him. I adored him then. I adored him while I was yelling at him, and I adore him now. So I never, never have one minute when I did not really like the man,"* before adding, "He is a charming, genial, grown-up child."

By that, he meant that Goldblum wasn't an easy actor to direct. "It's not that he doesn't listen. He does listen, but he listens through a filter and hears things the way he wants to hear it." Given the strange duality of his project (to both perform *The Music Man* and make *Pittsburgh* interesting), that shouldn't come as a surprise, especially considering some of the anecdotes the director enjoys doling out.

"One day Jim Walton, who was playing Marcellus, came up and said, 'You have got to get downstairs. I'm gonna kill him.' He was smiling. Not like 'I hate him' or anything, just 'He's driving me crazy,'" Sabellico said. So the director walked downstairs to find Goldblum's newest interpretation of Hill.

"He's doing the song 'The Sadder but Wiser Girl' and he wants to make rings around his nipples with his fingers. I said, 'Jeff, it's 1912! You can't do that!'

"He just said, 'Ohhh, okay.' He would never argue. He was just like a disappointed little kid: 'Oh, okay.'"

Things didn't get better by opening night, much of which appears in the movie. Not everything made the cut, though. For example, they had acquired the costumes from the Broadway staging of *The Music Man* that had just ended, which featured Rebecca Luker as Marian

---

*I completely believe he adores Goldblum, even if he didn't necessarily enjoy directing him. He said that Goldblum told him on more than one occasion, "'You could stand to lose a few pounds.' But, like, in a way you can't get mad at him," Sabellico said. "It was sincere that you'd probably be better off." It's a testament to how charismatic Goldblum is that the director didn't just haul off and slug him.

the Librarian. Wreford supposedly wasn't thrilled about having to wear the costume and, according to Sabellico, actively asked for a different wardrobe, but no one would budge.

"So it's intermission on opening night, and I'm in the lobby and Van Kaplan, the producer, comes over and says, 'You've got to get backstage. You've just gotta take care of this. This is ridiculous.' So I go backstage, assuming it's Jeff, which it was not. The problem was with her. She had wanted a different dress, and I kept saying to her, 'You're not getting a different dress. You are wearing the Broadway costumes.' And she's going on and on, and I just said, 'Look, here's the deal. You are either going to wear the costume, or you're not going to wear it and you're not going to go on. Then they would cancel the show and you'd be responsible for paying all the money back' or whatever. I was making up some bullshit.

"She and Jeff had dressing rooms that were right next to each other. So he comes out of his dressing room, and she starts complaining to him. He just puts his hands over his ears and starts to sing 'A Foggy Day (In London Town)' while she is screaming at him. And once again I look at him, and I just think, 'God, I love this guy.'"

For what it's worth Wreford doesn't remember this, but, God, don't you just hope it's true?

Of course, not every story has a conventionally happy ending. Goldblum's engagement with Wreford came to a sudden end soon thereafter, just after Goldblum's run in the Martin McDonagh play *The Pillowman*. Wreford said the actor became moody and dark, something she attributed to the material he performed almost nightly. When the end came, he essentially kicked her out of their shared Los Angeles home and told her not to contact him. Instead, he told her she could contact his lawyers, according to Wreford. Since Goldblum hasn't weighed in on anything in this book, he didn't weigh in on this, either, and Wreford, who lives with a terminal illness, seems like a reliable source. That said, she was quick to say she doesn't have any hard feelings, which is a true testament to her. Most of us, I daresay, would remain livid for a long, long time.

His relationship with his parents also apparently fell apart. Goldblum has alluded to the fact that he wasn't speaking with his mother toward the end of her life in several interviews, though he's always a bit oblique as to why. Instead, he usually gives some general sentiment about life's being mysterious and confusing or some such nonsense.

The people of Pittsburgh were significantly more pleased with Goldblum's return to the town than Sabellico, even if the project was (at least partially) a façade. "People loved it when Jeff came back. This is a city that embraces its alumni. There's a real sense of fantastic camaraderie here," Allan-Lindblom, who met him during the project, told me. At the same time, "there was kind of a twinkle in his eye of 'What the hell am I doing?'"

One of the charming aspects of the film is watching him interact with excited townies and old friends. These unscripted moments have the added benefit of offering a glimpse into how nonfamous people interact with Famous People. In one scene, a jogger stops to reminisce with the actor, clearly proud of having struck him out a few times in Little League.

The biggest surprise came when Shields decided to declare Tuesday, July 13, 2004, "Jeff Goldblum Day" in the city of Pittsburgh. One of the reasons, according to the official proclamation, was that "despite his fame and fortune, Jeff Goldblum has always remembered with pride his hometown and as such serves as an ambassador for Pittsburgh."

When he first pitched the idea, his staffers balked, telling him there was no chance that Goldblum would come to city hall. "I said, 'Are you kidding me?'" Shields remembered. "'Who wouldn't want a day named for themselves? Make the call.'" Goldblum's camp gleefully accepted, leaving Shields's staff "flabbergasted."

The actual meeting between the men in the movie is simple enough. Shields and his camp assumed that was that. Imagine Shields's shock when, months later, "[he got] in on a Monday morning, and [his] administrative assistant said, 'Doug, you have a really long message from Jeff Goldblum.'"

It was an invite to the Tribeca Film Festival, so Shields could see a screening of the movie. At the Q & A afterward, the actor even pointed to Shields, name-checking him. "And I see the movie for the first time. What a great scam!" he said, clearly still tickled by the idea. "It's a great trick."

One aspect of the production that was *definitely* real, much to Sabellico's chagrin, was the actual staging of *The Music Man*. In the movie, just before the show opens, Goldblum is overcome with nervousness, sitting in his dressing room, head in his hands. Unsurprisingly, the show played to packed houses, but the director's fears were realized. It didn't exactly earn rave reviews locally, to say the least. Wrote longtime theater critic Christopher Rawson for the *Pittsburgh Post-Gazette*: "In the local case of Jeff Goldblum, Hollywood star and Pittsburgh favorite son, the evidence of Tuesday's opening performance in Pittsburgh CLO's 'The Music Man' is clear: He's not quite ready for prime time on the musical comedy stage . . . if [only] he could just relax and let the role and his own charisma do their work. Jeff, do less! Leave the perpetual motion to Tommy Djilas. Start by dropping all those nervous hand-to-face gestures."

Rawson also grappled with the real-life implications of having Goldblum and his young fiancée onstage, writing, "The production also engages us in the drama of Goldblum's baptism by fire, and it complicates this by casting his young fiancée, Catherine Wreford, as Marian. I know actors should be allowed to leave their real lives off-stage, but few in Tuesday's audience can have been unaware of the leads' relationship. So which was more gripping: Whether Marian's integrity would settle Harold down or whether Wreford's profession-alism would stabilize Goldblum?

"As portrayed by Goldblum, there has never been a Harold so in need of Marian's love to rescue him from rootlessness, which does give the ending of the musical a surprising poignancy. When the two kiss passionately (twice!) at the footbridge, both plots are resolved—Harold is tamed and Goldblum has made it through."

That said, it's fairly telling that even Rawson was somehow so enraptured by Goldblum's status that he returned the next week to review the play a second time—an unusual thing for a theater critic to do. He only returned for an hour, but he wrote, "[Goldblum is] more at ease; dozens of small details are evidence. Now, the audience is more likely to relax and enjoy his goofy hyper charm. More at home, he's able to be even more himself, and while Jeff Goldblum may not be my idea of Harold Hill, he almost disarms that objection." Though Rawson added a telling jab that the actor's charms don't "deny the other limits, those of Goldblum's voice and acting."*

Since then, Goldblum has occasionally visited Pittsburgh, usually giving back in some small way. After a gunman killed eleven wor-shippers at the Tree of Life synagogue in an anti-Semitic massacre in

---

* Amusingly, Rawson suggested, "[He] could even see him making a go on Broadway, given the right role and lots of work. But I suppose he'll go back to being a movie star. Wouldn't you?" The irony therein, of course, being that Goldblum *started* on Broadway.

2018, Goldblum played a benefit concert at the Carnegie Library of Homestead Music Hall. Proceeds benefited the Tree of Life Victims of Terror Fund. Even at an event with such sober underpinnings, locals delighted in having him back. They mobbed him beforehand, but he remained good-natured. He "was pointing at people and saying things like, 'You used to swim in my pool,'" Eberson remembered.

Finally, in 2019, his presence in the city was cemented when he became the celestial voice of the Carnegie Science Center's Buhl Planetarium, which sits at the intersection of the Ohio and Allegheny Rivers. Like all things Goldblum, this unlikely marriage began with a whimsical idea, one with seemingly no hope of reaching fruition.

Ralph Crewe, the center's program development coordinator, had a thought similar to one many of us have from time to time: wouldn't it be cool to work with a celebrity? While putting together a new welcome message for the planetarium, he thought it'd be nice to have a famous Pittsburgh voice for it, something to "give [them] a little more gravitas."

"Immediately Jeff Goldblum came to mind," Crewe said. "He's instantly recognizable, such a unique and interesting guy and very much a Pittsburgher, who grew up going to the Buhl Planetarium."

Of course, getting in touch with a movie star, much less convincing one to do *more work*, feels like a pipe dream. But Crewe found himself with some time on his hands and dug up the name of Goldblum's agent from the depths of the Internet. He shot off an email, expecting not so much as a peep in response.

But this is Goldblum we're talking about.

"It caught me completely off guard when I got an email an hour later from his agent [asking for a script]. So I found myself writing a script for Jeff Goldblum, which is a very surreal experience. Like, I've written things before for other people to say, but usually it's a science presenter trying to explain how the sun works or something like that, never a script for a movie star."

Within two days, Goldblum sent Crewe an email from his personal account with the audio attached, an experience Crewe dubbed as "unreal."

"I was at home when I got the email, and I jumped up and down and was yelling. My wife was like, 'WHAT IS GOING ON?!' and I told her, 'IT WORKED!' It takes me longer to get a meeting with three colleagues together than it took to do this."

It was as simple as that. Now legions of Pennsylvania stargazers will begin their journey in the planetarium with that calming purr and the following message, delivered in Goldblum's dulcet, undulating tones.

"Hello. Uh, my name is Jeff Goldblum. Jeff Goldblum. And you know what I wanna say? Welcome. Welcome, welcome, welcome to you. 'Cause here you are at the Buhl Planetarium, which we like to say is a theater of the stars. Now, the stars you're about to see aren't movie stars. Some people call me a movie star. But these are profoundly large, brilliantly hot masses of gas and plasma. Well, some of that actually does describe me," he says in the clip, chuckling before continuing. "In any case, these ones are like the sun. Many of them are bigger and brighter than our own sun.

"Hey, you know, I grew up in Pittsburgh," he adds, as if he's just remembered and is thrilled by this fact. "And when I visited the Buhl Planetarium, I think that's where I, at least partly, located my sense of wonderment and curiosity. Gee, that's a wonderful thing. Now, I'm nothing if not a curious cat." Of course, he purrs here. "But really, curiosity, it's a real important part of the scientific process, a process which I highly esteem. C'mon. Facts and reason you can't get better than that!"

Then he gives some specifics, before offering a parting, "Bye, bye, bye."

Unreal is a good word for it. The classic story of an aspiring actor leaving his hometown for the big city usually ends there, but Goldblum, ever the gracious soul, continues to return. It's further proof that even after he achieved a larger-than-life A-lister status, Goldblum's default setting is humble and gracious.

So if anyone wonders why the Hollywood star would lend his voice to a local planetarium, and if anyone wonders why he would appear in a local production of an American stage classic, and if anyone wonders why he would make a low-budget docu(mocku)mentary with two early-career filmmakers, the answer, as always, is simple.

Because he's Jeff Goldblum.

The End

Beloved Hollywood actor Jeff Goldblum, best known for starring in films such as *Jurassic Park*, *The Fly*, and *The Big Chill*, died tragically on June 26, 2009, after falling more than sixty feet from the Kauri Cliffs while filming an episode of *Law & Order: Criminal Intent* in New Zealand. He was fifty-six years old.

Goldblum began acting in the 1970s, rising to fame with his role as a *People* magazine journalist in 1983's *The Big Chill*. Since then, he's appeared in dozens of blockbuster films and offbeat television shows and became one of the earliest known Internet memes. Author and culture journalist Travis M. Andrews expertly chronicled his career in *Because He's Jeff Goldblum*, potentially the greatest book ever written.

Perhaps the person most upset by Goldblum's death was beloved Hollywood actor Jeff Goldblum, who appeared on Comedy Central's *The Colbert Report* just days later to offer a few words about the iconic celebrity.

Somberly dressed for the occasion in a smart black suit, he wandered onstage during the show, began tapping his arms impatiently with his hands, and (confusingly) told Colbert, "I'm so sorry to interrupt, my friend Stephen. But look, I'm not dead. I'm not dead!"

Colbert, clearly annoyed with the interruption, fired back: "Do you mind, Jeff Goldblum? I'm reporting on the death of Jeff Goldblum."

Then Goldblum dropped the bombshell, announcing that the week during which he died, he "was not even in New Zealand." He then proceeded to text an unbelieving Colbert from beyond the grave. Eventually, Colbert showed Goldblum a news report of his death, finally convincing the deluded actor of the tragedy that had befallen Hollywood, the United States of America, Earth, and, let's be honest, the universe.

"Well, I guess I am dead," Goldblum admitted. "I owe you an apology."

He then offered a touching eulogy for the late thespian.

"No one will miss Jeff Goldblum more than me. He was not only a friend and a mentor, but he was also me. Jeff Goldblum's performances combined the muscularity of Brando, the pathos of Streep, and the musky sensuality of a pride of baboons. One former conquest raved that sleeping with Jeff Goldblum was like, quote, 'being caught in a flesh storm with a ninety percent chance of satisfaction,' unquote. That's verbatim. I cannot overstate how amazing Jeff Goldblum was in bed.

"When Jeff Goldblum passed away, a little bit of all of us died," he added. "I will be missed."

Goldblum's death so affected Goldblum that he continued to speak about it for weeks. "Before I got the word out and we could call everybody—yes, my mom called and was [saying,] 'J-J-Jeffrey? J-Jeffrey, are you all right?'" he later told television host Andy Cohen on *Watch What Happens Live*. "Then a friend of mine, oh, I don't remember who, tearfully, hysterically, left a message."

Of course, Goldblum was not the only person upset by the news. New Zealand police were not pleased to see reports on the Australian morning news that New Zealand police had confirmed Goldblum's death. In response, New Zealand police inspector Kerry Watson released the following statement: "Police at Kerikeri are receiving phone calls regarding a person falling from a cliff at Kauri Cliff. There is no such incident and police have no information to provide."

Goldblum leaves behind millions of adoring fans, all of whom require at least three copies of this book.

Each.

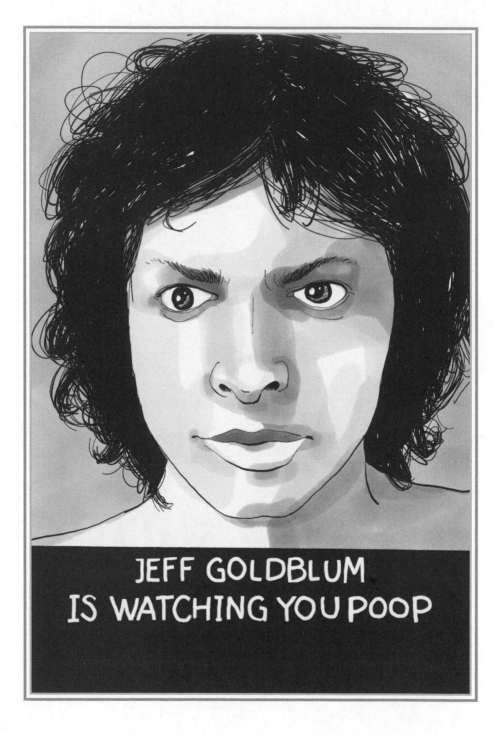

10.

Jeff Goldblum vs. the Idea of Jeff Goldblum

Before any of us truly understood what was happening, the basic way many (if not most) of us communicate with each other changed profoundly. I'm speaking, of course, of the Internet and the social media companies that would soon call it home. Suddenly, the barriers to being noticed by *everyone* disappeared to the point where a child stating, "I like turtles," on YouTube has been viewed more than sixty million times, which you can bet your bottom dollar means a hell of a lot more people saw it than saw *Adam Resurrected*.

Perhaps the most radical aspect of how the Internet altered our lives is how time became meaningless. There is suddenly no difference between old and new media. *Jurassic Park* came out decades ago, but clips and images from the film can be used as immediate currency. The only differentiation between a YouTube clip from a movie that came out forty years ago and one that came out four years ago might be the quality of the video itself. Everything now lives alongside everything else, accessible at all times. And if it's not free, a small fee will get just about anything for you. The Internet created a constant present. There is no longer any such thing as "the past" as we once understood it.

The meme, in many ways, is an encapsulation of this idea. And memes forever altered our relationship to Goldblum. But what, exactly, is a meme? There's a lot of confusion about exactly how to define it. Ryan Milner, an associate professor of communication at the College of Charleston and author of *The Ambivalent Internet: Mischief, Oddity, and Antagonism Online* and *The World Made Meme: Public Conversations and Participatory Media*, said there are multiple ways to do so. "There's one sense of *meme* that means 'Internet inside joke,' the funny little JPEGs [photos] that people share that require some sort of production," he told me. The most common version of these is a photo, often of a Famous Person, with funny text added above and below said photo.

Using that particular definition, Goldblum became the face of one of the earliest Internet memes in 2002. Unlike the memes we think of today, which are trafficked on social media sites by most of us and emailed by grandparents in triple forwards, this one's purpose was to creep offline. People were supposed to print the image out and tape it in bathroom stalls at hipster dive bars, rock clubs, and coffee shops.

The meme is simply a close-up of Goldblum's face from a scene in *The Fly* before he transforms, so he's got the crazy bug eyes and wild mane of black hair. His lips are pursed, and he looks deeply serious. In large white lettering under the photograph are the words "JEFF GOLDBLUM IS WATCHING YOU POOP." It's that simple, that stupid, and (somehow) that amusing.

Also sitting beneath the image is a link to a now-defunct Geo-Cities website, one of the old ones with black text on a bright red background, according to a version of the page archived by the Way-back Machine, which captures images of websites at various points in time. A crude map of the United States sat at the bottom of the page, marking cities where the meme was spotted. Populating the rest of the page was the meme and the following instructions:

DIRECTIONS:

1. RIGHT CLICK AAND SAVE PICTURES (YOU CAN CHOOSE COLOR OR BLACK&WHITE)
2. PRINT OUT COPYS
3. TAPE UP IN PUBLIC BATHROOMS BY THE TOILET
4. SEND IN PICTURS TO JGIWYP@HAIRDRESSER.NET

It also included a running captain's-log-style diary, spotted with what must have been purposeful misspellings, with supposed updates of the meme.

One such entry: 4/29/02—!!! SIGN THE GESTBOOK AND TELL JEFF HOW MCUH YOU LVOE HIM TO WACH YOU POOP!!!!

Another: 4/27/02—MORE JEFF! We havge rumored, but unconfirmed, sighhtings in West Vrigina! We will kep U up to date [*sic, for literally all of this, obviously*].

This original meme inspired a variety of imitations. Most just swapped out another person for Goldblum, including actors such as Kiefer Sutherland and Harold Ramis, or less desirable people, like Branch Davidian cult leader David Koresh and deformed Ohio sex offender Brian Peppers, whose face became associated with various memes of this type. In one of these, Christopher Walken watches you pee. It also inspired a meme called "Ceiling Cat is watching you masturbate,"* which features a photograph of a cat looking through a ceiling and . . . oh, never mind. You get the point by now.

And that's just the beginning. Know Your Meme, essentially the encyclopedia of these viral Internet jokes, has an entire section devoted to Goldblum.

Probably the best-known one is that image of Goldblum as Dr. Ian Malcolm, defined torso visible thanks to his wide-open black shirt, lying on his side and propped up on his elbow. Sometimes text is added above and below the image (what most people probably think of when they think of a meme), such as "Paint me like one of your French girls," a reference to Kate Winslet's Rose asking Leonardo DiCaprio's Jack to paint a nude of her from *Titanic.*† Sometimes, the image is superimposed over a famous painting. Or turned into a GIF, such as one with Sam Neill's Dr. Alan Grant hugging Malcolm's belly, which has been digitally manipulated to move up and down, up and down, up and down in perpetuity. (For his part, Neill [jokingly?] tweeted in 2016, "It is stomach churning.")

Another popular meme involves Photoshopping images of various flowers to replace their centers with the head of Goldblum (or, as the joke goes, Gold*bloom*), petals sticking out from his stubble-covered jaw.

Memes in video form also proliferated. You might have seen his

---

* Mama, please never go on the Internet. It is a terrible place.

† "Paint me like one of your French girls" is one of those great misremembered movie lines—it's really "I want you to draw me like one of your French girls"—along with "Play it again, Sam" from *Casablanca* (really, "Play it once, Sam. For old times' sake. Play it, Sam") and "Houston, we have a problem" from *Apollo 13* (really, "Uh, Houston, we've had a problem here"). It's a fascinating form of collective brainwashing, for lack of a better and less nefarious term. Someone who is smarter than me should write a book about why we do this. (Both my editor and my agent will surely remove that sentence, but I mean, you'd read that, *right*?!)

1999 Apple advertisement slowed down so it seems like he's slurring his words while talking about logging on to the Internet in a meme known aptly as "Drunk Jeff Goldblum." Or people reenacting his line reading of "Life, uhhh, finds a way" from *Jurassic Park*.

The list goes on, but these are much better seen than described. So if you're really interested, just log on to Google and take a peek around. The sheer number of them will overwhelm you. For example, on November 12, 2019, at 9:17 p.m., just after giving my new puppy her first bath, I searched Google for "jeff goldblum memes," which returned "about 1,610,000 results (0.92 seconds)." Since I doubt this had to do with the date, the time, or the fact that I gave a puppy her first bath, I think it stands to reason that the Internet is filled with goofy Goldblum memes.

But, why? Oh, let's ask Ryan Milner!

Hey, Milner, what's going on here?

Internet culture was shaped "about ten to fifteen years ago on places like 4chan, Reddit, and Tumblr, these Internet culture hotbeds where people would come together and share things that were funny or absurd," Milner said. "People are more inclined to make memes out of stuff that resonates, stuff that clicks with them at a personal level. And a lot of people producing that kind of content were people of a similar age and cultural background. There were a lot of people, in short, who were familiar with who Jeff Goldblum is . . . American millennials, we think back to our childhood, and he had a massive role in *Jurassic Park*, in *Independence Day*. So he's kind of this known entity and this known character to the millennials who then grew up to create Internet culture and do so by referencing their pop culture touchstones. I think this is the reason why SpongeBob SquarePants is also a massive meme."

Milner concluded with a tl;dr (Internet-speak for "too long, didn't read"): "In this case, what's resonating is the nostalgia of Jeff Gold-blum because he's this kind of endearing childhood character."

Of course, we can be (and likely are) both personally and collectively nostalgic for a tremendous amount of pop culture from our youth, but that doesn't mean we're going to memeify all of it. Who has the time? We'd never get anything done! So why, exactly, did Goldblum of all people rise to the top in the first place? How did he get tossed out as a piece of Internet currency? Our man might be ubiquitous now, but as we've discussed throughout this here tome, it's not like the guy carried all that many movies on his shoulders.

No, but those same qualities that made him so memorable in his early roles—that off-kilter intelligence, the unique speech patterns, his commanding yet unintimidating physical presence, his general otherness—those are what make a great meme. As Brandon Wink, the editor in chief of *Meme Insider* magazine, pointed out to me, "When picture memes started to take off, Goldblum was blessed with some very classic shots and great facial expressions, leading to him being one of the first widely used text-on-picture meme examples." He's weird but likable, interesting enough of a person that people enjoy considering him at a deeper level. And, on the Internet, that "considering" often means "turning into comedy."

"How he acts and performs is very unconventional," Milner said. "He's got the stutter and the *umm*s and the *uhh*s. He resonates as this unconventional character who is simultaneously larger-than-life, very funny, and relatable. He reminds me of Bill Murray in that way, and Murray is another celebrity who has risen to this kind of [meme status] because of these perceptions about who they are as a person and a character."

Plus, "early Internet culture was all about incongruity and stuff not quite making sense and the absurd and the nostalgic," he added. "Part of what resonates about him is that sort of uncanny nature, where you don't know how to place or categorize him. And that really works with Internet culture. People take different pop culture texts and make them their own. So any time somebody uses an animated GIF from a pop culture source to express something on Twitter, they're taking that moment and making it their own. They're reading a lot into a moment, taking it out of original context. And he's vague enough, versatile enough, but also striking enough that you can do that with him."

Milner suggested that, in a strange way, Goldblum is the living equivalent of an Internet adage known as Poe's law. A user named Nathan Poe originally wrote the "law" on ChristianForums.com in 2005 as this: "Without a winking smiley or other blatant display of humor, it is utterly impossible to parody a Creationist in such a way that *someone* won't mistake for the genuine article." In other words, and in a broader context, it's almost impossible to make a joke online because someone somewhere will assume you're being serious. On the other side, it's impossible to know if someone is making a joke online without knowing that person's intent. Milner said the "law" has evolved to mean "essentially, you can't know people's motives on-line. You don't know the difference between sincerity and satire, between earnestness and irony."

He continued, "[Goldblum's] face is that. His whole persona is that. Is he being ironic? Is he being sincere? So I think he maps really well because of that unknowableness."

The chasm between Internet fame and Hollywood fame is vast, though, and somewhat paradoxically, not everyone achieves both. "The nature of fame is always probably to some degree changing," Chuck Klosterman said. Now, with booming population growth and the rise of technology that allows us to seek out whatever niche thing interests us, "you can now be famous in these small silos." Klosterman continued, "You can be very famous to a chunk of the populace, which creates a real illusion of fame, even though outside that silo, you'd be nobody. If I walked around the audience of a Kiss concert, I could convince myself I'm a famous person because seven people recognized me, or whatever. But that's about the only place it could happen. Now the whole world is like that. If you're in a certain space, either in life or online, you can be a very famous person while to the rest of the world, not only are you not famous, you're unknown."

It gets murkier when you consider how there are generationally different definitions of fame. "Different people classify fame differently and would likely say that even though Logan Paul might have more views on YouTube videos than Tom Cruise has views of his movies in the past decade, Cruise is still a bigger star. Conversely, there are undoubtedly millions who know Logan Paul and his favorite ice cream flavor but can't pick Tom Cruise out of a lineup of him and Terry Crews,"* Wink said via email. "Because Jeff Goldblum WAS a big A-lister in the nineties, and he is a current A-list meme today, I would say he holds greater 'value' than either of the previous examples, for his value transcends both generational and media consumption barriers."

With the memes playing on his preexisting multiple decades as a popular actor, Goldblum became famous both in a standard-famous way and in the small-silo way. So while Goldblum the meme maybe was known to a more modest portion of the population than Goldblum the actor, the two began to meld as Goldblum the actor began leaning into Goldblum the meme. In other words, he began acting more "Goldblumy," be it in his movies, on late-night talk shows, etc. In their own strange way, these memes helped usher in a new era of

---

*I understand Wink's point, but I would very much like to meet the person who mixes up Tom Cruise and Terry Crews and ask them what life circumstances led them to that point.

Goldblum, one in which he transitioned from capital-A Actor to capital-C Celebrity,* at least in the public eye.

But, as Klosterman said, the "downside to becoming a pop culture figure is that you're taken slightly less seriously." He pointed to Philip Seymour Hoffman, someone who "never really moved into the category of being a figure in the popular culture because of who he was. So he could take on an extremely serious role, and people generally expected him to succeed at it." But now "if Jeff Goldblum does that, it would feel as though there's some element of gimmick here, that they want the audience to sort of recognize the character of Jeff Goldblum in whatever character he's portraying."

And sure enough, he began being cast more and more as variations on himself toward and into the 2010s, to the point where his appearance in a movie or a TV show always feels like something bordering on parody. That's not always bad. While it means he probably won't take on many of the types of roles he excelled in during his earlier days—like his roles in *The Fly*, *The Big Chill*, *Invasion of the Body Snatchers*, or *Deep Cover*—if used correctly, the fact that he comes to an audience with preconceived notions can be a strength.

Take his turns in *Portlandia*, which showcased the best work he's done to make people laugh from the small screen. Goldblum regularly appeared on Carrie Brownstein, Fred Armisen, and Jonathan Krisel's sketch show as a variety of different characters, generally artisans who work in specialty shops, such as the Pull-Out King (who owns a furniture store that only sells sofas, love seats, and such that pull out into beds), the Doily Shoppe Proprietor (who sells bespoke doilies, obviously), and the Knot Store owner.

Oh, the Knot Store owner.

---

*Sick of this little writer trick yet?

A signature Goldblum move on late-night shows, etc., is to pull out some arcane knowledge and try leading the conversation into oddly abstruse pastures. Often, it's about a work of art, a scientific theory, a woefully forgotten film. While he's serious in those moments, it's hard not to imagine his talking about something ridiculous. Like, say, lozenges. Or perhaps artisanal knots.

That's exactly why Krisel, Armisen, and Brownstein cast Goldblum as these ridiculous salesmen. "You know that he has the ability to talk about something in real life that's very absurd, but you know you'll be won over by his passion for it," Krisel told me. Those are the kind of sketches the *Portlandia* team "would bring him in for, selling these esoteric things. He plays a lot of really intense people, a lot of experts or specialists, and you always believe him. It's like, 'Oh, he's excited by this? Then it must matter.'"

In the *Portlandia* sketch, he does just that, playing the proprietor of the Knot Store, which sells various types of artisanal knots, from tangled iPhone cords to "the classic sailing bowline knot" in hemp. Alan, his character, rubs his fingers with his thumbs in excitement when discussing his knots, the same way Goldblum often does when talking about a film or a piece of music he particularly enjoys. When he pulls out the twisted white pair of earbuds, he says, "An artist that we work with makes these by jamming them into his pocket"—a pause for one of his now-expected long purrs—"and then he pulls it out. . . . You could pair this with a rosé, or even a white burgundy."*

The joke here is clearly on young, preppy hipster millennials who

---

*He also got to reuse that magic trick he pushed during *The Pillowman* and *Mini's First Time* and who knows how many other projects. In the sketch, he shows the customers what looks like a knot but—*he pulls the thread*—actually isn't! Abracadabra! While he pulled it out in *Adam Resurrected*, it's a lot more fun here, as you might imagine.

might buy such ridiculous products and those who hawk them. But there's a meta-joke here, as well, on Goldblum himself for having such a singular but really out-there personality. As one YouTube user pointed out, "No matter what role you give Jeff Goldblum, he plays Jeff Goldblum." It's a sentiment that fills the comments sections of these clips, and they're not exactly wrong.

Every time they had him on "[they] looked forward to his performance, because [they] knew he was going to make [them] laugh." The sketches always struck gold, in part because "he always comes from a real place, this real, genuine, authentic wonder and excitement. That can be both believable and funny at the same time. That's what makes great comedy: when it feels real but also broad at the same time. . . . He's a great actor. But he's also almost become this parody of himself because he's always going to make a meal out of it. But he can still do serious stuff. He's pretty reliable. He's always going to give you something great," Krisel told me. Becoming a meme is a bit like working with house money. Goldblum himself has become a commodity.

That might seem obvious. After all, aren't *all* performers a commodity in and of themselves? Sure, to a point. We go see a Tom Cruise flick because we want to watch this guy do death-defying (thus life-affirming) stunts. We catch the latest Meryl Streep or Daniel Day-Lewis film because we enjoy transformative acting the same way we're always curious how much Christian Bale will physically transform himself for each new project. We watch movies with Amy Adams and Glenn Close to see just how monumentally the Academy will screw them over this year.

It's slightly different with Goldblum. We often watch his more modern movies, TV shows, and talk show appearances because we want to hang out with *him*, or at least the person we perceive him to be. Many accuse him of exaggerating his eccentricities to craft a

certain Goldblum-esque* persona, and that theory carries some water. But the "truth" doesn't actually matter. If he goes home and turns
into Tom Hanks, it doesn't really matter. What does is that everyone
enjoys Goldblum as we've come to know him through interviews,
public appearances, and the Internet writ large. Goldblum-as-meme
is how we've come to understand him in the age of social media, and
it's what audiences want from him.

   And he knows it. Of course. While it's obviously unsurprising
he's hyper-aware of his image, it's surprising that he's completely
open about that fact in a way that somehow doesn't damage the very
image he's open about. Think about it like this: Say you're acting in a
play, and in the middle of the play, you turn to the audience and yell,
"I'm acting! I'm specifically presenting myself to you in a particular
manner to make you feel and think a certain way!" The play would be
ruined, right? Yet, when Goldblum sat down for a lengthy interview
with David Marchese for Vulture in 2018, he pulled back the curtain
and somehow only managed to strengthen that persona by doing so.

   "People write Jeff Goldblum–y parts and they want me to do them
and that's fine. I think I can even do a better version of it. So no, this
little Jeff Goldblum row that I'm hoeing is still adventurous," he said.
But he also added, "I would hope any interest in me or my work comes
from my aspiring to be authentic. I'm certainly not trying to pull the
wool over anybody's eyes about who I am. But when it comes to being
real and true, isn't trying to find that what acting's all about? . . . I
aspire to an ideal of authenticity in my public presentation and my
work. You want to be without delusion or illusion in what you're creating. You don't want to lie. 'The camera knows' has been said many

---

*I swear using his name as other parts of speech is like eating Pringles. It's nearly impossible to
stop.

times and maybe that applies here, doesn't it? No one is fooling any-body. Your real character will win out."

It's a tricky tightrope to walk, yet he manages to do so with grace. It certainly doesn't hurt that two of today's most visionary directors, Wes Anderson and Taika Waititi, noticed this quality about him and capitalized on it—something else he's transparent about.

"I've done a couple movies that have been well-received and widely seen—the *Thor* movie. And I remember a few years ago somebody said, 'You know there's this Jeff Goldblum's watching you poop thing.' This does seem to be a moment for me, doesn't it?" he said. "My as-sociation with Wes Anderson didn't hurt as far as the cognoscenti goes. And now when I do press—there's lots of content needed for our communicative infrastructure these days—people will ask me to do things like, 'Hey, Jeff, do all the parts in *Jurassic Park*' and then those things make the rounds online."

As for the part that's in his hands, he said, "I think what's hap-pened is that I've found my voice in a newer, more fun way. Things like *Thor: Ragnarok* and *Portlandia*, both of which had large elements of improvisation, were delicious experiences for me creatively. And they're similar to what I've been doing with the press—whether it's commenting on people's tattoos or reading tweets about myself. I feel like it's all creatively true. So yeah, the version of me that exists in so-cial media is quite congruent with my approach toward authenticity."

Anderson, whose movies are basically memeable treasure troves, if not long memes themselves, first tapped Goldblum to join his growing cabal of actors for 2004's *The Life Aquatic with Steve Zissou*. By 2020, the director had also used him in 2014's *The Grand Buda-pest Hotel* and (his voice in) 2018's stop-animated *Isle of Dogs*. Ander-son excels at using actors with offbeat looks and mannerisms, actors who seem to dance to their own beat. He's partially able to do this because he's an incredibly exacting director, insisting actors stick to the written script with just about no improvisation in costume, mannerisms, or dialogue. "I've gone to other movies and the director will go, 'Oh maybe you are wearing this,' and I'll go 'That's a good idea but how about this? What if I have a hat or a thing?' With him you don't do that. You go: 'What do I get to do in this?' And he goes: 'Here's the thing, here's the thing, here's the thing.' And you go, ok," Goldblum told the Daily Beast. "So, that's what you sign up for too. And his ideas are so good. And his taste is so good that you go: 'Oh, yes please.'"

"[Anderson] is terrifically meticulous, prepared, detail-oriented, knows what he wants. In *Life Aquatic* he said, 'You're going to wear this baby pink scarf that I have and Mark Mothersbaugh, my friend, has these glasses that we're going to borrow. You're going to wear those glasses.' Etc., etc., etc. It's great to be used in such a way, and you know it's going to be good. You're going to look interesting," he elaborated for Collider. Anderson even personally trimmed Goldblum's beard for *The Grand Budapest Hotel*. "After all of his preparation, it leaves [Anderson] to be wildly present. He is, like I say, a master appreciator. You feel connected with him. Within this, as if you're doing a play, he didn't want me to change a 'the' to an 'and.' I remember in a big speech in *The Grand Budapest Hotel*, and I was like, 'Oh, OK.' Then he does 27 takes and kind of within a particular range, there's beautiful detailing that he does with your behavior and his direction. . . . So it's very enjoyable, and within it, the final experience is a very kind of free, creative, little swim."

Anderson crafts his films so well that some of Goldblum's performances, particularly in his two live-action movies, feel at once naturally spontaneous while also feeling inevitable. And his characters always seem to toy with his public persona as a wildly eccentric but alluring member of the intelligentsia. In *The Life Aquatic with Steve Zissou*, he portrays Alistair Hennessey, the wealthy, cultured, and snooty oceanographer who serves as the rival to Bill Murray's Zissou. And in *The Grand Budapest Hotel*, he's a careful, meticulous, feline-obsessed lawyer who discovers some dark secrets that put his life (and his fingers!) at risk. The movies are so overwhelmingly insular, he fully becomes the character. But his public persona simultaneously looms so mightily, the viewer can't help but apply that second layer to the characters.

Culture critic Gavin Edwards pointed out that Goldblum and his fellow cast members so uniquely exhilarate in these movies because Anderson's films are "not melodramatic or operatic, but it's a slightly more saturated reality. You need people who either have that mythic persona where they fit right in or feel as if they belong in that world the whole time."

In Edwards's book, Bill Murray compares Anderson's scripts to music. The director requires actors who can read a script and hit certain unseen notes in it, the way a great trumpeter could view some sheet music, imagine what the song should sound like, and toot out a specific version of that tune, making it feel both polished and improvised. Said Edwards, "You've got these people who are just great stylists, like Gene Hackman, Anjelica Huston, Jeff Goldblum, and Bill Murray, who are incapable of doing it except in a way that is both true but in their own voice, and that's what this heightened Wes Anderson world needs."

But no director has weaponized Goldblum's public persona as a comedic tour de force for a film the way Waititi did in *Thor: Ragnarok*. Nearly every major living actor has appeared in the Marvel Cinematic Universe (MCU), though most played forgettable roles, wasting both their talents and what they represent. Michael Douglas appears in the *Ant-Man* movies as a father figure of sorts, for example, but really anyone over the age of sixty could have taken on the role and likely been just as successful. The issue with the MCU is, despite the variances in heroes and stories, there's a certain sameness to them, a certain rhythm you come to expect. They're pop songs as movies. And while there's nothing wrong with pop songs, they can grow tired after a spell.

As time, and Marvel's dominance, marched on, directors began using the universe as a canvas to tell more personal stories. Waititi's first entry in the universe upended everything we've come to know about it, much like Ryan Coogler later did with *Black Panther*. But while the latter homed in on the heartfelt spirit at the center of these films and used the MCU as a Trojan horse to shine a light on the African diaspora and its resulting injustices (stories that aren't often told in the mainstream), Waititi went in the opposite direction, applying his absurdist comedy sensibility to one of the more inherently ridiculous superhero stories.

Thor is an Asgardian god of thunder who carries a powerful enchanted hammer and somehow fights alongside both humans like Iron Man and Black Widow, wizards like Doctor Strange, and aliens like half the Guardians of the Galaxy. Without denigrating what these films mean to so many people, I think we can safely agree that sentence is a bit silly.

Waititi leaned into that silliness, directing Chris Hemsworth's Thor as a wisecracking, hyperattractive hardbody goofball who happens to be good at saving the universe. But every superhero needs a foil. In this case, it was the Grandmaster. He is "one of the ageless Elders of the Universe and has mastered most civilizations' games of skill and chance" and is "one of the oldest living beings in the universe, coming from one of the first intelligent races to evolve after the Big Bang.'"*

"When I met him, I realized that all of his characters are just him," Waititi told *Wired*. "So what else could I say to him besides 'Just be yourself'?"

The role excited Goldblum, seemingly for just that reason. As he told *Empire* magazine during the ramp-up to the movie, "[The Grandmaster is] a hedonist, a pleasure-seeker, an enjoyer of life and tastes and smells. I thought, 'I can do that, I'll bet!' I'm working on my part every day. I'm a sponge, researching." It's a solid joke, since "hedonist," "pleasure-seeker," and "enjoyer of life and tastes and smells" sounds like the summary at the top of the actor's résumé. He added, "[Waititi] is encouraging me to improvise and make it my own, and that's what I'm trying to do. I hope he doesn't throw me out on the first day!"

The director, of course, did not throw him out. Instead, as Goldblum relayed, he said, "This is a comic book. We'll put you in a funny costume. But I think there's something in your area, it's a character. It's not your straight behavior. I want a lot of you and a lot of improvisation." And that's exactly what he did, improvising his way through a Marvel movie, something that would have seemed implausible at best before Waititi took the reins.

And boy, did it work. The key seems to be that improvisation, the fact that the Grandmaster is so nakedly Goldblum in electric blue makeup. The character dominated the Internet when the movie hit

---

*For full transparency: As is likely obvious by now, I am by no means an expert in the MCU. This description comes straight from Wikipedia. I know, I *know*, but the main point here is that the character is totally ridiculous and Goldblum is totally ridiculous and so it makes sense for Goldblum to play the Grandmaster.

theaters. Much like his Dr. Ian Malcolm in *Jurassic Park*, Goldblum's Grandmaster serves as a Han Solo character, someone who points out the inherent absurdity of the story he's in using an endless barrage of quips. With gold, red, and blue robes; elegantly coiffed silver hair; and a silvery-blue painted-on goatee, he gleefully mocks the universe by mocking Thor himself. "I hear you call yourself the Lord of Thunder," he taunts him, later calling him "Sparkles" and letting him know what to do to get back to "Ass-place, uh, Assberg."

Though the approaches of Anderson and Waititi diverge, the result is the same—an incredible, memorable, memeable performance by Goldblum at his Goldblumiest. As Sean Fennessey said, "He brings the same thing to Wes Anderson movies as he does to the MCU, which is an overt eccentricity and oddness that communicates positively on-screen, that makes people feel not unmoored but weirdly safe and interested in what he has to say. There's an active oddity to his persona. He's so big, and his eyes are so big, and he has this very mannered speaking style in both movies that just demands your attention in a way."

Plus, Milner said, around the time the movie came out (likely *because* of it) there was "this explosion of him again into the popular consciousness, and it just kind of snowballs and escalates from there, only increasing his prominence and only increasing the fun people have with him. [He participates in] more media appearances in which he leans into a certain personality that's been working for him as he's aged."

That a director might consider the way Goldblum is culturally perceived while casting shouldn't come as a surprise. In some ways, playing on Goldblum's Goldbluminess has been a director's trick from the beginning, even if we (and perhaps even the director) didn't realize it. To be fair, there were so many misses throughout his career, that's an easy fact to forget. But consider this: The humor of "I forgot my mantra" exists in the line, the setting, and Goldblum's delivery, of course. But when we look back on the clip through the lens of having watched this oddball for twenty years, its hilarity grows exponentially.

Just because directors weaponize his public persona to add extra layers to their films or late-night hosts use it to sell their show to more viewers, it doesn't mean his various eccentricities aren't genuine, which is exactly what he was driving at in the Vulture piece. I mean, what makes a persona real anyway? As Milner said, "His persona is his persona." Think of it like modern currency. Money is merely an idea we all agreed on. It's not real, but it is because we say it is. By all of us collectively agreeing that it's real, it becomes real.

Talk to enough people about the guy, though, and it's difficult not to believe him when he says that the person we see is the person he actually is. Let's take the filming of *The Life Aquatic with Steve Zissou*, for example. This is long before he became a fashion icon, an Instagram like generator, really even before he became a meme. During the production in Italy, he was just beginning to watch people here in the United States poop, a fact of which he was probably only vaguely aware, if at all.

Upon arrival, "he started asking everybody their name, introducing himself to literally every crew member who was in the room . . . then as [they] prepared to start filming, he started improvising a jazz song using the names of everybody he met," Inti Carboni, a first assistant director on the film, told me. He did this in the tense moments just before Anderson called action, and the second he did, "he stopped the song and went immediately into the scene." Carboni said, "So, that was, you know, strange. And he did that for every take. . . . I think it was a way to get himself concentrated." At one point, he began reciting a monologue from *The Pillowman* between takes, stopping just as Anderson called action. When the scene ended, "he would pick up exactly where he left off. This went on for a half hour."

Carboni said the film felt like a "fun student film" even though it was clearly a larger-budget production with an all-star cast.

Or consider the "fond memory" he left with Sam Hoffman, another first AD, which Hoffman recounted via email: "We were in Rome and I was being visited by my wife, her parents, my sisters, and their husbands and so we were throwing Thanksgiving in Rome. It was a bit of an ordeal because even though we thought ahead and ordered a turkey in Rome, the oven in my apartment was too small to fit it.* Anyway, we had someone smuggle cranberries in their luggage and we managed to put together a wonderful, homey Thanksgiving at my place. Before I left work, I mentioned to Jeff that if he didn't have a place to go, and if he was jonesing for an American Thanksgiving, he should come by my place. I never thought he'd come, but he did, with his girlfriend.† Well, that Thanksgiving became the most memorable in my family's history. Jeff, who is by nature a raconteur, entertained everyone and was singing Christmas carols with other cast members and my in-laws before the night was through."

Or consider the fact the learning-everyone's-name thing isn't a random or stunt-y move of his. Everyone from the producers of *Law & Order* to every director I spoke with told a story that included some version of his learning everyone's names. To keep it in the Anderson world, here's what Katharina Hingst, the assistant director runner on *The Grand Budapest Hotel*, said of that shoot: "When he first arrived, he asked me for a crew list. The next day he came to set

---

* A local butcher cooked the bird for them and sent over one that was more size-appropriate for their oven.

† That would be Catherine Wreford, whom you may remember from the chapter on Pittsburgh and *Pittsburgh*.

trying to put faces to all of the names on the list. He continued greeting everyone by their name, making it a priority to arrive on set early to walk around and say hello to the entire crew. From craft service to producer he'd literally memorize everyone's name. Sometimes he'd pull me aside, point at someone, and ask me who that was again, then he'd go over and say hello. I always thought that was very charming. Though as an AD it could be a nightmare getting him to go anywhere on time as he'd always make so many stops to chat to the crew. I saw him years later in L.A., where he was handing out an award at an event for best location manager, I think it was. I was attending with Tony Revolori, and he invited us to come see his band play. I never did but he still remembered my name."

These stories exist outside the Internet, which seems obvious but remains an important distinction to make these days. One of the most troubling aspects of celebrity journalism (something I do) and Internet culture (something that provides endless fodder for what I do) is how quickly said celebrities are, depending on your view, reduced or heightened to some godlike status, their humanity erased. While Goldblum-as-meme is fascinating, and something we're about to discuss much more, these stories from that set resonated deeply with me and, I hope, will with you. All of life's a stage and all that, I know— thanks, Billy Shakespeare. But if that's true, then the play is pretty much all that's real.

Which brings us back to something vital Milner mentioned: the broader definition of *meme*, i.e., the original definition "going back to when the term was coined by Richard Dawkins, the evolutionary biologist. In this sense, the meme is essentially culture that people create, circulate, and transform as they make it their own. So ideas are memes in this way. Any time somebody takes an idea and applies it to a new context, they're furthering the meme, this idea people share."

The image—shared through Hoffman's telling me and now

through my writing this and my editor's leaving the anecdote in and my publisher's sending it out into the world and the talk shows to promote it, and so on and so forth—of Goldblum sitting in a small Italian apartment eating smuggled cranberries and singing Christmas carols and enjoying an American Thanksgiving abroad, that image filtered through my lens and now yours, is essentially a meme now, too. It's both real in that it happened and imagined in that you and I must re-create something we weren't part of. In that way, memes are like that old game of telephone, where one person whispers a message to the person sitting next to him, and that person passes on the message, and so on and so forth until the message becomes so distorted, it only marginally resembles the original.

The difference is Goldblum has some—not a ton, but some—agency over his own memeability.

"In this sense, Jeff Goldblum as quirky fashion icon is itself a meme. So any new photo you're sharing of him dressed up that way, any time you like one of his Instagram posts, you're possibly affirming that meme, that persona, that bit of culture that Jeff Goldblum has become and is leaning into," Milner said. "This happens a lot around Keanu Reeves, too. The idea of Keanu being ageless or incredibly naïve and nice or whatever kind of persona people map onto Keanu Reeves and then share images or photos online to back up that persona, that's them participating in a meme. They might not be capturing a photo or making a GIF, so in that narrow sense it may not be a meme, but that very idea of Sad Keanu or Nice Keanu or whatever is a meme. Jeff Goldblum, the aging, quirky fashionista, however you want to label it, that idea is a meme that he's been leaning into."

This all circles back to the idea of what makes someone truly authentic. Maybe Goldblum sees that people like his personal quirks, so he's accentuates them. Or maybe he spent most of his career hiding them, trying to be the old Hollywood ideal of a star, until he felt more comfortable. Does it matter either way? Would either make him less human, less "authentic," especially considering authenticity is an invented construct in the first place?

In other words, how different are Jeff Goldblum and the idea of Jeff Goldblum?

INTERLUDE #10

The Recipe for
Jeff Goldblum's Instagram Account

The only social media platform Goldblum deigns to be part of is Instagram. You know, the one where he can post endless photographs of himself. He's done a fine job of it, one many may wish to replicate. While the ingredients for this recipe might prove difficult—if not impossible—to obtain, the steps themselves are fairly simple.

INGREDIENTS

- The body of Jeff Goldblum
- The face of Jeff Goldblum
- The acting skill of Jeff Goldblum
- Two heaping cups confidence
- One cup sense of humor
- Three dashes self-deprecation

- One Andrew T. Vottero (Note: Another stylist may be substituted in an emergency, but expect a decline in quality)
- More money than you have right now

STEPS

1. Spend four decades as an extremely successful character actor with a few memorable leading roles.

2. Remain in terrific shape.

3. Create an Instagram account.

4. Combine all the ingredients in the account, and share a mixture of photos showcasing:
   a. The fashion Vottero suggests you wear.
   b. Your children.
   c. Random bits of nature, such as two whale fins sticking out of the water.
   d. Shots from your old movies.
   e. The odd memorabilia your fans create, such as a mousepad bearing a close-up of your face.

5. Enjoy.

11.

A Living Meme

Ideas must originate somewhere. If Internet jokesters (along with accomplished directors like Anderson and Waititi) are playing with Goldblum's public image, then the image must first exist. The old adage about every joke or rumor's containing at least a kernel of truth also applies to memes. There's a reason John Oliver isn't considered a fashion icon. It's not that he dresses poorly—to the contrary, he usually has on a smart suit and looks well put together. But nothing particularly stands out about his sartorial choices, which is probably an intentional decision on his part. Goldblum, on the other hand, clearly wants you to notice what he's wearing.

But aspects of his fashion, as with aspects of his personality, always seem to tie back into one thing: his obsession with jazz music. Ever since those early lessons in Pittsburgh with Frank Cunimondo, Goldblum has lived a musical life.

He continued playing piano even as he became an established actor, often sitting at the keys in his film roles. Which adds a bit of irony
to the fact that although he doesn't play with Peter Weller's rock band
in *The Adventures of Buckaroo Banzai Across the 8th Dimension*, the
two made an off-screen musical connection anyway, getting together
for jam sessions during filming.

Then, as the story goes, Weller, who plays the trumpet in his spare
time, ended up working with Woody Allen in 1995's *Mighty Aphrodite*.
Allen, a jazz clarinetist, spent nearly three decades playing regular gigs
at Michael's Pub in New York City before moving to Café Carlyle, so
the two got to chatting, and Allen offered Weller a simple bit of advice
that ended up changing Goldblum's relationship to music. As Goldblum told the *New York Times*, "Woody says: 'You should do what I
do, have a weekly gig, and you'll get better. And it'll be fun.' When
Peter came back to L.A., we started to play out and about. And we got
other musicians. In the years since, Peter's living all over the world, but
I've maintained this group. It's Woody Allen's fault, in a way."

Eventually, Goldblum played with Allen at the Carlyle. He even
named the red-haired poodle he and his family got in 2013 "Woody
Allen."[*]

That advice paid off, with Goldblum eventually starting a weekly
gig (whenever he's in town) with his Mildred Snitzer Orchestra sometime in the 1990s, though Goldblum's admitted to being foggy on exactly when. The group, which was playfully named for his family
friend back in his childhood in Pittsburgh because he found the name
amusing and unique, includes a rotating band of jazz cats and plays at
the Rockwell Table and Stage in Los Feliz. There, Goldblum plays

---

[*]Despite allegations from Dylan Farrow that he sexually abused her when she was a child,
Goldblum has stuck by the director, saying in late 2019 that he'd consider working with him
again.

piano and occasionally sings, but mostly he's something of an MC. Even so, he seems to take his piano playing as seriously as his acting.

Despite his strict routine of waking up each day at around five thirty a.m. to practice, he tickles the keys loosely and playfully, his variety-esque jazz show taking nontraditional turns. He told the *Hollywood Reporter,* "It's sort of become this living room happening kind of thing where there's much involvement with the audience. We play games of one kind or another and we talk, and I have nothing planned."

In *Los Angeles* magazine, writer Tim Greiving described one such show: "As a pianist, he's an unshowy showboat, providing sunny accompaniment and taking the occasional solo that usually ends in a high glissando. He bops and smiles while he plays with a kidlike energy, sometimes turning his head away from his hands for a while with a giant Cheshire grin as he surveys faces in the crowd. . . . But jazz plays second fiddle to the Goldblum Factor, and he serves it in heaping spoonfuls. For 45 minutes before the downbeat, he mills around the room with a mic, asking people where they're from, relaying news of upcoming weddings and babies, making people laugh and feel dizzily touched by fame. He does a dramatic reading of a text exchange on one man's phone, and signs another man's leg next to a *Jurassic Park* tattoo."

His shows even begin dipping into a bit of audience-participation improv comedy. As Greiving continued, "He plays a game where, with the audience's help, he connects one film or actor to another through a human-IMDb wormhole. He plays 'Would You Rather?,' asking the crowd to register their vote with applause on the bangability of Paul Newman versus Robert Redford. Between songs . . . he queries the audience on things like what hypothetical statements would constitute dating deal-breakers, and ways to 'pornify' famous movie titles."

For years, he played these shows to little fanfare outside of the in-the-know Hollywood crowd, which only served to make him even more appealing. Nearly every director I spoke with shared fond memories of seeing him play in that small room, often highlighting the lack of self-centeredness he seems to have onstage.

"The idea of celebrities playing in bands, of actors playing in bands in particular, has a probably righteous bad rep. It often is a fairly brazen ego trip. Jeff's version of it is the complete opposite," Drew Pearce, who directed him in 2018's *Hotel Artemis*, said, adding that when he'd see him play in Los Feliz, the only criticism anyone ever had was that Goldblum didn't speak enough. "I don't think he's there to show off. I think he's there to be a part of it, to be a part of his orchestra. It's not about a bunch of people backing him, which is what you usually find with actors playing music. Even if they're on second guitar, they're going to make sure there's a solo in it to spotlight them. With Jeff, I feel like he'd be just as happy to pull the brim of his hat down and just play in the back."

For Pearce, the anecdote serves as synecdoche for Goldblum's general popularity in today's world. As he explained, "Today's audience, a social media audience, requires a level of authenticity that's very difficult to fake. And I think Jeff is authentically himself, authentically original and authentically singular, as well. I think that's why this feels so much like his moment."

The circumstances leading to his transition from lounge player to bona fide *Billboard*-charting recording artist fit with this theory, along with the idea of his not being a careerist. Once again, chance intervened. If any of you have half the luck of this guy, I recommend buying a lottery ticket *immediately.* Hell, buy two.

Goldblum counted himself as a longtime fan of Grammy-winning jazz baritone Gregory Porter. Then, one day, fate or chance or whatever you want to call it reared its head. Fate/chance/whateveryoucallit often chooses an airport as its venue of choice, and it had no interest in trying something new on this particular day. So they met in an airport. LAX, to be specific, when Goldblum spotted Porter from across the lobby. The two later discussed the moment on the inaugural episode of Porter's podcast *The Hang*, which led the host to become a little emotional.

"You came and you got about six inches away from my face. Your breath was pleasing, and you smelled like some beautiful cologne. And you expressed the charm that you have. You looked off to the side and were like, 'Gregory' . . . and you listed the songs that you liked. And you spoke of me in a warm way,'" Porter recalled. "In my head, I'm like, 'This is Jeff! This is the Fly!† This is the man!'

"You have no idea where the music goes and who it touches. And it's such a beautiful thing when it happens to touch the people who are your idols as well, and they come back to you with admiration and love," he added. "At that moment, I hadn't left the ground in the plane, but I was already thirty thousand feet in the air from the inter-action that we had. It was so cool for me."

They shared more than just a fleeting admission of admiration. Later, they appeared together on *The Graham Norton Show* and Goldblum ended up tickling the ivories while Porter sang the Ray Evans and Jay Livingston jazz standard "Mona Lisa," made famous by Nat King Cole. Though Goldblum normally becomes the center of the universe every time he appears on-screen, here he slips into the background. As should be the case, Porter's voice, thick and sweet as warmed gooey caramel, takes center stage. Goldblum isn't even intro-duced until *after* the segment, and the camera doesn't spend much

---

* This might be the easiest scene to picture in the history of human imagination.

† While Goldblum gives an incredible performance in this movie, I'm not sure if the titular character is whom I'd like to be referred to as. Like, "Hey, you're the egotistical dude with the fingernails and ears falling off and everything. But you're really good at sex and arm wrestling, I guess."

time with him during the tune, but every once in a while a little melodic flourish slips out of his piano as Porter finishes a verse, until just
after the middle of the song, when he plays a small solo as he hunches
over the keys, back arched like a cat methodically hunting its prey.
His musical tangent's nothing flashy, just enough to fill an empty
space with a twinkling smile, a few notes you want to reach out and
catch between your fingers.

Some UK-based Decca Records execs, along with just about everyone else on the island, caught the performance. It struck such a
chord,* they rang up Larry Klein and asked him to go check out his
show at the Rockwell. Klein is no nobody. Quite the opposite. The
multi-Grammy-winning producer has polished records by Herbie
Hancock, Madeleine Peyroux, and his ex-wife Joni Mitchell, and he's
played bass with titans like Bob Dylan, Warren Zevon, and Randy
Newman. Which is to say, Klein knows his stuff, and he knew what a
cultural atom bomb a solid performance on Norton's show could turn
out to be.

"It's a TV show in England that is distinctive in that to a large
extent, people actually still watch it at the time it comes on," Klein
said. "It was almost like when he did this duet, the country woke up
the next day and everyone was raving about it. It was like a cultural
event all through England."

Though he harbored reservations, knowing this could turn out to
be nothing more than an actor's vanity project, he went to the show
and "was knocked out by it." He found it to be both a type of "performance art," what with Goldblum's crowd interactions and pausing to
take selfies, and a warm invitation to the world of jazz for audiences

---

*Pun obviously intended, because career suicide is my jam, apparently. Plus, I promised many,
many pages ago to bring this back.

who might not be particularly familiar with the genre. In fact, he guessed about 95 percent of the audience weren't jazz fans "and left the club that night wanting to listen to more jazz," he said. "I thought that was a great thing for all considered. Especially jazz. Jazz needs to open up to new audiences. It's in danger of becoming something that only lives in academia."

Mostly the band played standards from classic artists like Charlie Parker, and while Goldblum didn't display some prodigal proficiency at the keys, his show didn't require it. The other musicians more than carried the weight, while the bandleader's charisma, charm, and sense of showmanship kept the audience focused. "It was a delightful evening," Klein concluded, one that could be re-created as an interesting live album. "I thought it was a very interesting idea to try and make a record of what he was up to there."

Execs floated the idea of recording at Rockwell, but Klein pushed for his idea of combining two soundstages in the studio and "creating a little nightclub in the Capitol building," complete with patrons, just like the real things.

Soon enough, Decca signed him to a record deal. After decades of playing jazz as a hobby, Goldblum would now get to do it as part of his career. To say the famous actor needed a big break would be an exercise in saying ridiculous things, but jazz isn't exactly the most popular genre these days. It probably falls somewhere between "my friend's cover band" and "wedding funk crew."

Of course, those execs probably glommed on to the fact that a major actor could likely sell more jazz music than a major jazz musician. As Chuck Klosterman pointed out, "Success in the very, very small world of jazz is a reflection of his success as an actor." It's akin to the fact that Steve Martin "probably made more money playing banjo than anyone else over the past fifty years" and that Jewel is "one of the bestselling poets in the past fifty years."

Now he's released two records with the Mildred Snitzer Orchestra.

That Klein-produced debut album, 2018's aptly titled *The Capitol Studios Sessions*, attempts to re-create the loose, familiar atmosphere of his cabaret-style weekly shows, and it's generally successful in its mission. As in those, his piano doesn't take center stage so much as his guests and his personality as the band progresses its way through jazz classics like Duke Ellington's "Caravan" and the King Cole Trio's "Straighten Up and Fly Right," often with the assistance of trumpeter Till Brönner.* Other featured guests feel a bit more like stunt casting. *American Idol* alum Haley Reinhart appears on a few tunes, such as when she's flirting her way through Walter Donaldson and Gus Kahn's old standard "My Baby Just Cares for Me," swapping "baby" for "Jeffy." ("Can I call you Jeffy?" she asks with her throaty drawl, to which he replies, "Oh, you can call me Jeffy, or Jeff, or Jeff Goldblum.")

For the most part, we only hear Goldblum's voice in spirited quips both between and during songs, when he's chatting with the audience or his fellow performers. He sings only once, on the album's comic center, a duet with Sarah Silverman, of all people. They sing "Me and My Shadow," the classic twenties tune popularized by Frank Sinatra and Sammy Davis Jr., with her as the latter. The jokes fall incredibly flat—they trade these lines at one point: "Before we get finished, we'll make the town roar / We'll change the name 'Redskins,' is that such a chore? / Then we'll tackle climate change, hats off to Al Gore"— something Klein attributes to the fact that the powers that be at Decca felt uncomfortable letting everyone improvise and hired comedy

---

* "Not very well-known [in the US] because he hasn't spent much time playing here, but a big star in Germany. He's one of the best trumpet players in the world," Klein said.

writers to provide a script, clearly an unfortunate move. "They made the mistake of not trusting fate," Klein said. "I think that really made the comedic aspect of things, in a big portion of both nights, somewhat flat."

Much of the rest of it is successful, with credit due to Goldblum's openness to Klein's input throughout the process. "I loved working with Jeff," the producer said, echoing so many before him. "I always look for people who are curious, and he is honestly and obsessively curious."

Goldblum followed the record up a year later with his sophomore effort, *I Shouldn't Be Telling You This*, which removes all pretenses of being a live album. Instead, it wanders into more conventional pop territory, which is why Klein chose not to be involved with it. Saying the record received the "big circus" treatment, he told me, "[It] felt crass to me [to fill it with pop artists], and intentional to me that [it] doesn't reflect what [Goldblum] does live. He doesn't have that crass attitude."

Indeed, it feels more *Independence Day* than *Between the Lines*. It features a litany of pop and rock artists—such as Miley Cyrus (umm . . .), Inara George of the Bird and the Bee, and various other indie darlings, such as Anna Calvi, Sharon Van Etten, and even the indie rock queen Fiona Apple—all of which can't help but feel like a cheap ploy for attention. Which made the run-up to the album a little painful. At one point, Goldblum posted to his Instagram stories a telephone conversation with Van Etten in which the two discussed the record, but it was tough not to feel like Goldblum expected some sort of thanks from the singer, when in reality *he* was lucky to work with one of rock's greatest living artists in the midst of a legendary hot streak.

Even if the guest list feels a tad cynical, the record is a lovely listen. Perhaps that's what's needed to bring a nearly defunct genre to the widest possible swath of listeners, particularly those whose listening habits were molded by pop radio and Spotify easy-listening rap play-lists. Plus who cares what Klein or I think? It earned the ol' silver medal on the *Billboard* jazz charts, while his debut earned the gold. He played jazz music—*jazz music!*—on *Jimmy Kimmel Live!* and *Today* and you-name-it. Hell, he even performed at Royal Albert Hall for Queen Elizabeth II for the Royal British Legion's annual Festival of Remembrance.[*]

The true paradox at the heart of his jazz career is how much doing something that no one would care about in another context has made people care about him again. The fact that his playing jazz is benefi-cial to the genre is practically a given, since he shines a brighter spot-light on something many people don't often consider. That it shines a spotlight back, though, is at once complexly obvious and completely unpredictable. It's like if the moon somehow threw the sun's light back to the sun, illuminating it more, rather than wasting it on us mere Earthlings.

"It is much more interesting for a late-night talk show host to in-terview Jeff Goldblum about his jazz music than it would be to inter-view Jeff Goldblum about his okay movie that just came out," Klosterman said. "So even though he's doing things that would seem counterproductive to fame, it is probably serving the opposite role. It is a kind of weirdness that works."

What's a jazz cat without the look, though, particularly if that jazz career has placed you in front of an audience that has preconceived notions about what a jazz cat is supposed to look like? His music might be part of the persona Milner mentioned, but his turn as a fashionista is a vital ingredient in the recipe that (re)captured the

---

[*] They sadly didn't meet, though he spent the day thinking they might.

world's attention. And, perhaps fittingly for someone who insists he's not a careerist who planned anything out, he essentially stumbled into his embrace of high fashion. As the story goes, during a *GQ* shoot for a fashion story in the September 2014 issue, he met Andrew T. Vottero, a Brown-educated stylist who wrote his college thesis "about the language of fashion and how there's sort of an unwritten language of clothes and we use clothes to communicate."*

Clearly, Vottero is someone who deeply considers clothing and what our fashion choices communicate to the world. Goldblum, meanwhile, always liked clothes without possessing any particular expertise. He enjoyed them "not so much as trophies or things like that, but the power they have over the image one can project of one-self to the world. It's like costumes for a film. 'Who do I want to be today?' Although it's not so much smoke and mirrors, as just trying to be true to one's inner monologue," Goldblum told *GQ*. "I remember as a kid I would go to these painting classes and I would do sketches of collars and ties—I have no idea why. That was in the mid-Sixties and shortly after that I went out to get the appropriate hippie attires. I was in seventh grade, so about 13, and I would go to school in the Navajo jacket, the black rollneck, the John Lennon little round glasses and the medallion around the neck. Whoa! I was the only person dressed like this at school, let me tell you."

He was also an enormous fan of the jumpsuit, even wearing one when he met Woody Allen for his non-audition for *Annie Hall*. As a younger man, he also loved uniforms of all sorts, prancing around in

---

* He continued: "Sort of like the design of the Margiela label on the back of a sweater and how those four little stitches are really small. And they actually communicate to a really small audience. But it's like self-selecting for, like, the people that I want to know that I'm wearing Margiela. They'll see that and they'll know, you know. And so for like that language of clothing in that way of forming identity."

those striped pants made for members of marching bands. Needless to say, his fashion instinct wasn't exactly killer early on.

By the height of his film career in the 1990s, he essentially dressed like his *Jurassic Park* character: black leather jacket, button-down opened halfway down his chest, and some tinted sunglasses. In a more formal setting, expect a smart suit. Nothing that would stand out fashion-wise but something that would just help accentuate his handsomeness. As Rachel Tashjian, who writes about fashion for *GQ*, told me, "He was definitely someone who was wearing cool and interesting stuff. . . . He was paying attention to looking good. Not necessarily fashion, but he was a guy who looked good." It certainly didn't hurt, she added, that "he has a perfect body to wear a beautifully made suit."

Nice as he may have looked, Vottero wouldn't have counted himself as a fan of Goldblum's style at the time. As he told *Vice*, "It's so funny to me now because he's getting all this press that's like 'Jeff, he's always had the best style,' but I think if you look back at some old photos, it was a mess." His theory is that Goldblum loved clothing but didn't have the right guidance, which may have led to some unfortunate choices.

But that's where Vottero comes in, a vital link between the world of high fashion and Goldblum's passion for it. The stylist likes "to celebrate masculinity and classic menswear while at the same time gently pushing at the borders of what we're used to seeing men wear." He said, "I think that Jeff and I are kind of like a match made in heaven. The thing that I think I sort of can't overstate enough is the importance of Jeff's energy and personality before clothes even enter the conversation."

After that fateful meeting in 2014, Vottero quickly became Goldblum's personal stylist. Vottero said, "We've been in cahoots ever since."

"When I used to go [shopping] by myself I'd spend hours trying things on. I used to pester girlfriends and wives, telling them about T-shirts, asking them, 'What do you think?'" Goldblum told *GQ*, but now his stylist is a quick text message away. "I can't wear [him] out and [he] can't wear me out. We're both equally excited."

"He wanted a stylist not because he needed help getting dressed but because he wanted, I think, someone to guide him through the best of what was available and to find things that maybe would be difficult to find or even [to convince designers to] make things that weren't available," Tashjian said. "It's funny. What he's doing is how you might think of a socialite from the fifties or sixties or seventies creating her persona through clothing and just giving herself over to a designer and saying, 'Just put me in what you will.' He's just giving himself over to this clothing and having so much fun with it. It's a personal expression maybe he hadn't been able to make before or hadn't felt comfortable making before."

A vital step, as any Marie Kondo fan will tell you, is out with the old (if, of course, it doesn't spark joy). Soon after they started working together, the pair dug through Goldblum's closet and threw away most of what they found there, which wasn't much since he's always been a self-described "minimalist," even when it came to clothes. Which makes sense, given how often he seems to enjoy wearing as few as possible, unless they come from a fashion house whose name has appeared in a Kanye West song.

His clothing these days tends toward the eye-catching, the loud, and the surreal. Think big patterns, often with little winks to their absurdity, such as when he donned a zebra-print sweater with matching zebra-print pants, or when he kept those pants and went with a leopard-print short-sleeve shirt when attending Southern Decadence in New Orleans, or when he and his wife, Emilie, donned matching floral-print Prada button-ups to dinner. His clothes are meant to be seen and celebrated—and, yes, memed.

His fashion "is an interesting combination of 1950s jazz cat with extremely cerebral high fashion," Tashjian said. "He is pulling from his own recent jazz music career, but he's also someone who's gotten really into fashion, and he's sort of combining that interest in fashion with this Chet Baker–esque West Coast jazz look."

Meanwhile, he manages to make it wholly his own. When the clothes are described, they don't make sense. Or, worse, they sound atrocious. But Goldblum manages to make them look unattainably cool. "It kinda says that he doesn't give a fuck about growing old gracefully, but by that very token, he's growing old gracefully and memorably and he's having more fun, with his clothes at least," Murray Clark, a London-based digital editor for *Esquire* who often covers fashion, told me. "It seems like he's having more fun now than he's ever had."

Josh Sims, a fashion writer who has penned several books on the subject, including *Men of Style* and *Icons of Men's Style*, told me via email that he thinks Goldblum's "style is wholly his own" or perhaps "a reflection of what can seem to be his studied oddness, even his lankiness; and perhaps not entirely his own in that, refreshingly, he seems quite open about using a stylist," and added, "I think that makes him an especially modern celebrity, [especially] among men.

"There are plenty of men who have reinvented themselves stylistically from 'bad' to 'good' (or at least better)—Chris Pratt, Jonah Hill, John Travolta, kind of—and I'm not sure JG's age is all that relevant (other than via the stereotype that older men should give up their interest in clothing). Though I think it's interesting (or blindingly obvious) that women have carte blanche to reinvent themselves stylistically, whereas in men it's considered something of a crisis moment. Men are expected to reinvent themselves in career terms, not aesthetic ones."

For his part, Sims thinks Goldblum might represent a modern and growing trend. He wrote, "I think male celebs probably get more of a free pass to not be stylish, but that's a pass that's soon going to see its cancellation date. Even male academics are expected to be kind of chic now—just part of that visual world/personal brand thing."

Since such stylistic gambles haven't become mainstream yet, though, there's a deep and important interplay between his clothes and his personality that allows him to pull off wearing such outlandish pieces and to be praised instead of dragged by the Internet mobs. "If Jeff Goldblum was the kind of guy who stood at the Oscars, really posing, and practiced in front of cameras, taking himself incredibly seriously as a Hollywood star, and you paired that with the kind of clothes he wears, he'd be a laughingstock and everyone would think, 'This guy's a bit of an arsehole,'" Clark said. "He's pretty irreverent, and he's pretty joyous. That translates into his wardrobe because it matches up with the person that he is, or at least the person we see through the lens of fame. And I think that's why he pulls it off."

Vottero and Goldblum seem to prefer Prada, which Tashjian kindly informed me "is the cerebral fashion brand. That's what they stand for. . . . So he is such a perfect person to interpret that on a larger scale. Prada is not a brand that has many official spokespeople. . . . I think he's in this perfect way for Prada serving as this unofficial spokesperson [as] this thinking man's fashion hunk." Goldblum and designer Miuccia Prada have so hit it off that they've collaborated with the brand.

"For a guy that age to pick up Prada is a pretty confident thing. I'm twenty-eight, and there are guys [my age] who I know who would be wary about wearing today's Prada," Clark said. "I can't think of anyone who has evolved as they've gotten older to that degree. It's pretty remarkable."

One of his more popular looks has been a Prada camp shirt "with archival prints from the nineties, which is an interesting way for him to build this resonance and joy around what he's wearing, because this really cerebral brand is kind of resurfacing some of their most popular looks from the nineties—a moment when he was also in his prime," Tashjian said. "It creates a fun Easter egg narrative for people who like fashion and nineties icons." Before that, it was seventies prints. As she wrote, "Goldblum has certainly solidified his place in the menswear pantheon—most recently, in his wardrobe of Prada shirts. For the past two years, Goldblum has made an art of wearing the Italian brand's mixed-up, boxy, sleazy printed shirts, which combine two or even three of the brand's retro seventies prints with flames, monsters, flowers, and other icons of oddness. Last year, the preference cemented into a full-blown partnership, with Goldblum wearing the shirts almost exclusively on his jazz tour. Most recently, he wore a cornflower-blue shirt in the rose print from the brand's fall/winter 2019 Frankenstein collection with a gray fur collar; in a studious and sly bit of meta-commentary, that collection was Frankenstein-themed. The shirts, for the most part, are now pieces the brand has made custom for Goldblum."

The brand even collaborated specifically with Goldblum on their fifty-fifty shirts, which look the way they sound: two mismatched patterns on either side of what can best be described as a bowling shirt à la *The Big Lebowski*, but far more colorful.

"There's a certain irreverence that [Goldblum and Prada] both have," Vottero told Tashjian. "[The partnership] does seem like a perfect match: Jeff is super handsome, super classic, but also an intellectual, and also a little bit adventurous, and I feel like he has that spirit of constantly moving forward and being excited and enthusiastic about the future. And I see that all in Prada as well."

There's a solid chance you've seen at least one of these shirts, paused, and whispered something to yourself about not understanding the world anymore. The shirt that likely caused this existential crisis is the one fittingly referred to as the flame shirt. Oh, dear Lord, the flame shirt. It's the kind of shirt that invites the phrase "Bless his heart." For any Northerners among us, that's a kind way to say a cruel thing down South. Sweet as sugar but sure to cause diabetes.

One half is striped from top to bottom with thick Hawaii-ocean blue, dark brown bloodstain red, and white bars. Flames, the color of the melted American cheese atop a Whopper, race up the side like some car decal that somehow slipped off Guy Fieri's old El Camino. Or, as *New Yorker* fashion writer Troy Patterson put it, "the flames might have leaped to the print from a shirt owned by a driver whose rear window features a decal of a urinating cartoon character, or from the uniform of a bygone bowling team."

The other half of the shirt features a series of red and black interlocking U's, like a particularly ugly pattern that would play in the background of a cheap commercial for a (cheap) local electronics store. As Patterson wrote, the "shirt resembles an elevated version of an embarrassment perpetrated by one's father at a backyard barbecue. Its ugliness is impudent."

Accentuating the seizure-inducing patterns is the fact that the shirt is perpetually boxy, meant to hang widely around the body. If you want one of your own, expect to drop around a grand on it. And, before you chuckle, people want it. Despite, or probably because of, the shirt's ugliness, it isn't favored only by Goldblum. It also appealed to rapper Pusha T, who donned the exact same flame-covered buttondown, a fact that became known thanks to Jimmy Kimmel's featuring photos of the two in his segment "Who Wore It Better?"

"Let me say publicly that Pusha T and I are in no competition, and I sit at your feet, Pusha T," Goldblum conceded to *Vanity Fair.* "I think you wore that shirt absolutely beautifully and I did the best I could."

That quote exemplifies the importance of clothing in returning Goldblum to the public consciousness. The Goldblum personality and the Goldblum style: part and parcel. The former allows him to experiment with the latter, while the latter allows him to continue showcasing the former. Articles dissecting his various looks abound and keep him relevant in the stretches between big projects—which are growing longer and longer as he continues following his own muse. His turn to high fashion served as friendly ammunition for bloggers, meme makers, and social media mavens. It's no accident that Instagram is the only online platform Goldblum uses. It's helped him become relevant. Quite simply, it's given him something to talk about.

"He's a bit of an anomaly in himself that he's come back, but it's not really pinned to anything. It's not like Mickey Rourke in *The Wrestler*. There was never a defined, specific film that brought him back," Clark said. He thinks it's because "Jeff Goldblum is still Jeff Goldblum. The guy that we remember from the eighties and the nineties, he still seems to be the same guy. He's not that affected by Hollywood. He doesn't seem to take himself too seriously. Many people have seen no change in this guy, apart from his clothes. So there's a sense of authenticity to him. He's quite unusual and he's quite odd. Look at the jazz piano thing he's doing. But he's odd in a cool way."

These essential elements combine to make Goldblum a compelling "living meme." When it all collides—his jazz-daddy bona fides, his fashion choices, his offbeat line readings, his good looks—it's like Earth, Fire, Wind, Water, and Heart coming together to create Captain Planet. Only, instead, they create Goldblum the Living Meme. As Milner said, "What's really interesting is this kind of reciprocal thing between his Internet culture persona and his performances, and how they're kind of amplifying each other as he's gone this more eccentric route with his persona and his performances."

What began occurring in Anderson's and Waititi's films has only continued, to the point where it feels almost expected. Imagine going to see a movie featuring Goldblum and getting the serious, actorly version of him. *The Mountain*, which featured Goldblum as 1950s lobotomist Dr. Wallace Fiennes and was released in select theaters in 2019, offers potential insight into that scenario. No one should expect such a small indie to make much money, but its total box office return was $61,035. No, it wasn't in many theaters—not even close. But given the seemingly near-universal love for the movie's top-billed star, it boggles the mind that the movie didn't pull in a bit more dough. I'm sure it'll have a nice run on VOD, and it's impossible to pin a movie's not doing well at the box office—pretty much a guarantee at this point if it doesn't feature men in tights—on any one factor. But it's tough to imagine a movie where Goldblum is giving the Full Goldblum not earning enough to purchase a Ford F-150.

People want the meme. More specifically, people want some variation on the meme. And these days, that's usually what they get.

Take 2018's dystopian action-thriller *Hotel Artemis*, a movie also featuring Jodie Foster, Sterling K. Brown, Sofia Boutella, Brian Tyree Henry, Jenny Slate, Zachary Quinto, Charlie Day, and Dave Bautista. On the poster, Goldblum is the fourth-billed actor, despite the fact that he's in the movie for maybe five minutes. Five minutes full of Goldblum being Goldblum, sure, but five minutes nonetheless. He's become that kind of actor.* And screen time aside, the movie showcases Goldblum's living-meme status as well as Goldblum's general status as a working actor.

Let's set the scene. It's 2028. Water's been privatized, causing riots

---

*This marketing strategy was also used, though much more cynically, around *Jurassic World: Fallen Kingdom*, a yawn of a movie that came out the same year as *Hotel Artemis*. There was much fanfare about his reprising his role of Dr. Ian Malcolm, which he does—for about three minutes at the beginning and end of the film.

from desperate masses across a burning Los Angeles, riots that career criminals happily exploit. When injured, the latter seek solace and care at the members-only Hotel Artemis, which has everything needed to treat the most severe wounds, but which comes with a few ground rules, such as no guns and no killing of other guests. Here, Jean "the Nurse" Thomas (Foster), a recluse who hasn't left the premises in twenty-two years, is queen. Outside, Orian "the Wolf King" Franklin (Goldblum), an exceedingly suave kingpin, sits atop the pecking order.

Throughout the movie, we hear tales of the Wolf King, including the bone-chilling fact that he's injured and en route to the hotel, which has just about everyone on edge. Given how heavily his shadow hangs over most of the film, director Drew Pearce knew he needed someone special. But he had a problem in that he was making a movie "in thirty days . . . for fuck-all money." And it's not like it was probably going to be some runaway hit. "If you go around telling everyone that you're making a movie inspired by films like *Repo Man* and *Diva*," Pearce said, "then you shouldn't be too surprised if it doesn't blow the doors off the box office."

Not to mention that "the character is supposed to be the smoothest talker in the room, and it's only in his turn right towards the end that you see his absolute true colors. You'd heard about his true colors, but you're entirely taken in by the power of his personality," Pearce said. "I just needed someone with infinite supplies of charisma, and that's why I thought of Jeff."

Know how Walter Gretzky, or Wayne Gretzky, or Michael Jordan (or maybe even Michael Scott) once said you miss 100 percent of the shots you don't take? Well, wittingly or not, Pearce heeded that advice and pitched Goldblum on the movie. Next thing he knew, Goldblum asked him to meet at the bar of the Chateau Marmont, where they "chatted for four hours and . . . talked about everything from plays to music to fashion." And, of course, "the character."

Pearce described something he immediately noticed: "On some levels, he's Sinatra now. When he walks in a room, it's *Jeff Goldblum*, you know, and there's a cool that comes with that, there's a suaveness that comes with that, there's an expectation of esoteric humor. And the thing is, that's very much of him. And I suspect it's always been of him, but he's one of those people that, as he's gotten older, he's become more and more comfortable with his own esoterica."

Surprised he landed the big fish and eager to get to work, Pearce then had to figure out how to direct the actor, generally a jovial guy, to be the kind of murderous sonofabitch he hadn't played in years. "Jeff is a really wonderful person who doesn't usually go to that darker place. So we did a few takes, and it was nearly there, and it was a darkness there I still wanted to push him towards. And the note that got him to the take that I used every part of and that was his favorite, I said to him, 'Have you ever met one of those Celtic drunks, one of those Irish drunks that is the heart and soul of the room until that one drink too far, and then their voice changes, and a darkness comes over their eyes, and suddenly they are a different human being?' And he did that tap with his fingers.

"Then we rolled, and he managed to get there instantly. But that is a far longer, more eclectic note than I would usually give any actor. Weirdly more specific as well, but that's partly how he works, is in stories, is in rhythms, is in the music of stuff. That's the language he works in.

"He did two days on a fuckin' tiny sci-fi, noir indie movie, but he didn't just show up. He was on set, bonding with people. He and I have stayed in touch ever since. There are some people who have a special energy, and, yes, I've lived in California a long time and I just said 'special energy,' but he's just so fierce."

Much like Goldblum himself, the Wolf King presents himself as a dapper gentleman with a penchant for designer brands and the sort of clothing that almost certainly costs more than my DC English-basement apartment, which posed a bit of a problem for Pearce.

"We were making a tiny-budget indie movie, so there was an instant and gigantic divide between what the character would be able to afford to wear and what I could afford to buy, which was exacerbated all the more by the fact that Jeff's character has been sliced in the ear and his expensive outfit would be covered in blood," Pearce said. He had found these "amazing Gucci loafer-sandals that had a wolf emblem on them, but they were pretty much the cost not just of his outfit but all the costumes. And Jeff just bought them in order to use them in the movie."

But, of course, that's all the behind-the-scenes shit that often doesn't mean squat to the rest of us. What does is the performance, which is brief but memorable—maybe because of its brevity. We get a Goldblum–as–Wolf King full of swagger and menace who just seems . . . fun to be around? Sure, he's a murderous, selfish sociopath who would probably kill children without a second thought, but he's an enjoyable hang when he's trading quips with everyone for a few minutes, a perfect seasoning, as Nayman had observed, but also memorable and absurd enough to become a meme.

And that's what people want. So much so that Disney capitalized on his living-meme persona as part of the launch of its streaming service, Disney+, by completely throwing pretense out the window and creating a show named *The World According to Jeff Goldblum*. Think an Anthony Bourdain travel show with less ambition but more whimsy. It follows Goldblum as himself—and at his most Goldblum-y—as he visits various locales and speaks to experts on a variety of popular everyday subjects that supposedly interest him. These range from tattoos to sneakers to ice cream. "I'm very curious, but I think curiosity is our birthright," he told *USA Today* of the show. "I have a 4-year-old boy and a 2-year-old boy, and I don't think it's just my genes. I think kids and all sapiens must be curious; we need it to survive." In particular, he examines "science and the unexpected and surprising aspects of ordinary things around us"; he said, "I'm not teaching anybody, but kind of (inviting) people to come along with me and learn things."

As he said during the D23 Expo panel preceding the service's launch, the show brings out his spontaneous side, since we watch him explore these subjects in real time, adding a certain immediacy. "The premise of the show is, because it's *The World According to Jeff Goldblum*, it's me with all the information and experience that my life has entailed up 'til this point. . . . It's not as if I do some extra homework/research/bone up on it so that I tend to know something about it and then tell you about it. No, it's not like that," he said. "I have whatever associations I have or past experiences with it, and that's it, and then I kind of encounter interesting people around these subjects and you see me, you go along with me, if you're so inclined, and we have this experience together. That's the idea. It's all a surprise to me. I don't even meet the people, see the places, before they turn on the camera. It's all me kind of like a chick popping out of its shell."

The show isn't just a natural extension of the persona that has dominated the Internet; it was almost inevitable thanks to *who* embraced him. Namely, the supposed intellectual elite who see him as something of a kindred spirit, someone beyond irony, someone who is both in on the joke and wondering if there's any joke to be in on.

There are two categories of celebrities in the Internet age: "The people who seem to be beloved on social media are often people who are hugely famous and have this sort of rabid, idiotic fanbase . . . who see it as, like, their job to keep these people famous," Klosterman said, citing Beyoncé's fans (known as the Beyhive), which just goes to prove his point. Then "there's this sector of famous people who, for whatever reason, are seen as acceptable among the sardonic, intellectual elite of Twitter. [Meaning] the people who are on Twitter all day long but don't see themselves as advocates of these people so much as a certain kind of tastemaker. Jeff Goldblum seems to fit in this category. He seems to have been adopted by people who see his weirdness as something that should be championed."

As a result of the show's feeling inevitable but also like a testament to Goldblum's charisma, critics (the very people who often fit into that second category) offered warm reviews overall. Mike Hale of the *New York Times* smartly wrote, "It feels like a fairly extreme case of a star parachuting into the scenes his producers have set up, dispensing charisma and charming non sequiturs (twice in four episodes he declares he's having the best time of his life) and not forgetting to find a backdrop for the 15-second philosophical wrap-up. When you get past the Goldblumishness* of it, there's probably nothing you need to go out of your way for." The key, of course, is enjoying the actor. Critic Brian Tallerico resides on the other side of that coin, writing that while he enjoys Goldblum's acting, "his leaning into his eccentricity in interviews [has] kind of made him the new Christopher Walken, and a little bit of that goes a long way." He considers these episodes "really just vehicles for the actor to refine his new image," adding, "Imagine a half-hour Apartments.com commercial and you have some idea what to expect here. I found it mostly annoying."

While your mileage may vary, one thing's clear. Like it or not, Goldblum's become a living meme, and whatever else happens, you can't exactly erase an idea.

---

*SEE! OTHER PEOPLE DO IT TOO!

EPILOGUE #1 (& ONLY)

Life Finds a Way and Goldblum Finds a Life
(i.e., the Chapter We "Need")

On the eighth of November, two thousand fourteen, millions of yearning hearts shattered due to the occasion of the intertwining of two lives in marriage: that of Jeffrey Goldblum and that of Emilie Livingston.[*] The two wedded at the Chateau Marmont in Los Angeles before a gathering of friends and family, thus taking the famed actor, jazz pianist, and Internet sensation off the market—seemingly for good. At the reception, our man serenaded his new bride with his piano and own dulcet voice.

The Internet proceeded to explode.

See, celebrity couples tend to be a dime a dozen, and Goldblum's dating life certainly never left a void in the tabloids. But their coupling dazzled fans for the same reason Goldblum himself always has: their

---

[*] Livingston now goes by "Goldblum," at least in public-facing media profiles. But to differentiate between the two throughout the chapter, and to make sure none of you think I'm referring to the ABC sitcom *The Goldbergs*, I'll be (respectfully) referring to her by her maiden name.

love feels real. It doesn't hurt that they have a love story that's at once both simple/relatable while also being nearly impossibly aspirational, one that he enjoys telling (and retelling (and retelling . . .)).

First, the meet-cute: "We were at Equinox on Sunset Boulevard," he told *Wired*. "I saw her from across a crowded room and I marched up to her, entranced, and began some kind of conversation."

"Wait," you might be thinking, *"that's it?"* But hold on a moment and consider the short story, one that rivals "For sale: Baby shoes, never worn" for brevity and far surpasses it in positive emotion. How many times have you seen someone cute across the gym and daydreamed about asking for their number, maybe how easy it would be to "bump into" each other by the water fountains or the smoothie line and let things play themselves out from there? Now consider how many times you've actually followed through.

Now imagine if that cute person who caught your eye happened to be a contortionist and rhythmic gymnast who represented her beloved Canada in the 2000 Olympics and would soon serve as a body double for Rihanna in the pole-dancing scenes in the 3-D sci-fi movie *Valerian and the City of a Thousand Planets*, and for Emma Stone in the aerial dance scenes in the Oscar-nominated *La La Land*? Kind of complicates things, doesn't it? Not for our man, who not only asked her out but asked her *to come watch him play the fucking piano*. Oh, Lord, to have the confidence . . .

Second, the first date: Their first date arrived two days after that fateful meeting at the gym, as a gaga Goldblum giddily gushed on *The Graham Norton Show*. There she was in the crowd watching him play piano, a date that feels reminiscent of what a sixteen-year-old boy would think is really sexy—come hear my band play! But Goldblum's Goldblum, so he began singing that old standard "Emily," the Johnny Mandel/Johnny Mercer tune that Frank Sinatra covered a few times. "Emily, Emily, Emily / Has the murmuring sound of May . . ."

As if that's not enough, he continued: "And then I say, 'Hey, Emily, you want to come up and do contortion on our piano?' We had a grand piano," Goldblum recalled. "She said, 'Yeah.' She came up, and I said, 'What do we play?'" So, thinking of the scene from *The Fabulous Baker Boys* in which Michelle Pfeiffer, wrapped in a skintight red dress, crawls over a piano and sings the jazz standard "Makin' Whoopee," they launched into exactly that. ". . . Another season, another reason / For makin' whoopee."

"She got up and did this amazing routine. That was two days after we met!" Goldblum said, adding, "We're still very much in love."

I mean, *come on.*

Third, the therapist: After the pair dated for a couple of years, Livingston raised the idea of having a child together. Goldblum already saw a therapist named LaWanda Katzman, whom Garry Shandling introduced him to, and he decided to bring Livingston to a session to explore the idea and to ensure it was the right move. "And over the course of that next year, we excavated all my fears, considerations about it," he told Conan O'Brien on his podcast. "And after a year, I said, 'Yeah, this could be peachy. And we'll get married and have a baby.'"

And so they did.

Fourth, the wedding: A small group of friends and family gathered to witness their vows, and Katzman even got licensed so she could officiate the wedding. The best part, though, happened before the festivities even took place, as he told the London *Sunday Times*. "We had already started to try to get pregnant and the day before the wedding she presented me with a sonogram, saying, 'Look what happened,' so it made the wedding sweet and romantic," he said.

Fifth, the happily-ever-after: For a person who basically defines that silly Internet term *zaddy*, who expected Goldblum to actually become a da—... oh, God, I'm not gonna say it. A father. There. Who expected Goldblum to actually become a father?

He certainly doesn't sound particularly prepared for the new phase of life in that *Sunday Times* profile, though he clearly adores the journey: "I was a bachelorly kind of guy in the way I never had food in the house. The first time she opened my refrigerator I had a bottle of water and some Chinese takeout. Now it's a family fridge with abundance all over. It's great."

As of this writing, the pair has two sons. Throughout his life, Goldblum considered names for his future children, which he often shared with various publications while doing press for different projects. "I spent years before I had kids fantasizing about what their names would be," he once said. "What would go with Goldblum?" It shows. They named the eldest Charlie Ocean, after Goldblum's uncle, a budding college basketball star who volunteered to fight in World War II and likely lost his life there—he was never found. They named their younger son River Joe, which feels like the yang to Charlie Ocean's yin. As is often the case, Charlie had to adjust to having a younger brother. "Charlie had dark feelings about the introduction of his younger brother, so we keep them safe and say you can hit the floor. You do not have to suppress your feelings. You can say you don't like him, but you can't hurt him," Goldblum told the *Times*. "And now there are many moments of friendship and sweetness. They bathe together and Charlie helps and protects his younger brother. River always wants to know what his brother is doing. He's just started to walk. He's a bit wobbly but he follows Charlie around."

The couple, meanwhile, bestowed each other with sweet little nicknames: she's Peaches and he's Patches, as he said on *Conan*. "She's sweet, like a peach, juicy and sweet," he said. As for him: "I have a lovely distribution of hair on my torso." Across his middle, "I have a couple little adornments of fluff. . . . I've got something here that occurs, it's a nice couple of patches." But "one is inconsistent with the other . . . it's asymmetrical. I used to try to even it up, but she said, 'Don't! I like you, sweet Patches. I like you, Patches.'"

But, enough! Family is sacred—though the self-righteous bloggers of the world certainly didn't think so when they took to the Internet to decry the fact that he was sixty-two and she thirty-one at the time of their nuptials—and we should leave it at this: the pair seem truly happy, something Goldblum takes every chance to announce.

"I feel right on schedule and I love our two boys," he told *Us Weekly* in 2018. "Everything seemed to happen perfectly. I appreciate it wildly."

A celebrity gushing about his or her family on late-night television might not seem cause for much more than a tweet, especially when the love life of the celebrity in question has been tabloid (and glossy!) fodder for decades. But, as we know by this point to often be the case, there's something different about Goldblum's love for Livingston and their children.

He would previously discuss his personal life, such as in that 1989 *GQ* profile, though it usually seemed like he was simply playing along at the celebrity game, doing what was expected of him. When he speaks of his family now, however, it's like he can't help himself, like something inside him will simply explode if he doesn't mention their names. A cute giddiness seems to overtake his body.

So mourn if you must. But we're better off celebrating. Because, look, life's hard. As if any of us need a reminder of that. It's become particularly difficult in these divided times. Being able to cheer for someone just makes us happy. It gives us hope. I pray these words won't be thrown back in my face with some awful revelation down the road, but at the moment, Goldblum seems like a really solid dude with a really nice life. Who wouldn't want to take some comfort in the life of such a guy? Is this all pretty sophomoric? Well, yeah. Caring about any of this shit is sophomoric.

But since the dawn of humanity, we've put certain people in certain fields on public pedestals and followed their lives. And we'll do it until the last one of us breathes his final breath and this whole absurd experiment of humanity comes to an end. So who cares if it's sophomoric? It makes us happy. It gives us something to aspire to. We can't become Jeff Goldblum, no. We can't suddenly spring up to six foot four, and we can't wander our way into a successful movie career and suddenly fix our broken relationships and go to the gym for hours a day and buy absurd $1,000 shirts and actually wear them well and have everyone who meets us fall head over heels for us. But we can use him and his life as inspiration.* We can say that the world's a little bit better for having him in it.

And there ain't nothing wrong with that.

Speaking of which, shall we segue into the end of this here book?

There's a common refrain on the Internet, a bit of digital-speak I've always abhorred: _____ *is what we need right now.* Generally some uplifting news story—video of a dog doing something outrageous like

---

*If you're somehow still reading this book, then you *know* this will pay off. Right? (Please say yes. I can't handle bad reviews.)

balancing a watermelon on its snout while riding a unicycle, or a photo of a celebrity casually enjoying themselves in some normal setting or maybe complaining about how tough things like working out and eating healthy are (they're just like the rest of us!)—fills that blank. And sometimes a celebrity doing something *none of us* could imagine doing fills that blank. Naturally, Goldblum—what with his energizing style sense, good-natured attitude, and exciting unknowability—is often "what we need right now."

When I started writing this book, my feelings toward the idea that we "need" Goldblum "right now" can be best described as overwhelmingly cynical. And I won't pretend like I like the Internet-speak any better now than when I began. But! But but but! As it turns out, there's something tremendously uplifting about speaking to dozens and dozens of people who interacted with someone over the course of his life, only to find that every single one of them glows warmly when discussing that person. That someone is so beloved, even if someone tells a *slightly* negative story about him, it's immediately told with the caveat: "But he's wonderful."

Michael Shamberg, the producer of *The Big Chill*,* put it simply: "The reason Jeff is adored is there's no one else like him. And he's never burned his contract, his relationship with the public, because he is just inherently likable. He's a really decent guy in person. [Plus] nobody can do on-screen what he does, so as business shifts from being a star who can open a movie to simply an actor who people want to work with because they're an actor's actor, he'll always have a career. . . . Movie stardom is all about essence, and he has an essence that hasn't faded. It will always endure."

It's certainly not eye-opening to say we live in tumultuous times, that

---

*Everyone, flip to chapter 5.

people are perhaps more divided than they've been in nearly half a century. No one *needs* anything but food, water, and sleep, of course. But to see everyone, on either side of any aisle you can imagine, agree on something—even if that something is admiration for an actor who appears to be aging in reverse, like some sort of Benjamin Button—well, that's a pretty special feeling. Maybe we don't *need* Goldblum, but we're sure as hell happy to have him. Not to overstate, but I'm going to overstate. He's a soothing balm on the wounds we constantly inflict on one another. Much in the same way seeing a puppy eating ice cream or a duckling befriending a kitten can suddenly make everything feel like it's going to be all right, just for a moment, even if it isn't, bringing up Goldblum in conversation brings most everyone a momentary feeling of joy. And, really, what else is there to want from a celebrity?

We'll never really know what makes the man tick, what motivates him to be openhearted and kind or exactly how he manages to pull off leopard-print suits. We'll probably never really be able to pin down why we love how much he loves throat lozenges or why we're just good with it when he's flirting with Conan O'Brien. We'll never really come up with a better word to describe his whole persona, other than transforming his name into a different part of speech, like an adverb (*Goldblumly*) or a verb (*to Goldblum*).

No, all we can really know with 100 percent certainty is we're lucky to have him. And whatever indelible qualities he exudes, well, it's just . . .

. . . because he's Jeff Goldblum.

The End*

---

*Of the book, obviously, not like the end of Jeff Goldblum. Though there's the whole acknowledgments section where I tell my mom, agent, and editor both thanks and sorry, and then a bibliography and all that, so it's technically not even actually the end of the book. Oh well.

ACKNOWLEDGMENTS

Here: I would be remiss if I did not, first and foremost, thank Jeff Goldblum for existing and being a fascinating subject and not demanding that I do not write a book about him. So, thank you!

After that, I owe more people thanks than I will probably recall. Please accept my deepest apologies in advance, and I will accept any awkward run-ins we may have in the future during which you say, "I see you forgot to acknowledge me in your book," and I turn beet red and start stammering and probably put my foot in my mouth by coming up with some cockamamie story about how your name was actually cut from the final transcript for reasons beyond my control, and then our friendship ends, and I grow very sad about it.

OK, let's do this.

My deepest, deepest thanks go to my mother, Mindy/"MamaBear," who has always supported my dreams as I embarked on the quest to become a writer and a journalist during a time in which neither seemed particularly employable. Without her, I wouldn't be doing any of this. Equal gratitude goes to my younger brother, Tyler/"Bouge," who sincerely remains my hero. Without you two, none of this would hold any meaning whatsoever.

To my dearest Maoria, who not only dealt with my constantly blabbering on about 1990s movie star Jeff Goldblum for the better part of a year and a half but scoured the libraries—her domain—for everything from old movies to half-inch newspaper clippings. Without you, Snail, this project would never have come to fruition. Not only because I wouldn't have the actual materials I needed but because I would have lost my mind long ago.

To Stevie Nix, well, you didn't actually help me in this process at all. You actually distracted me constantly and on more than one occasion chewed through the cord of my laptop charger. But you're a puppy, and you're awfully cute, so I guess it's okay.

To my agent, Laurie Abkemeier, the debt I feel is insurmountable. If she calls any of you and suggests you write a book, I highly recommend doing everything she says. She's a genius and isn't even mean when you ask the dumbest possible questions. Thank you, Laurie, and everyone else at the DeFiore and Company.

To my editor, Jill Schwartzman, it means the world that you took a chance on this book and didn't even throw it out of the window when I turned it in, which is probably good because your office is pretty high up and that easily could have hurt a passing tourist. Thank you, Jill, and everyone else at Dutton and Plume who has been so helpful in this process.

I also owe special thanks to so many of my *Washington Post* colleagues. To Fred Barbash, who called me up to DC in the first place: You changed my life. I cannot overstate that. To my colleagues Beth Butler, Geoff Edgers, Ben Guarino, Derek Hawkins, Susan Hogan, Elahe Izadi, David Malitz, Caitlin Moore, Sonia Rao, Zachary Pincus-Roth, Mitch Rubin, Samantha Schmidt, Liz Seymour, Kyle Swenson, and Emily Yahr—thank all of y'all for your unwavering support.

Then there's Abby O., Brett L., Colin, Elmeaux, Gamby, H. Wells, Mal, Maya, Mears, Meegs, Mims, Mook, Murph, Saj, and Willa. Thanks! Finally, to The Hold Steady, thank you for making the music that served as a constant soundtrack through the penning of this book.

WHEW! If I forgot you, please know it's because you probably didn't text me as I wrote these two pages, so that's kinda on you. And to everyone who bought and read and shared this book, thank you so very, very much.

BIBLIOGRAPHY

CHAPTER 1

Interviews with Ronald Allan-Lindblom, Chris Bradley, Bruce Broglie, Craig Kilborn, Helen McClory

Cochrane, Kira. "Jeff Goldblum: The Buddha of Hollywood." *Guardian*, July 12, 2010. https://www.theguardian.com/stage/2010/jul/12/jeff-goldblum-prisoner-second-avenue.

Marcus, Lilit. "Giant Jeff Goldblum Statue Appears in London." CNN, July 19, 2018. https://www.cnn.com/travel/article/jeff-goldblum-statue-london/index.html.

Nordyke, Kimberly. "Huge Statue of Dripping Wet Colin Firth Erected in London Lake." *Hollywood Reporter*, July 8, 2013. https://www.hollywoodreporter.com/news/huge-statue-dripping-wet-colin-581865.

CHAPTER 2

Interviews with Ronald Allan-Lindblom, David Beistel, Frank Cunimondo, Sharon Eberson

Barlow, Eve. "Jeff Goldblum: 'I'm Like One of Those Yogis Who Wanders the Earth with a Diaper.'" *Guardian*, June 12, 2016. https://www.theguardian.com/global/2016/jun/12/jeff-goldblum-actor-interview-fatherhood-independence-day-film-eve-barlow.

Cochrane, Kira. "Jeff Goldblum: The Buddha of Hollywood." *Guardian*, July 12, 2010. https://www.theguardian.com/stage/2010/jul/12/jeff-goldblum-prisoner-second-avenue.

Coelho, Saroja. "Jeff Goldblum on the Importance of Pursuing Your Dreams at Any Moment." CBC Radio, October 23, 2018. https://www.cbc.ca/radio/q/tuesday-october-23-2018-jeff-goldblum-tanya-taylor-jason-moran-and-more-1.4873317/jeff-goldblum-on-the-importance-of-pursuing-your-dreams-at-any-moment-1.4873319.

Eberson, Sharon. "Jeff Goldblum Jazzed to Be Coming Home." *Pittsburgh Post-Gazette*, February 12, 2019. https://www.post-gazette.com/ae/music/2019/02/07/Jeff-Goldblum-jazz-Homestead-Pittsburgh-Hollywood-music-movies-Snitzer/stories/201902070138.

Bibliography

Edutopia. "Celebrity Q&A: Jeff Goldblum on Theater and Arts Programs." May 17, 2007. https://www.edutopia.org/pop-quiz-jeff-goldblum.

Evening Standard. "What Jeff Loves About London." January 29, 2008. https://www.standard.co.uk/go/london/theatre/what-jeff-loves-about-london-6682423.html.

Haga, Evan. "Jeff Goldblum: Not a Hollywood Square." *JazzTimes*, December 26, 2018. https://jazztimes.com/features/interviews/jeff-goldblum-not-a-hollywood-square/.

Itzkoff, Dave. "Playing Piano, and Blaming Woody Allen." *New York Times*, September 12, 2014. https://www.nytimes.com/2014/09/13/arts/music/jeff-goldblums-orchestra-debuts-at-cafe-carlyle.html.

Marchese, David. "In Conversation: Jeff Goldblum." Vulture, June 2018. https://www.vulture.com/2018/06/jeff-goldblum-in-conversation.html.

Maron, Marc, host. "#721: Jeff Goldblum." *WTF with Marc Maron*, podcast, July 4, 2016.

Myers, Marc. "Jeff Goldblum Fulfilled a Teenage Dream Written on Steamed Glass." *Wall Street Journal*, November 20, 2018. https://www.wsj.com/articles/jeff-goldblum-fulfilled-a-teenage-dream-written-on-steamed-glass-1542727843.

Nelson, Jim, host. "Jeff Goldblum." *Mad Influence*, podcast, December 10, 2018.

O'Brien, Conan, host. "15: Jeff Goldblum." *Conan O'Brien Needs a Friend*, podcast, February 24, 2019.

Perry, Kevin E. G. "The Big Read—Jeff Goldblum: Sex and Drugs and Jazz Piano." *NME*, November 9, 2018. https://www.nme.com/big-reads/big-read-jeff-goldblum-sex-drugs-jazz-piano-2400542.

Rawson, Christopher. "Jeff Goldblum Resurrects Fond Memories with a Journey Through His Hometown Haunts." *Pittsburgh Post-Gazette*, July 4, 2004. https://www.post-gazette.com/uncategorized/2004/07/04/Jeff-Goldblum-resurrects-fond-memories-with-a-journey-through-his-hometown-haunts/stories/200407040197.

Rosen, Marjorie. "More than a Contender." *People*, May 11, 1992. https://people.com/archive/more-than-a-contender-vol-37-no-18/.

Rouvalis, Cristina. "Mentored by the Masters." *Carnegie Magazine*, Spring 2019. https://carnegiemuseums.org/carnegie-magazine/spring-2019/mentored-by-the-masters/.

Silicon Valley Historical Association. "Jeff Goldblum's the Mildred Snitzer Orchestra Named After Silicon Valley Centenarian." YouTube, January 29, 2009. https://www.youtube.com/watch?v=W67Is7NZOFY.

Svetkey, Ben. "The Lizard King." *Entertainment Weekly*, May 23, 1997. http://www.goldblum.com/magazine/entertainment/ew.html.

Bibliography

INTERLUDE #2
Interview with Ranjiv Perera
Doob, Nick. *American Masters: Sanford Meisner: The American Theatre's Best Kept Secret.* YouTube, August 27, 1990. https://www.youtube.com/watch?v=K6q7 dxwa_PM.
Ideas Tap. "Jeff Goldblum." YouTube, October 26, 2010. https://www.youtube.com /watch?v=KkbgQzAkJM4.
Lyman, Rick. "The Lives They Lived: Sanford Meisner; The Proof Is in the Protégé." *New York Times*, January 4, 1998. https://www.nytimes.com/1998/01/04/maga zine/the-lives-they-lived-sanford-meisner-the-proof-is-in-the-protege.html.
Meisner, Sanford. *Sanford Meisner on Acting.* Vintage, 1987.

CHAPTER 3
Interviews with Jonelle Allen, John Guare, Mel Shapiro
Associated Press. "In the First of a Series Looking at First Auditions, Jeff Goldblum Recalls His 'Lucky' Early Career." AP Archive on YouTube, September 18, 2018. https://www.youtube.com/watch?v=c3Wo7LIMGsQ.
Bhattacharya, Sanjiv. "Jeff Goldblum: What I've Learned." *Esquire*, June 20, 2016. https://www.esquire.com/uk/culture/film/a10164/jeff-goldblum-what-ive -learned/.
Maron, Marc, host. "#721: Jeff Goldblum." *WTF with Marc Maron*, podcast, July 4, 2016.
Myers, Marc. "Jeff Goldblum Fulfilled a Teenage Dream Written on Steamed Glass." *Wall Street Journal*, November 20, 2018. https://www.wsj.com/articles/jeff -goldblum-fulfilled-a-teenage-dream-written-on-steamed-glass-1542727843.
Perry, Kevin E. G. "The Big Read—Jeff Goldblum: Sex and Drugs and Jazz Piano." *NME*, November 9, 2018. https://www.nme.com/big-reads/big-read-jeff-goldblum -sex-drugs-jazz-piano-2400542.
Rafanelli, Stephanie. "How Mr. Jeff Goldblum Stays Forever Young." *Mr. Porter*, December 22, 2016. https://www.mrporter.com/en-us/journal/fashion/how-mr -jeff-goldblum-stays-forever-young-700910.
Svetkey, Ben. "The Lizard King." *Entertainment Weekly*, May 23, 1997. http://www .goldblum.com/magazine/entertainment/ew.html.

CHAPTER 4
Interviews with Gary Arnold, Adrian Danks, Stephen Dunn, Chuck Klosterman, Sean Fennessey, Philip Kaufman, Adam Nayman, Richard Pearce, W. D. Richter, Alan Rudolph, Juliet Taylor, Ken Van Sickle, Ben Vereen
Arnold, Gary. "'Between the Lines': A Most Appealing Comedy." *Washington Post*, May 18, 1977, B1.
Associated Press. "Jeff Goldblum Stays Calm amid Fireworks." Nwitimes.com, July 5, 1996. https://www.nwitimes.com/uncategorized/jeff-goldblum-stays-calm-amid -fireworks/article_eb250db5-4fd0-5d9b-874d-1b08e9a1b16e.html.

Bibliography

Blume, Lesley M. M. "Jeff Goldblum Is a Jazz-Playing Smoothie King Devotee." *Vanity Fair*, October 30, 2017. https://www.vanityfair.com/hollywood/2017/10/jeff-goldblum-jazz-smoothie-king-thor-jurassic-park.

Ebiri, Bilge. "Adam Resurrected's Jeff Goldblum on His First-Ever Movie Accent and Forgetting His Secret Mantra—TV." Vulture, December 15, 2008. https://www.vulture.com/2008/12/jeff_goldblum.html.

Editors of *GQ*. "Jeff Goldblum on Being a Pencil Salesman." *GQ*, December 10, 2018. https://www.gq.com/story/mad-influence-ep-6-jeff-goldblum.

Evans, Melissa. *Jeff Goldblum and Keith Carradine (Nashville 1975)*. YouTube, April 13, 2019. https://www.youtube.com/watch?v=Ewxsr2QSbBw.

Fetterman, Mindy. "Lessons Learned: Students and Their Teachers." *Washington Post*, August 21, 1977, 113.

Heldman, Breanne L. "Christopher Walken Told a Funny Story About How He Met Jeff Goldblum." *Yahoo! Entertainment*, December 4, 2014. https://www.yahoo.com/entertainment/christopher-walken-told-a-funny-story-about-how-he-104359856352.html.

King, Susan. "Classic Hollywood: Jeff Goldblum's Long, Strange Hollywood Journey." *Los Angeles Times*, July 25, 2019. https://www.latimes.com/entertainment-arts/story/2019-07-24/classic-hollywood-jeff-goldblums-long-strange-hollywood-journey.

Knight, James. "Michael Winner." *Vice*, September 1, 2009. https://www.vice.com/en_us/article/5g5b4k/michael-winner-143-v16n9.

Laurent, Lawrence. "Ben Vereen's Tongue Goes as Fast as 'Tenspeed' Role." *Washington Post*, June 22, 1980, TV6.

Making of "Nashville," The. IMDb, 2013. http://www.imdb.com/title/tt7223384/.

McCarthy, Kevin, and Ed Gorman, eds. *"They're Here" . . . Invasion of the Body Snatchers: A Tribute*. Berkley Boulevard trade paperback edition. New York City: Berkley Trade, 1999.

Nataloff. *Robert Altman on Casting and Directing*. YouTube, 2009. https://www.youtube.com/watch?v=9OiHq3HyQMQ.

O'Connor, John J. "TV VIEW; Detective Series Are in Hot Pursuit of New Gimmicks." *New York Times*, March 16, 1980, 39.

Peele, Anna. "Jeff Goldblum: An Oral History of Hollywood's Most Charming Eccentric." *GQ*, November 1, 2017. https://www.gq.com/story/jeff-goldblum-the-oral-history.

Thorn, Jesse, host. "Jeff Goldblum." *Bullseye with Jesse Thorn*. NPR, August 6, 2019. https://www.npr.org/2019/08/05/748432437/jeff-goldblum.

Vanity Fair. Jeff Goldblum Breaks Down His Career, from "Jurassic Park" to "Isle of Dogs." YouTube, 2018. https://www.youtube.com/watch?v=py9lrUq7cOU.

Weiner, David. "Why 'Invasion of the Body Snatchers' Still Haunts Its Director." *Hollywood Reporter*, December 20, 2018. https://www.hollywoodreporter.com/heat-vision/invasion-body-snatchers-ending-still-haunts-director-1170220.

Winner, Michael. *Winner Takes All: A Life of Sorts*. Portico, 2005.

Ziegel, Vic. "Not Just Another Funny Face." *New York* 16, no. 38 (September 1983): 78–90.

CHAPTER 5

Interviews with Gary Arnold, Stephen Dunn, Sean Fennessey, Lawrence Kasdan, Philip Kaufman, W. D. Richter, Johanna Schneller, Michael Shamberg, Harry Shearer, Lewis Smith

Attanasio, Paul. "Murkily 'Into the Night.'" *Washington Post*, March 11, 1985.

Barlow, Eve. "Jeff Goldblum: 'I'm Like One of Those Yogis Who Wanders the Earth.'" *Observer*, June 12, 2016.

Bouzereau, Laurent. *The Big Chill: A Reunion.* Columbia TriStar Home Video, 1999.

Canby, Vincent. "Film: John Landis's Into the Night." *New York Times*, February 22, 1985, C8.

Feldman, Paul. "John Landis Not Guilty in 3 'Twilight Zone' Deaths: Jury Also Exonerates Four Others." *Los Angeles Times*, May 29, 1987, 1.

French, Alex, and Howie Kahn. "An Oral History of the Epic Space Film The Right Stuff." *Wired*, November 2014. https://www.wired.com/2014/11/oral-history-of -right-stuff/.

Gordinier, Jeff. "A Time to Chill." *Entertainment Weekly* 457 (November 1998): 36–41.

Nixon, Rob. "The Big Chill." Turner Classic Movies. http://www.tcm.com/this -month/article/115768|0/The-Big-Chill.html.

"Roy London, 50, Dies; Actor and a Director." *New York Times*, August 12, 1993, D21.

Schneller, Johanna. "Married . . . with Chicken." *GQ*, June 1989, 222–27, 268, 284.

Shout Factory. "Jeff Goldblum Goes Into the Night." *Shout!Takes*, podcast, December 8, 2017.

Thompson, David, ed. *Altman on Altman.* New York: Farrar, Straus and Giroux, 2006.

Weintraub, Steve "Frosty." "The Collider Interview: John Landis, Part II." Collider, September 2, 2005. https://collider.com/the-collider-interview-john-landis -part-ii/.

CHAPTER 6

Interviews with Gary Arnold, Adrian Danks, Stephen Dunn, Stephan Dupuis, Sean Fennessey, Lawrence Kasdan, Gillian Richardson, Johanna Schneller, Chris Walas

Cerone, Daniel. "Jeff Goldblum: Still Looking for His Niche." *Los Angeles Times*, June 24, 1990, U1.

Durang, Christopher. "Film and TV Writings." ChristopherDurang.com. http:// www.christopherdurang.com/filmtv2.htm.

Ebert, Roger. "Earth Girls Are Easy." RogerEbert.com, May 12, 1989. https://www .rogerebert.com/reviews/earth-girls-are-easy-1989.

Farber, Stephen. "Carson Outfit Gains." *New York Times*, March 6, 1984, C18.

Maio, Kathi. "Earth Girls: A Good Man Is Hard to Find." *Sojourner* 14, no. 11 (July 1989): 34–35.

Morton, Jamie, James Cooper, and Alice Levine, hosts. "Footnotes: Dame Emma Thompson." *My Dad Wrote a Porno*, podcast, November 14, 2018.

"Roy London, 50, Dies; Actor and a Director." *New York Times*, August 12, 1993, D21.

Schneller, Johanna. "Married . . . with Chicken." *GQ*, June 1989, 222–27, 268, 284.

Siskel, Gene. "Oscar Swats 'The Fly.'" *Chicago Tribune*, February 18, 1987.

Smith, Liz. "Liz Smith." *Toledo Blade*, June 2, 1989, 5.

Sun-Sentinel. "Jeff Goldblum & Geena Davis: The Press Has Paired the Two Since Transylvania 6-5000. They Leave Their Personal Life Off-Camera but Still Bring Their Friendship to the Screen." September 13, 1986.

Thompson, David, ed. *Altman on Altman.* New York: Farrar, Straus and Giroux, 2006.

Travers, Peter. "Earth Girls Are Easy." *Rolling Stone*, May 1989.

Valero, Gerardo. "David Cronenberg's 'The Fly.'" RogerEbert.com, January 13, 2014. https://www.rogerebert.com/far-flung-correspondents/the-fly.

Vallely, Jean. "Jeff Goldblum, Who Still Forgets His Mantra." *GQ*, July 1985, 106–9.

CHAPTER 7

Interviews with Bryan Curtis, Bill Duke, Sean Fennessey, Chuck Klosterman, John T. Kretchmer, Adam Nayman, Sean Pelligrino, Brandon Smith, Bradford Tatum, Johanna Schneller

92nd Street Y. *That Time Jeff Goldblum Joined Aerosmith Onstage.* YouTube, 2018. https://www.youtube.com/watch?time_continue=4&v=PTRBkVK2J4U&feature=emb_title.

Appelo, Tim. "Laura Dern Is Not a Lesbian." *Entertainment Weekly* 376 (April 1997): 36–38.

Associated Press. "Jeff Goldblum Stays Calm Amid Fireworks." Nwitimes.com, July 5, 1996. https://www.nwitimes.com/uncategorized/jeff-goldblum-stays-calm-amid-fireworks/article_eb250db5-4fd0-5d9b-874d-1b08e9a1b16e.html.

First We Feast. *Jeff Goldblum Says He Likes to Be Called Daddy While Eating Spicy Wings.* YouTube, 2018. https://www.youtube.com/watch?time_continue=940&v=TMfVEkfXEV8&feature=emb_logo.

Frankel, Martha. "Laura Dern: What She Does for Love." *Redbook* 189, no. 3 (July 1997): 60–63.

Hoban, Phoebe. "The Outsider as Hollywood Favorite." *New York Times*, June 15, 1997, 19.

Jerome, Jim. "Riding Shotgun." *People Weekly* 35, no. 24 (June 1991). https://people.com/archive/cover-story-riding-shotgun-vol-35-no-24/.

Lee, Luaine, and Scripps Howard News Service. "Laura Dern Finds Love Amid Horror in 'Jurassic Park.'" *Chicago Tribune*, June 18, 1993.

Maron, Marc, host. "#721: Jeff Goldblum." *WTF with Marc Maron*, podcast, July 4, 2016.

O'Toole, Lesley. "Smart, Sexy, Nerdy, Funny Jeff Goldblum—Archive, 25 July 1996." *Guardian*, July 25, 2019. https://www.theguardian.com/culture/2019/jul/25/smart-sexy-nerdy-funny-jeff-goldblum-archive-1996.

Bibliography

Peele, Anna. "Jeff Goldblum: An Oral History of Hollywood's Most Charming Eccentric." *GQ*, November 1, 2017.

Perry, Kevin E. G. "The Big Read—Jeff Goldblum: Sex and Drugs and Jazz Piano." *NME*, November 9, 2018. https://www.nme.com/big-reads/big-read-jeff -goldblum-sex-drugs-jazz-piano-2400542.

Rosen, Marjorie. "More Than a Contender." *People Weekly* 37, no. 18 (May 1992).

Sears, Rufus. "How Jurassic Park Became the Biggest Movie of All Time." *Empire Magazine* 50 (August 1993).

Stack, Tim, and Keith Staskiewicz. "'Welcome to Jurassic Park': An Oral History." *Entertainment Weekly*, April 4, 2013. https://ew.com/movies/2013/04/04/jurassic -park-oral-history/.

CHAPTER 8

Interviews with John David Coles, Billy Crudup, Robert Fox, Nick Guthe, Martin McDonagh, Pat Mendelson, John Roman, Dick Wolf, Graham Yost, Doug Zanger

Boriboj. *Paul Schrader Adam Resurrected Interview Karlovy Vary*. YouTube, 2009. https://www.youtube.com/watch?v=dofnOwWfPxk.

cinematographos. *Jeff Goldblum on "Adam Resurrected."* YouTube, 2010. https://www .youtube.com/watch?v=aGX9xlhZU1Q.

Elliott, Matt. "Let's All Relive That Time Jeff Goldblum Played Dracula in an Fmv Goosebumps Game." *PC Gamer*, October 28, 2019. https://www.pcgamer.com /lets-all-relive-that-time-jeff-goldblum-played-dracula-in-an-fmv-goosebumps -game/.

Holden, Stephen. "Treated Like a Dog, in War and Madness." *New York Times*, December 11, 2008, C12.

McGrath, Charles. "'The Pillowman' Audience: Shocked and a Bit Amused." *New York Times*, April 26, 2005, 1.

O'Brien, Conan, host. "Jeff Goldblum." *Late Night with Conan O'Brien*, April 27, 2006.

Siegel, Tatiana. "Producers, Director Say Alec Baldwin Lies in Memoir's Claim of Sex Scenes with Underaged Actress." *Hollywood Reporter*, April 5, 2017. https://www .hollywoodreporter.com/news/dana-brunetti-claims-alec-baldwin-is-lying-memoir -claims-regarding-nikki-reeds-age-991315.

Simmons, Bill, host. "The 2018 Masters and Jeff Goldblum Reminisces on His Career." *The Bill Simmons Podcast*, podcast, April 4, 2018.

Wilson, Chuck. "Jeff Goldblum and Paul Schrader on Their Strange Holocaust Fable." *LA Weekly*, December 1, 2008. https://www.laweekly.com/jeff-goldblum-and-paul -schrader-on-their-strange-holocaust-fable/.

CHAPTER 9

Interviews with Ronald Allan-Lindblom, Chris Bradley, Ralph Crewe, Sharon Eberson, Kyle LaBrache, Richard Sabellico, Doug Shields, Catherine Wreford

Leydon, Joe. "Review: Jon E. Edwards Is in Love." *Variety*, April 21, 2003. https://variety.com/2003/film/reviews/jon-e-edwards-is-in-love-1200542113/.

Rawson, Christopher. "Stage Review: Goldblum Opens 'Music Man' on a Jittery Note." *Pittsburgh Post-Gazette*, July 7, 2004. https://www.post-gazette.com/uncategorized/2004/07/07/Stage-Review-Goldblum-opens-Music-Man-on-a-jittery-note/stories/200407070191.

CHAPTER 10

Interviews with Inti Carboni, Gavin Edwards, Sean Fennessey, Katharina Hingst, Sam Hoffman, Chuck Klosterman, Jonathan Krisel, Ryan Milner, Drew Pearce

Carico. "Big Contradictions in the Evolution Theory." Christian Forums, August 10, 2005. https://www.christianforums.com/threads/big-contradictions-in-the-evolution-theory.1962980/.

"Grandmaster (Marvel Comics)." Wikipedia, https://en.wikipedia.org/w/index.php?title=Grandmaster_(Marvel_Comics)&oldid=930444883.

Hines, Nico. "The Cast of 'The Grand Budapest Hotel' Says Wes Anderson Is a Genius Hardass." Daily Beast, February 16, 2014.

Horseeater. "Jeff Goldblum Is Watching You Poop." Know Your Meme, 2009. https://knowyourmeme.com/memes/jeff-goldblum-is-watching-you-poop.

Krisel, Jonathan, director. "One Moore Episode." *Portlandia*, season 2, episode 2, January 13, 2012.

Marchese, David. "In Conversation: Jeff Goldblum." Vulture, June 18, 2018. https://www.vulture.com/2018/06/jeff-goldblum-in-conversation.html.

Neill, Sam (@TwoPaddocks). "Yes I am. It is stomach churning." Twitter, May 27, 2016. https://T.Co/OEUoEy5dUB.

Semlyen, Phil de. "Jeff Goldblum Talks Thor: Ragnarok's Grandmaster." *Empire*, June 6, 2016. https://www.empireonline.com/movies/news/jeff-goldblum-talks-thor-ragnarok-grandmaster/.

t-bone and ribeye. "Jeff Goldblum Is Watching You Poop!" GeoCities, October 10, 2002. http://web.archive.org/web/20021010190500/http://geocities.com/jeffgoldblumiswatchingyoupoop/.

Watercutter, Angela. "A Few Thor: Ragnarok Updates, Straight from Its Director." *Wired*, June 2016. https://www.wired.com/2016/06/taika-waititi-thor-ragnarok/.

Weintraub, Steve "Frosty." "Jeff Goldblum on Isle of Dogs, Wes Anderson and Goldblum-Isms." Collider, March 23, 2018. https://collider.com/jeff-goldblum-interview-isle-of-dogs/#greenwich-village.

CHAPTER 11

Interviews with Murray Clark, Larry Klein, Chuck Klosterman, Ryan Milner, Drew Pearce, Josh Sims, Rachel Tashjian

Greiving, Tim. "Jeff Goldblum's Semi-Regular Jazz Night Has Returned to Los Feliz." *Los Angeles Magazine*, April 6, 2018. https://www.lamag.com/culturefiles/jeff-goldblum-jazz/.

Bibliography

Hale, Mike. "Review: On Disney Plus, a Show That Goldblumsplains the World." *New York Times*, November 11, 2019. https://www.nytimes.com/2019/11/11/arts /television/jeff-goldblum-disney-plus-review.html.

Heaf, Jonathan. "How Jeff Goldblum Became the Coolest Guy in Hollywood (Again)." *GQ*, July 5, 2018. https://www.gq-magazine.co.uk/article/jeff-goldblum-interview -2018.

Itzkoff, Dave. "Playing Piano, and Blaming Woody Allen." *New York Times*, September 12, 2014. https://www.nytimes.com/2014/09/13/arts/music/jeff-goldblums -orchestra-debuts-at-cafe-carlyle.html.

Katz, Evan Ross. "How One Stylist Turned Jeff Goldblum into a 'Fit Savant.'" *Vice*, April 2, 2019. https://garage.vice.com/en_us/article/mbzzwq/jeff-goldblum -style.

Keveney, Bill. "The 'Very Curious' Jeff Goldblum on His New Disney Plus Show and Latest 'Jurassic' Sequel." *USA Today*, November 20, 2019. https://www.usatoday .com/story/entertainment/tv/2019/11/20/world-according-to-jeff-goldblum -disney-plus-jurassic-world/4205214002/.

Newman, Jason. "Jeff Goldblum Has a Number One Jazz Album. It Only Took Him 50 Years." *Rolling Stone*, December 18, 2018. https://www.rollingstone.com /music/music-features/jeff-goldblum-jazz-album-mildred-snitzer-orchestra -interview-759895/.

Patterson, Troy. "The Prada Flame Shirt Is Performance Art." *New Yorker*, July 22, 2018. https://www.newyorker.com/culture/culture-desk/the-prada-flame -shirt-is-performance-art.

Porter, Gregory, host. "Jeff Goldblum's Lucky Break." *The Hang with Gregory Porter*, podcast, August 6, 2019.

Riefe, Jordan. "Jeff Goldblum Brings Cabaret Act to Beverly Hills." *Hollywood Reporter*, December 18, 2015. https://www.hollywoodreporter.com/news/jeff -goldblum-brings-cabaret-act-850203.

Schube, Sam. "Jeff Goldblum Explains How to Talk to Your Wife About Her Outfit." *GQ*, June 24, 2015. https://www.gq.com/story/jeff-goldblum-interview-gq.

Tallerico, Brian. "Disney Plus Launches with Original Shows in the Shadow of Its Massive Library." RogerEbert.com, November 11, 2019. https://www.rogerebert .com/demanders/disney-plus-launches-with-original-shows-in-the-shadow -of-its-massive-library.

Tashjian, Rachel. "In Prada, Jeff Goldblum Found Shirts as Perfectly Weird as He Is." *GQ*, April 22, 2019. https://www.gq.com/story/brand-loyalty-jeff-goldblum -prada.

Bibliography

EPILOGUE

Iley, Chrissy. "The Magazine Interview: Actor Jeff Goldblum on His Jazz Album and Becoming a Dad in His Sixties." *Sunday Times*, August 5, 2018. https://www.the times.co.uk/article/the-magazine-interview-actor-jeff-goldblum-on-his-jazz -album-with-gregory-porter-and-becoming-a-dad-in-his-sixties-0hxmvmbxf.

"Jeff Goldblum's Wife Is a CONTORTIONIST!" *The Graham Norton Show*, You-Tube, October 20, 2017. https://www.youtube.com/watch?v=0VzsalqoLcY.

Lee, Chris. "How Rihanna Ended Up in That Strip-Club Scene in *Valerian*." *GQ*, July 21, 2017. https://www.gq.com/story/rihanna-valerian.

Takeda, Allison. "Jeff Goldblum Is Married!" *US Weekly*, November 11, 2014. https://www.usmagazine.com/celebrity-news/news/jeff-goldblum-married-actor -62-weds-emilie-livingston-31-20141111/.

Team Coco. "Jeff Goldblum on His Wife's Sweet Nickname for Him." *Conan*, You-Tube, June 22, 2016. https://www.youtube.com/watch?v=wA-SelKRSu4.

Wired. "Jeff Goldblum Answers the Web's Most Searched Questions." YouTube, March 27, 2018. https://www.youtube.com/watch?v=_l4xtcmrT6g.

ABOUT THE AUTHOR

Travis M. Andrews is a features writer for the *Washington Post*'s Style section, where he covers the Internet, pop culture, and the ways we live now. Previously he was an associate travel and culture editor for *Southern Living* and a contributing pop culture reporter for Mashable and *The Week*. He has also written for *Time, Esquire, GQ,* and the *Atlantic,* among others. He lives in Washington, DC, where he acquiesces to the every wish of his puppy, Stevie Nix, and misses his native New Orleans.